75 Brexit Benefits:

Tangible Benefits from the UK Having Left the European Union

By Gully Foyle

With a foreword by Rt Hon. Sir John Redwood

ISBN: 978-1-917743-11-2

The Bruges Group Publications Office
246 Linen Hall, 162-168 Regent Street, London W1B 5TB
www.brugesgroup.com

Twitter  @brugesgroup, LinkedIn @brugesgroup
GETTR @brugesgroup, Telegram t.me/brugesgroup, Facebook @brugesgroup
Instagram @brugesgroup, YouTube @brugesgroup

SCAN FOR MORE BOOKS

For My Partner

For the many evenings you have suffered through, listening to me excitedly explain how I had written something that really 'got traction', when all you really wanted to do was listen to your stories. Thank you for tolerating me through these last few years.

For My Kids

All of this will have gone by without your knowledge or involvement, but everything I have done and continue to do, is for you. I hope one day to sit you down and run you through it all.

For My Supporters

Those of you who were there from the start, when I only had a few thousand followers. Those who missed me when I was gone during the pre-Elon dark ages of de-platforming right-wing voices. Those who supported me and broadcast my content to a wider audience. Those who disagree with my position but still engage with the content respectfully and have the courage to defend its truthfulness with their peers. Those who are no longer with us but fought right to the end.

Thank you. From the bottom of my heart.

Contents

Foreword 1
Preface 7

Why I Voted to Leave the European Union 8
Benefits, Disbenefits and Tangibility 10
The UK-EU Summit: 19th May 2025 11
The Seven Brexit Benefit Types: 12
An Introduction 12
Quick Reference List...14

Section 1: Brexit Has Saved Us Billions in EU Fees and Membership Costs 17
1. Same-Same, But Different 18
2. Emission Impossible 21
3. The Bill Comes Due. Always. 23
4. Plastic Fantastic...25
5. It's All About the Benjamins, Baby! 27
6. The More the Merrier? 29
7. Removing the Lion, Keeping the Lion's Share 31
8. Banana-Rama...33
9. I Have a Semillon 35
10. Get Them While They're Young...............................37
11. Bring Me the Horizon 39
12. Quads Out, Quids In..41
13. Less is More 43

Section 2: Brexit Has Returned Our Independence in Fishing, Farming, Animal Welfare and the Environment 44
14. Huffin and Puffin..45
15. My Chemical Romance..47
16. (Don't) Bring Your Daughter to the Slaughter 49
17. The Fin-al Countdown 52
18. Skin in the Game...54
19. Plenty More Fish in the Sea................................56
20. Do Sheep Dream of Electric Androids?.......................58
21. Poppin' a CAP in Your Ass 60
22. Wet Wet Wet 63
23. Honk Honk..65
24. Hush Puppies...67

Section 3: Brexit Means Better Trade **69**

25. Harder, Better, Faster, Stronger **70**
26. How Low Can You Go? **73**
27. Common People **75**
28. Epic Berne **77**
29. Competency? What Competency? **79**
30. Through the Barricades **81**
31. In It for the Long Haul **84**
32. Feed the World **86**
33. Ill Customs are Seldom Forgotten **90**
34. Perfect 10 .... **92**
35. Time to Make the Chimichangas **95**
36. Digital Killed the Analog Star **97**
37. Rotterdam or Anywhere, Liverpool or Rome **99**
38. Rock, Paper, Scissors, Blockchain **101**
39. Liberalisation, Across the Nation **104**
40. A Stay of (Tariff) Execution **106**
41. Oh (Antipodean) Brother, Where Art Thou? **108**

Section 4: Brexit Means We Run Our Own Country Again ... **110**

42. Some Are More Equal Than Others **111**
43. Rise of the Machines, Interrupted **114**
44. (No Longer) Arrested Development **117**
45. Running Up That Bill **119**
46. I've Got the Power(s) **121**
47. Cellophane, Mr Cellophane **123**
48. School's Out for Starmer **125**
49. The Return of Democracy **127**
50. Approaching Artificial Intelligence, Intelligently **129**
51. Trainer, Trailer, Saver, Drive **131**
52. Not So Super, Super League **133**
53. High Stakes Make or Break for Fake Steak **135**
54. Respect My Authoritah! **137**
55. Rules Are Made to be Broken (or Made Better) **139**

Section 5: Brexit Means a Better Economy **144**

57. A Crescendo of Contactless **145**
58. No No, There's No (Commodity Position) Limit! **147**
59. Hire Locally, Higher Salary **149**
60. The Nuclear Option **151**
61. Just Be Good to Me **153**
62. The Revolution Will Be Subsidised **155**
63. All Around My Cap **158**

Section 6: Brexit Means We Control Our Own Borders 160
64. Go Your Own Way 161
65. Crime Doesn't Pay 163
66. I'm Picking Up Good Migrations................................... 165
67. Freeport Convention 167
68. Fake It Til You Make It... 169

Section 7: Brexit Has Strengthened Our Defences and Our Standing in the World.. 171
69. You Down With 'TPP, Yeah You Know Me 172
70. Service(s) With a Smile 175
71. Slava Ukraini 177
72. How Do You Take Your Power? Hard or Soft? 179
73. Who Ya Gonna Call?... 181
74. Take Me Down to the Acronym City 183
75. Through the Fire and the Flames 186

Acknowledgements 188
Notes   190
Index   215
About the Bruges Group 222

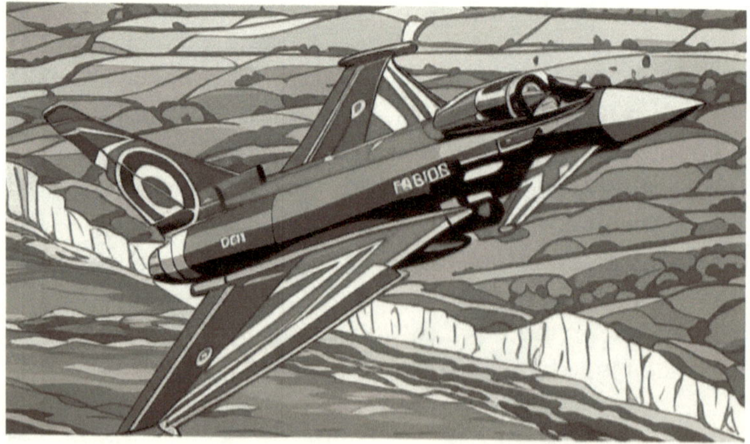

Foreword
The Rt Hon. Sir John Redwood DPhil, FCSI

This is an important book. At last, after nine years of propaganda from anti-Brexit spinners, here are the facts. These pages show how the UK has already enjoyed many wins from Brexit. This has occurred despite many parts of the UK establishment working hard to prove they were right to oppose Brexit, by stopping us making changes for the better.

At times Parliament, senior officials, judges and quangos often worked to prevent the UK using its newly acquired freedoms. Remain lost by being pessimistic about our country. Its forecasts of economic and trade harm from leaving proved to be wrong. Its attitude that the EU knows best was not widely shared by businesses and families that had suffered from EU laws and taxes. This book helps put the record straight.

Freedom is a huge win

People voted to restore our freedoms and our right to self-government. We are free of the large and fast-growing bills imposed on member states. We can negotiate our own trade deals. We can amend bad laws, repeal bad taxes and get closer to non-EU allies and friends.

Brexit brought the most precious prize of all, the prize of freedom. Our great country had pioneered the rule of law, setting Parliament above governors who broke the rules. Home to the Mother of Parliaments, the UK played a big role in the evolution of democracy. We exported it to others around the world. Our nation confronted the slave trade and used Royal navy ships to intercept its traders. We took pride in how individual liberty came to be central to our constitution. We advanced to universal suffrage, so all adults had an equal share in choosing or dismissing the government.

The UK spent much blood and treasure in wars to help oppressed nations be self-governing. Freedom was advanced and defended with the help of our ships and our armies. We often saved European countries from tyranny and from conquest. We stood up to tyrants and formed freedom coalitions of the willing to stop domination of the continent by autocratic governments based on violent invasions.

Our global seafaring reach was damaged by our membership of the EU. Our freedom loving instincts were suppressed by the need to accept laws and budgets we did not like, imposed on us from Brussels. Our democracy buckled as law after law passed by the EU behind closed doors had to be adopted by our once sovereign Parliament even where we did not want it or where it would do us harm. I voted to leave the European Community in 1975 in one of the first votes I cast as an adult. We were told we were voting to stay in a common market which would not harm our sovereignty. I read the Treaty of Rome which made clear this was a project to create an ever-closer union, with ever more governing power passing from the member states. I didn't like being lied to by the establishment.

We can do better than the slow-lane Single Market
After losing the vote as a good democrat I vowed to try to help create this common or free market most voters wanted. Appointed Single Market Minister in 1989 I was told to work to 'complete' the single market by 1992. I saw from the inside what a dangerous con it was. Far from being the free liberated market that would promote greater prosperity which people wanted, I saw it was a big power grab by the EU institutions. Law after law claimed power to legislate and regulate everything from employment to trade, from farming to industry, from health and safety to taxes and subsidies. A so-called market was a government in the making. No free market, this was a customs union with tariffs and other barriers to keep goods and services out from non-EU sources to the cost of UK consumers. It stifled innovation, was often harsh on small business and the self-employed. It buttressed the position of some established large European companies, embedding in law their way of doing things.

One of the myths this book busts is the idea that the single market was crucial to economic success. Our growth slowed after joining the EEC and slowed some more after 1992 and the single market. The UK went into permanent large trade deficit with the rest of the EU as rules, tariffs and taxes hit us but often helped France and Germany who had more influence over designing them. As readers will see in many examples, out of the EU we have able to get rid of unhelpful policies that hindered our economic growth. The UK 's farms can develop and adopt new technology which the EU bans. VAT on green products can be lifted in the UK. We have taken down tariffs on imports of things we cannot make for ourselves and removed tariffs from imports we need to transform into more valuable products.

We save plenty of money from Brexit
Saving the £12bn a year membership charges was an important feature of Brexit success. Despite a bad exit deal inflicted on us by Remainer negotiators, we are now saving more than that. The NHS has received a bigger injection of extra cash than that proposed in the referendum. This has been helped by the big EU saving. We have left an organisation that is borrowing on a large scale. This frees us from any responsibility to pay interest on the debt and means we do not in due course have to help them repay it. The EU has increasingly expensive tastes in common policies needing bigger member state payments and new EU taxes.

We have spared ourselves the need to accept these additional EU taxes. They are looking for more ways to raise money from EU citizens through carbon levies, emissions trading, plastics and waste taxes and a wide range of other options. The present UK government often wants the UK to have similar taxes, but they are now our taxes which we could abolish or vary. The UK state can choose how to spend the money.

We can be a better force for good
The UK wants to be kind to animals. Out of the EU we have been able to end the export of live animals which could cause them harm. We can ban imports of meat and poultry if the animals and birds have not been well looked after, setting higher

standards than we were allowed in the EU. We can regulate the fur trade properly.

There are more trade opportunities with Brexit
The UK wants to trade globally, not just with the EU. The USA is our largest single national trade partner. The rise of a much larger and faster growing market in Asia points to a future where the EU share of our trade will continue to decline. It was falling whilst we were still in the EU despite EU laws and tariffs to keep more non-EU products out. It is well under half of our trade. Since we left the EU the UK has enjoyed a surge in service exports, especially to non-EU countries. The UK has gone from being the world's fourth largest exporter of services to being the second. Service exports are now bigger than goods exports.

One of the problems with submitting to EU trade policy was the lack of attention they gave to services when negotiating trade agreements. A Brexit win has been to let the UK develop service market additions to trade agreements we rolled over from the EU. We can now make services an important part of new trade agreements.

A clear Brexit win has been the ability to negotiate and conclude our own trade agreements. Because the EU is more Customs Union than free trade exponent it has no free trade agreement with India, with the Trans-Pacific Partnership grouping or with the USA. The UK is now signing an Indian agreement. The UK has joined the CPTPP. The UK got the first mini agreement with the USA to abate new US tariffs. These are good wins. Remain said the UK would lose the trade agreements the EU had managed to sign. Instead, the UK transferred all these by agreement and was able to add improvements in some cases. Meanwhile CPTPP and India gives us access to a far bigger market opportunity than the EU offers.

Brexit has restored the UK to our own place at the World Trade Organization with our own vote, after years of relying on EU membership of that body. The UK is a more reliable voice for free trade there than the EU. The UK can once again offer international leadership for freer trade. Out of the EU the UK has abolished lots of tariffs and barriers to its own trade.

We can grow faster and be more prosperous outside
Much of the debate about Brexit outcomes so far has been dominated by the claim that Brexit has cost us 4% of GDP loss because it has hit our exports and damaged our productivity. This is all based on a forecast made before the vote and related to the longer term. The forecast said there would be a small shortfall in annual growth of around 0.25% compared to staying in, adding up to 4% less growth over 15 years. It is difficult to detect this in annual growth so far. Since we left our exports have performed much better than predicted and contrary to the model used for this forecast. There has been further good growth of exports with non-EU, especially in services. The forecast of slightly less growth has sometimes been misrepresented as a one off 4% reduction in our GDP which is clearly false.

Our GDP growth rate has been better than Germany's and shows no sign of a one off loss relative to the EU average. Like the EU our growth rate remains poor compared to the US. One of the big reasons for leaving was the way EU laws, taxes and energy costs were putting the EU in the slow lane, losing out badly to the US all this century to date.

The wish of some to go back to copying more EU laws and taxes and paying to be more involved in EU policies and programmes will make matters worse. We know from our experience in the EU and from the poor performance of the EU since we left that membership does not boost growth. It adds to budget stresses with extra costs and charges, and limits innovation and competitive business at a time of fast economic change.

75 great wins
This book sets out 75 Brexit wins. There are so many more available for the taking. I hope it will be widely read and referred to. I hope it will lead to a national search for all the other wins

there if we want them. I hope it will enthuse more people to see the opportunities.

Whatever governments do over laws and taxes in the short term there is one big Brexit win that is of inestimable value. The UK can now elect governments that want change and do believe in our country. Parliament does once again have full powers to be a force for the good. EU laws that hinder, taxes that damage, and policies which impede can now be swept aside.

Time for many more Brexit wins
MPs dipping into this book will be able to see they have already approved things that we could only do outside the EU. It will make them more popular if they try more of them. This book can show them the way. The UK showed the world how to be self-governing and democratic. It is time to try it for ourselves again.

The Rt Hon Sir John Redwood DPhil, FCSI
Conservative MP for Wokingham (1987 – 2024)
Government Minister incl. Secretary of State for Wales (1989 – 1995)

Preface

I am not the creator of these benefits, nor have I been even tangentially connected to any avenue or medium of government that would allow me to be such a thing.

I am an observer and an avid researcher. Someone who reads a headline, and then actually reads the article. Then reads the source material that the article refers to. Then the article on the same subject but published by the newspaper that leans the other way on the political spectrum. I know, right, shock horror. I spent years being subjected to ridicule at best, derision and hatred at worst, for making a decision that I was asked by my government and my country to make. A responsibility that I took very seriously, and one in which I deployed my efforts of research into equally seriously.

One can quite reasonably make different decisions in life on the same set of data, due to one's own outlook in life, one's own priorities and values. But what one cannot do, is deny that that data exists.

The only reason I felt compelled to bring this list into existence is because there are those who deny that the contents of this book exist. They clearly do. I present this book as Exhibit A: The evidence that tangible Brexit benefits demonstrably, and undeniably, exist.

Why I Voted to Leave the European Union

(The following text is based on that originally posted as a thread on X/Twitter in 2017, having been asked on numerous occasions at the time to defend my reasoning behind my vote to leave the EU in 2016)

Firstly - I consider myself European. I am lucky to have been able to travel to and through nearly all the countries of continental Europe. If I were to choose a foreign city to live in, it would probably be Strasbourg. I am a Francophile. I bear no ill will at all towards the rest of Europe.

Secondly - I accept a few things about the UK's relationship with the EU:

- That the UK chose to join on mostly economic reasons, in contrast to the primarily political motivations of the continent (to prevent war through interdependency)
- That the UK has always acted as a reluctant member

I make no judgement on whether it was right for the UK to keep the rest of the EU at arm's length, staying out of Schengen and the Euro. People have their opinions of course, as I do - but the fact of the matter is we will never know. As we are where we are. When it came to deciding how to vote I tried to think of the long term and not just the current status quo of remaining. The EU has made it very clear that their trajectory is an 'ever closer union'. The UK has made it very clear that it is in no way interested in that long term aspiration.

If you accept the position that the UK and EU want different things in the long term, then two things are almost guaranteed:

1. That the UK will veto things that the rest want to do
2. That the UK will suffer in some small or large part over time, from being politically tied to a bloc that it is ever increasingly not a part of

The above all led me to a simple conclusion - that leaving the EU, rightly or wrongly, is inevitable. At some point in the future a line will be crossed that the UK cannot countenance, and we will choose to leave. Once that thought had emerged, the decision was easy.

That once you accept that leaving is inevitable, then the next thoughts are:

1. Does leaving get more difficult, the longer you are in? YES
2. Does leaving after a certain point become so complex as to make it almost impossible? Probably as that is the whole point of the EU

Then it is a case, for me at least, that if it is going to happen anyway then better to do it now while it is still possible. That way the pain can be lessened and sit on my shoulders, rather than for it to happen in 10-20 years and sit on the shoulders of my children.

Now you will note that none of that is about immigration or economic policy or freedom of movement or the ECJ. I write this knowing that my opinions are far from the expectation of the stereotype, but my opinions are not unusual. They just do not fit the lazy argument typically used, that Leave voters are ignorant racists and xenophobes.

Benefits, Disbenefits and Tangibility

The call goes out, time and time again, 'can anyone give me just a single tangible benefit of Brexit'. As if the request is an impossible one to answer. As if any change can be singularly good or bad.

For example - in 2007 a smoking ban came into effect in pubs and bars across the UK. Ten years later, it was found that over 7,000 pubs had closed their doors – with the smoking ban cited by many as a primary factor in their reduced business and eventual business closure. The smoking ban is now looked upon as a net positive measure overall but denying that there were negative effects to the action would be to deny reality. With any change, there will always be positives and negatives to assess in retrospect. Benefits and disbenefits.

This book is not intended to provide a balanced picture of the pros and cons. That is not the purpose. There are plenty of mainstream commentators who have wasted many a column inch over the past nine years, extolling their perceived disbenefits of having left the EU. They have made no attempt to 'both sides' the debate. No attempt to present a reasoned and balanced viewpoint. So, neither will I.

As for the notion of tangibility. As the war cry of the remainer specifically calls for examples that are 'tangible', we need to deal with what it means to have a tangible benefit. For this I have required every benefit to pass two basic tests:

1. Is it demonstrable, rather than theoretical

2. Was it not possible, rather than not plausible

What do I mean, when I say that something was not possible rather than not plausible? Well, there is a reason that I have intentionally left out the UK Covid vaccine rollout from this book – as it was possible to do, just not remotely plausible.

The UK-EU Summit: 19th May 2025

As this book was in the final stages of review and amendment, the outcomes of the first post-Brexit UK-EU Summit were announced on May 19th, 2025. Though mostly given as an outline of an intended landing zone for multiple agreements yet to be codified let alone signed, the summit gave strong indication that several of the benefits outlined within this book could well be undermined or even removed completely subject to the final text of the agreement.

As those final terms are yet to be agreed and may well change radically as has been the case with the current UK government, I have opted to not update the contents of this book on a per-benefit basis – as those updates would purely be speculation. However, given that one of the major statements of the agreement was that the UK would 'dynamically align' with EU law as regards Sanitary and Phytosanitary (SPS) regulations, it is fair to assume that those benefits which relate to animal welfare, livestock, animal testing, gene editing and novel foods could all be at risk. With the sacrifice of UK fishing waters for a further 12 years, those benefits related to fishing are also undermined.

When former Prime Minister Harold Macmillan was asked what the greatest challenge was for a statesman, he famously replied 'Events, dear boy, events'. There is more yet to play out in the story of what has been dubbed as the 'Surrender Summit', but that will come to pass long after this book has gone to print.

The Seven Brexit Benefit Types:
An Introduction

The 75 benefits that I have detailed and evidenced within this book, have been broken out into seven broad categories as an aid to navigating the vast amount of information included within. These seven categories are as follows:

1. Brexit Has Saved Us Billions in EU Fees and Membership Costs

For those benefits where the UK has avoided or removed a fee, levy, contribution or cost directly associated with the former terms of our membership – including those that have been introduced since we left but would have been subject to had we not

2. Brexit Has Returned Our Independence in Fishing, Farming, Animal Welfare and the Environment

These benefits all directly relate to changes made within the UK since leaving, that were unable to be done independently from within the EU, in relation to the UK's fishing and agriculture sectors alongside environmental and animal welfare concerns

3. Brexit Means Better Trade

This section focuses on the 'Global Britain' concept of the UK being able to conduct trade on the international stage in a freer, faster, cheaper and fairer manner from outside of the EU, rather than battling with protectionist tendencies from within it

4. Brexit Means We Run Our Own Country Again

This section focuses on the return of sovereign power to implement laws and regulations within the UK that better suit the nation, as well as examples of where leaving the EU has enabled the UK to be a demonstrably more democratic nation

5. Brexit Means a Better Economy

There are many areas within the financial services sector and wider economic policy and approach, where the UK as a global capital of finance can operate better and quicker from outside of the EU - this section focuses on those benefits

6. Brexit Means We Control Our Own Borders

For good or bad, the UK is now fully in control of its own borders – and any issues that arise are now the responsibility and burden of the UK Government to resolve, and their cross to bear if their decisions lead to praise or pressure

7. Brexit Has Strengthened Our Defences and World Standing

This final section focuses on the false premise that the UK's standing in the world would be diminished by leaving the EU, when the evidence shows that what has happened has been the opposite

Quick Reference List

1. **Trade:** All the EU's trade deals without having to pay for them
2. **CBAM:** UK gets all revenue instead of 25%, and can adjust at will
3. **Covid Recovery:** UK cost would have been over €90 Billion
4. **EU Plastics Levy:** Over €1 Billion a year saved from EU coffers
5. **Core EU Budget:** €14-16 Billion in a year in contributions saved
6. **EU Expansion:** 21% increase in budget contributions avoided
7. **Customs Duty:** UK keeps 100% not 20% - Billions extra per year
8. **Cheaper Food:** UK now has the cheapest bananas in Europe
9. **Cheaper Wine:** Removed expensive and pointless packaging regulations
10. **Education:** EU Erasmus+ scheme is much worse for UK students than Turing
11. **Science Research:** Horizon losses now limited in relation to contributions
12. **Motor Insurance:** Repealed ridiculous ECJ lawnmower insurance decision
13. **Bureaucracy:** Ending the additional costs of European Parliament elections
14. **Wildlife:** Can ban sand eel fishing in the North Sea, for environmental gain
15. **Animal Testing:** Removal of cosmetics testing loopholes
16. **Livestock:** Banning live animal exports for slaughter or fattening
17. **Marine Life:** Tougher rules on preventing vile shark fin trade
18. **Fur Trading:** Can ban the sale of animal furs in the UK
19. **Fishing Industry:** Overall improvement of fishing quotas and opportunities
20. **Animal Sentience:** Stronger welfare measures for all animals
21. **Agriculture:** Replaced the despised Common Agricultural Policy
22. **Microplastics:** Banned the sale of wet wipes made with plastic fibres
23. **Animal Cruelty:** Can finally ban the sale of traditionally produced Foie Gras
24. **Pet Smuggling:** Can halt the illegal EU pet breeding and smuggling gangs
25. **Trade Links:** New trade agreements that the EU were unable to secure
26. **Trade Influence:** UK retook seat at the WTO, abolished nuisance and pointless tariffs

27. **Trade:** More trade with our Commonwealth allies trade delivered by tariff cuts
28. **Stock Exchange:** London can trade in Swiss equities again
29. **Trade Deals:** Full competency over international agreements, so better deals
30. **Trade Leadership:** Negotiated removal of hundreds of non-tariff barriers
31. **Haulage:** Allowing longer trucks making haulage more efficient
32. **Aid Through Trade:** Introduced new Developing Countries Trading Scheme
33. **AVRS:** Binding advance rulings on import costs and valuations
34. **US Trade:** UK better dealing with new US administration directly
35. **Financial Markets:** Removed limits on size of dark pool trades in stock market
36. **Digitalisation:** Fully digital goods shipment transaction enabled
37. **Shipping:** Removed the 'Rotterdam Effect'
38. **Digitalisation:** Introduced digital trade documentation, saving UK businesses
39. **Trade Facilitation:** A net lower level of combined trade barriers across the world
40. **Tariffs:** Targeted temporary tariff removal at business request
41. **Art Resale:** Artist royalties for UK art resale over a certain value in Australia
42. **Sovereignty:** Full sovereign control over UK laws within Parliament
43. **Motoring:** No mandatory rollout of driver intervention and assistance tech
44. **Medicines:** Better regulatory environment for drug innovation
45. **VAT:** Removal of VAT on green energy products and female sanitary goods
46. **Petitions:** Government regained the authority to action public petitions
47. **Transparency:** EU reduced business ownership transparency, UK did not
48. **Labour Manifesto:** Adding VAT on private school fees possible
49. **Democracy:** Increase of democratic legitimacy in British system of government
50. **AI:** Avoid damaging and overbearing EU restrictions and regulations
51. **Motoring:** Scrapped extra licence required to drive with a trailer
52. **Football:** Avoid ECJ judgements on legality of Super League

53. **Novel Foods:** More scope for food innovation outside of the EU
54. **Competition:** UK Markets Authority can make UK-centric decisions
55. **Procurement:** Better public procurement rules to benefit British businesses
56. **Critical Industries:** UK can use golden shares again, to protect British interests
57. **Payments:** Can use cards for contactless payments without EU limit
58. **Finance:** Can abolish commodity trading limits further growing the financial services industry
59. **Salaries:** Ending freedom of movement boosted wages e.g. for hauliers
60. **State Aid Options:** UK can flex state aid rules to back investment
61. **Welfare:** Equalised access to welfare instead of better terms for EU citizens
62. **State Aid:** Quicker and more flexible decisions for smaller subsidies
63. **Banking:** Removal of bonus cap on pay, meaning more tax revenue
64. **Immigration:** Removal of biased preferential treatment of EU migrants
65. **Immigration Security:** Easier to keep EU criminals out without freedom of movement
66. **Immigration Options:** Full control to implement and adapt meritocratic migration system
67. **Freeports:** Total freedom to rollout full-throated freeports across the UK
68. **Border Checks:** Remove need to accept easily forged EU identity cards
69. **CPTPP:** Joined trade deal in the fastest growing part of the world
70. **Services:** Top ranking for UK in OECD Services Trade Restrictiveness Index
71. **Ukraine:** Allowed faster response on trade and tariffs to help Ukraine
72. **Soft Power:** Top global rankings in global soft power index
73. **Defence:** UK more advanced in intelligence/ security not held back by EU
74. **AUKUS:** Deeper partnership with the USA and Australia
75. **Defence:** Bleeding edge military innovations in the field years earlier

Section 1

Brexit Has Saved Us Billions in EU Fees and Membership Costs

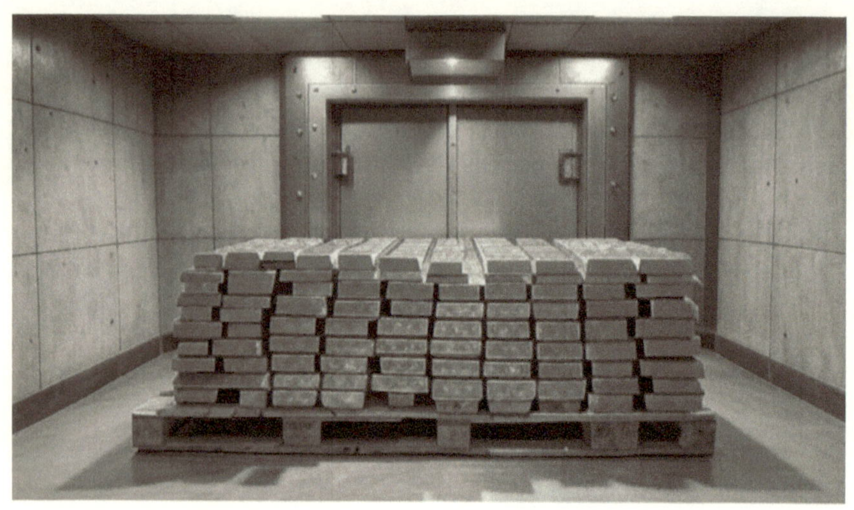

1. Same-Same, But Different

The UK left the EU with fundamentally the same trade deals with non-EU countries available to it as it had as an EU member, but without having to pay an annual membership fee to have access to them - and with full legislative control to renegotiate them in the future should they wish to.

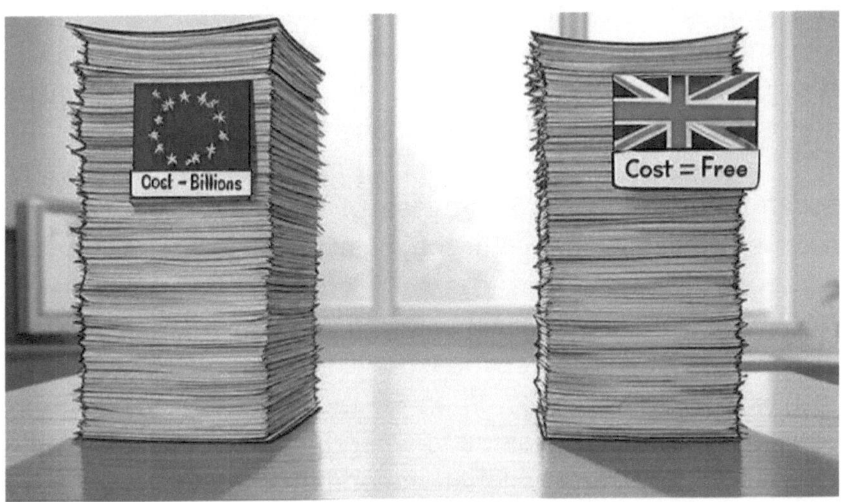

EU membership requires the delegation of many sovereign powers away from national governments, one of which is the ability to negotiate international trade agreements.[1] Being in a customs union requires centralised control of trade policy, as all members must control border crossings of goods in the exact same way, charging the same tariffs for the customs union to work.[2] A customs union is essentially a single policy wall surrounding the entire membership, with the same rules in place for crossing the wall – irrespective of where you happen to cross it.

The UK's membership of the EU Customs Union (EUCU) was as a member of the EU, and so when the UK left the EU, it also left the EUCU as a necessary consequence. From a UK perspective, the membership of the customs union and the access to EU negotiated trade deals – taking advantage of the size and heft of the EU to secure better terms – was often used as one of the major selling points of EU membership and one of the benefits worth paying for through the budget contributions.

At the point of leaving the EU in 2020, there were 45 free trade agreements or FTAs recognised by the WTO as having been notified to them as being agreed and in place (though worth noting at this stage that the WTO refers to them as Regional Trade Agreements or RTAs). Of those 45, 43 were seen to still be active / not suspended by one of the parties to the agreement.[3] The EU Single Market is itself an FTA/RTA, so this is the 46th agreement in place, which shows against EU member states within the WTO's RTA database.[4]

At the point of commencing Brexit preparations, the UK government instigated a process of trade continuity, which involved discussions with the signatories of all EU trade agreements, to attempt to secure continuity of those same trade agreements on the same terms, but with just the UK. This was seen to be a stop-gap measure to smooth the transition, as the UK was still considered an EU member until the point at which its membership came to an end, so was not legally able to conduct any trade negotiations or agree any terms different to those agreed centrally by the EU.[5] This meant that it was not possible for the UK to negotiate any different terms with those countries, until after the departure was complete. It was also of course not realistic to renegotiate that volume of trade agreements within the available time.

At the time of writing this (May 2025), the only active EU FTAs in place in 2020 that had not been either replicated or replaced by other means were those with Bosnia, Montenegro and Algeria – this means that the UK was able to take advantage of the same trade deals on the same terms, but without the membership cost for being within the EU.[6] There are few as easily demonstrable benefits, as getting the same thing you used to pay for but now getting it for free.

The first UK Trade Minister in the Brexit era, Sir Liam Fox, was routinely mocked and derided by those campaigning against leaving the EU, for his confidence in being able to replace the EU's trade deals prior to leaving. This mockery and derision has in the fullness of time been proven to be undeserved, and history now shows his confidence to have been well placed.

It is also worth noting that, as part of the replication of these deals, the UK agreed to what was seen to be its historical share of quotas agreed within the original EU texts. For example, if an EU FTA allowed for 1000 tonnes of a particular good to be exported to the EU on a lower tariff before a higher tariff would apply, and the UK historically saw 100 tonnes of that annual import, then the UK agreed as part of the replication to continue to allow 100 tonnes per year at the lower tariff. From the FTA partner perspective, the other country the UK agreed the deal with, this was a great win – as for them the EU deal doesn't change and so still includes 1000 tonnes of lower tariff quota, but they get an additional 100 tonnes with the UK. So, with the replication of EU trade deals on fundamentally identical terms, the EU was the only party to really come out of the endeavour with worse terms.

2. Emission Impossible

The UK Carbon Border Adjustment Mechanism (CBAM) is better catered to the UK economy than the EU version that preceded it. 100% of the revenue generated by it will be spent on the priorities of the British Government, instead of 75% going on EU debt repayments.

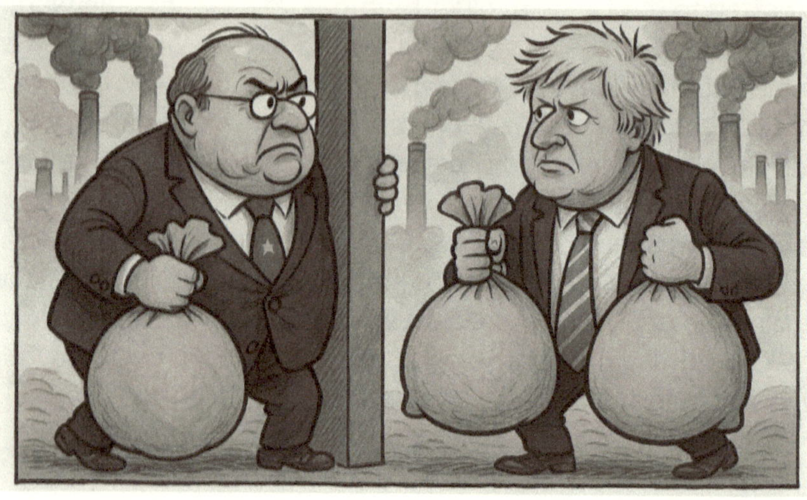

The EU operates an Emissions Trading Scheme (EU ETS), where domestic producers of carbon-intensive goods (goods that produce a large amount of carbon emissions as a by-product of their manufacture) must purchase vouchers in order to offset the amount of carbon emissions they produce, over and above an allocated allowance which reduces over time. This scheme, though well intentioned, only affects domestic producers (those within the EU) - so they become uncompetitive when compared to non-EU producers that do not have such taxation burdens. This means that businesses or consumers look overseas for cheaper imports, and in some cases 'greenwash' their business by moving their production overseas where their carbon emissions are not considered to be a problem.

The EU Carbon Border Adjustment Mechanism (EU CBAM) is a scheme designed to ensure that those domestic producers are not undercut by producers overseas, by requiring importers to be aware of the carbon emitted by the producers in the exporting nation, and making the importer pay the same cost as a domestic producer would face for those emissions on a per tonne basis.

The EU CBAM is being implemented by the EU as a new source of budgetary revenue, so-called 'EU own resources', with 75% of the total revenue from CBAM each year going toward the EU budget - and only the remaining 25% going to the member states.[7] The exact method by which the EU will divide the 25% between the member states has not been explicitly outlined at this time.

Meanwhile the UK is implementing its own Carbon Border Adjustment Mechanism (UK CBAM), to accompany its own Emissions Trading Scheme. However, the UK scheme will be subtly different in terms of impacted sectors, designed to better suit the UK economy as opposed to the wider EU economy. The real benefit however is that 100% of the revenue will go to the UK government to spend as it sees fit.

The UK scheme will commence in January 2027 and is expected to bring in up to £1.8 Billion in annual revenue.[8] Assuming a similar annual yield for the EU scheme would mean that nearly £1.5 Billion a year more revenue is being retained for spending in the UK instead of going on EU schemes and EU debt repayment. This is without mentioning the revenue from the EU Emissions Trading Scheme, which similarly has a proportion siphoned off from the member states to go toward EU projects.[9]

The UK gets to benefit from 100% of revenue from both the ETS and CBAM schemes, which it would not be able to do if it were still within the EU.

3. The Bill Comes Due. Always.

By leaving the EU, the UK has avoided being used as a guarantor for ever-growing EU debts for Covid regeneration loans and the purchasing of defence equipment, and having the EU cap on member budget contributions increase by two-thirds up to a maximum of 2% of annual Gross National Income (GNI).

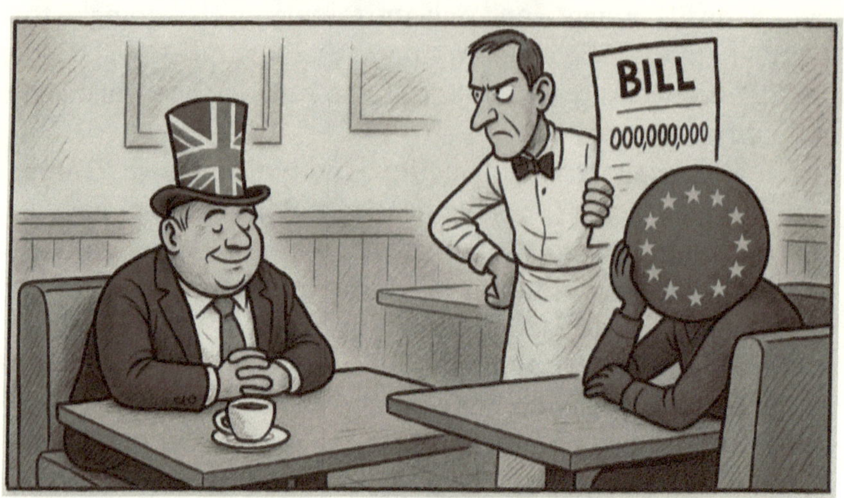

During the Covid pandemic, the EU27 took the collective and highly controversial step to allow the EU to take on its own debt and allowed borrowing of up to €800 Billion to be made through the issuing of EU bonds, to provide member states with grants and loans to help cover the impact of having fought the pandemic.[10] This debt is effectively given with the member states as guarantors, and the net contributors having to cover any funds not paid in time by the net recipients.

The NextGenerationEU (NGEU) programme was initially intended to be a €750 Billion recovery package but was later adjusted upward to €800 Billion in current prices. The €800 Billion was carved up into two separate pots, that member states could apply for:

Pot 1: €421 Billion in grants - these would not have to be paid back by the member state, but instead paid collectively by the

EU through the budget, which in turn is funded by all member states

Pot 2: €379 Billion in loans - these would be paid back by the member state directly, with the EU effectively passing on the bill for the loan when it receives it, for the member state to then be responsible for paying

To be able to guarantee the security of repayment on the issuance of these loans, the EU collectively agreed to increase the ceiling on how much of the EU's Gross National Income (GNI) it could demand in budgetary contributions, by 0.8 percentage points (from 1.2% of GNI to 2.0%). This quite literally uses the national incomes of the wealthier member states as guarantors for debts taken on by all 27 member states.[11]

The EU intends to introduce new 'own resources' mechanisms to increase revenue, to start paying back this debt - and the debts come due from 2027 until 2058. If those new revenue streams are unable to be agreed and put in place, then it is the net contributing member states who will see their budget contributions each year increase to foot the bill.

The UK would have effectively been on the hook for 12% of this debt, as its share of the EU budget – around €90 Billion.

In March of 2025, the EU announced the intent to issue additional collective debt, to finance loans for expanding defence spending. The proposals included allowing up to €150 Billion of collective debt, using the same mechanisms allowed for in the NGEU programme. Again, this debt is ultimately underwritten by the economies of the wealthier member states, who would ultimately be responsible for their repayment.[12]

Between the NGEU and ReArm Europe Plan, that would be almost €1 Trillion of collective debt, that the UK was ultimately the guarantor of around 12% of, were it not for having left the EU.

4. Plastic Fantastic

The EU introduced another source of funds to top-up their budget, over and above core contributions. This source of funds is based on the amount of plastic produced by a member state and not recycled but does not go towards combatting non-recycled plastics. This money is better off staying in the UK.

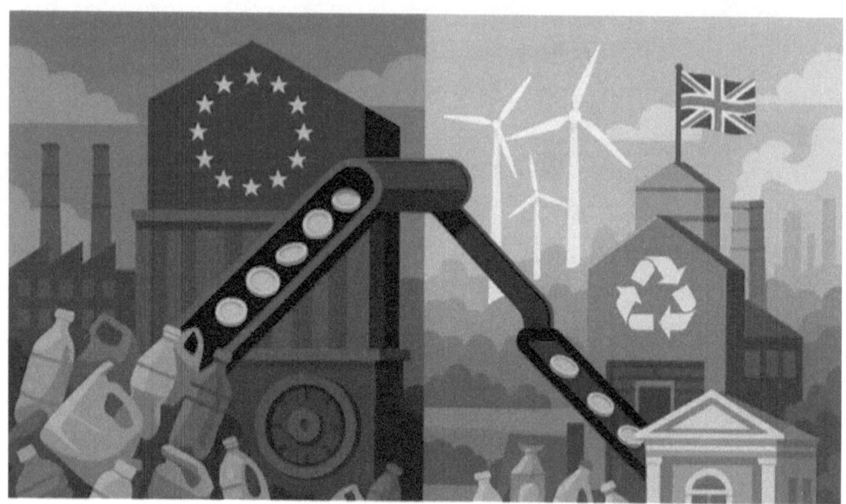

In January 2021, the EU introduced a new source of funds for financing the ever-growing EU budget, in the form of an annual fee to be paid by all member states. This fee was to be paid for plastic packaging estimated to have been created / manufactured within the member state but not recycled, at a rate of €0.80 for every kilogram of waste.[13]

In 2021, the UK is estimated to have produced around 2.5 Million tonnes of plastic packaging - with 1.4 Million tonnes believed to have not been recycled.[14] So were the UK to still be a member of the EU, this would have meant that for 2021 the UK would have had to contribute an additional €1.12 Billion to the EU budget, on top of its core contributions.

Your initial reaction to this may well be 'well, I want the UK to produce less plastic waste, so surely this additional cost is a good thing'. Except this money is not going towards any incentives to reduce plastic waste, or to increase consumer awareness, or anything else for that matter that could be seen to contribute to the efforts to reduce overall plastic waste production. If that were the case, then it could be argued that the additional contribution had some sort of intrinsic value. These funds however simply went straight into the EU coffers, to be spent on whatever the EU wished to spend it on.

Data on plastic packaging waste is published with a two-year delay, so we only have data for 2021-2023 at the time of writing – but for these three years combined, the UK would have paid the EU an extra €2.9 Billion.

5. It's All About the Benjamins, Baby!

The UK as an EU member would be giving in the region of €24 Billion a year to the EU just in core budget contributions. Though about a third of that got spent within the UK, it was on EU priority projects, not UK priorities. From outside the EU, the UK gets to decide what to spend that money on

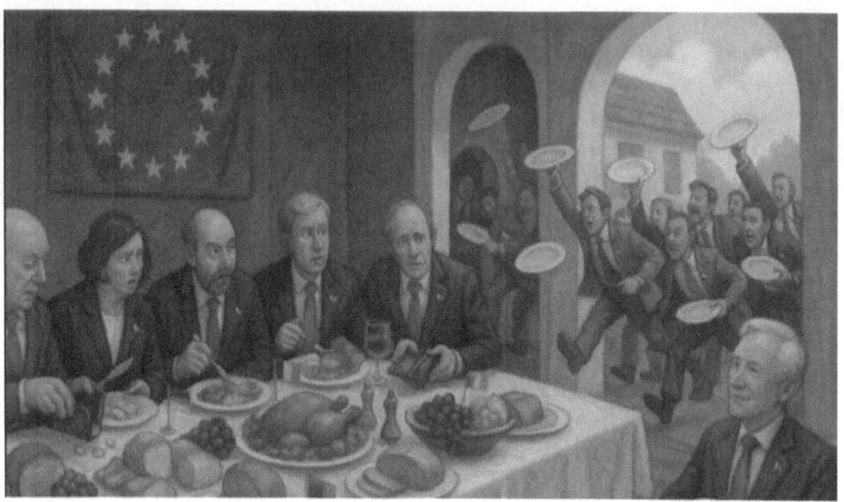

As one of the larger economies of the EU (second largest by GDP, third largest by population in 2016), the UK was also one of the largest net contributors to the core EU budget – which means that it would contribute more to the EU budget each year than it would receive back in expenditure by the EU within the UK.

The UK was responsible for roughly 11.5 – 12.5% of the annual core budget of the EU, which in 2024 was €189 Billion - which would in turn have resulted in a gross contribution from the UK of around €24 Billion, were it still to be a member.[15] This figure would have been higher though had the UK still been a member, as there would have been the additional spend within the UK as well. Working from previous ratios of gross and net contributions, and assuming an annual gross contribution of €24 Billion (which as we've already said would have been higher), the UK would have had a net contribution each year in this budgetary period of at least €14-16 Billion.

From outside of the EU, the UK government not only gets to decide, in line with the wishes of the UK electorate, where €8 Billion of UK contributions gets to be spent – but also has an additional €14-16 Billion to allocate to the priorities of the electorate as well. These figures do not include the billions of additional financial commitments to the EU foreign aid programme or other EU projects that were billed to the UK separately.

6. The More the Merrier?

There are nine additional European countries lined up to join the EU in the coming decade – all of whom would be net recipients (would be given more money than they contribute). This is estimated by the EU to require a 21% increase in the overall EU budget. The UK doesn't have to stomach this massive cost thanks to Brexit.

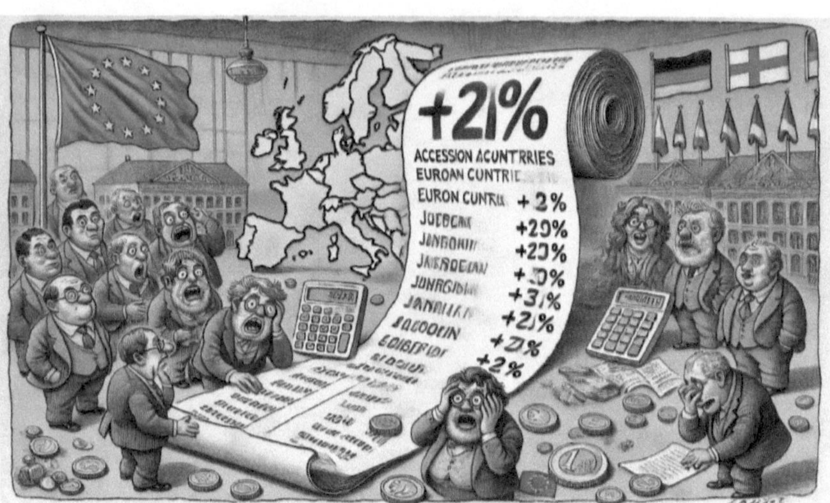

In October 2023 an internal EU report was leaked to the Financial Times, regarding the budgetary and cost implications of nine new countries acceding to the EU. This report found, as reported by the Financial Times (FT), that the EU annual budget would have to increase by 21% to accommodate these nine countries, who would all be net recipients (would get out more than they put in).[16]

As the leaked paper reportedly states, 'all member states will have to pay more to and receive less from the EU budget'. The UK would of course not have been spared from this calculation, making EU membership more costly and of less value in one fell swoop.

As covered in the previous benefit, the UK annual budgetary contribution would have already reached the region of €24 Billion a year by 2024 - so a 21% increase in the overall EU budget would see this balloon to nearly €30 Billion before taking into account any year-on-year increases, let alone any recalculation of the total percentage of EU budget that the UK would be expected to follow - which would also need to increase under this scenario. That's a further €5+ Billion a year of post-expansion budget contributions, that the UK can rest easy knowing it has completely avoided.

7. Removing the Lion, Keeping the Lion's Share

The EU kept 80% of customs tariffs collected at the UK's borders, as it considers tariffs to be its 'own resources' to spend as it sees fit. Outside of the EU, the UK can keep 100% of that revenue and allocate it to the priorities of the British electorate instead of the whims of the EU.

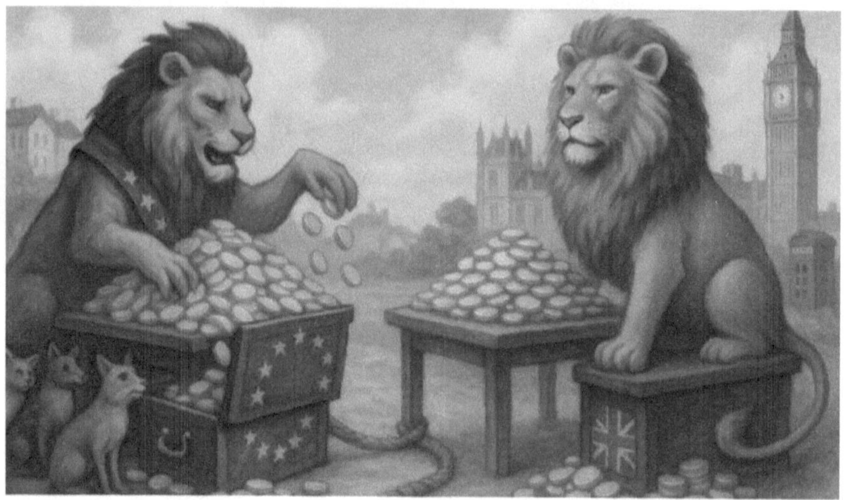

In one version of Aesop's Fable 'The Lion's Share', the lion would hunt with the wolf, fox and jackal – and would keep 75% of the spoils to himself. When it comes to the revenue from imports into the EU Customs Union, the EU behaves in much the same way as the lion in the story.

When it was still a member of the EU, the UK would pay – in addition to the core budget contributions mentioned earlier in this book – 80% of the revenue gained from the charging of import tariffs from international partners, straight into the EU's coffers.[17] The EU considers this to be one of the four 'own revenue' streams and uses it to bolster the EU budget over and above that paid in by member states as a percentage of their relative Gross National Income (GNI). With the UK having left the EU, the UK's Revenue and Customs service (HMRC) now keeps 100% of the revenue at the border, going toward paying for public services within the UK instead of wherever the EU deemed suitable for spending the money. To quote Simon Sutcliffe, a partner at the Blick Rothenberg tax and accountancy advisory firm, 'Pre-Brexit much of the Customs Duty collected by HMRC would have been sent to the EU Commission as part of our EU membership responsibilities. However, this revenue now stays in the UK and goes directly to the Treasury.'[18]

In the ten years before the UK left the EU, annual customs revenue at the UK borders varied between £2-3 Billion – and the UK HMRC got to keep 20% of it. Now outside of the EU, customs revenue in 2022/23 was £5.5 Billion, and 100% of that went to HMRC for use on UK public services.[19]

Note: In the next Multiannual Financial Framework (MFF) after the UK departed – 2021 to 2027, the EU reduced the amount of customs duty that the EU would keep, from 80% down to 75%.[20]

8. Banana-Rama

Brits are one of the biggest consumers of bananas in the world – and consume over five Billion a year. The EU agreed to artificially uphold prices, to protect former French and Belgian colonies from fair competition. From outside the EU, the UK now has the lowest retail prices for bananas in the whole of Europe.

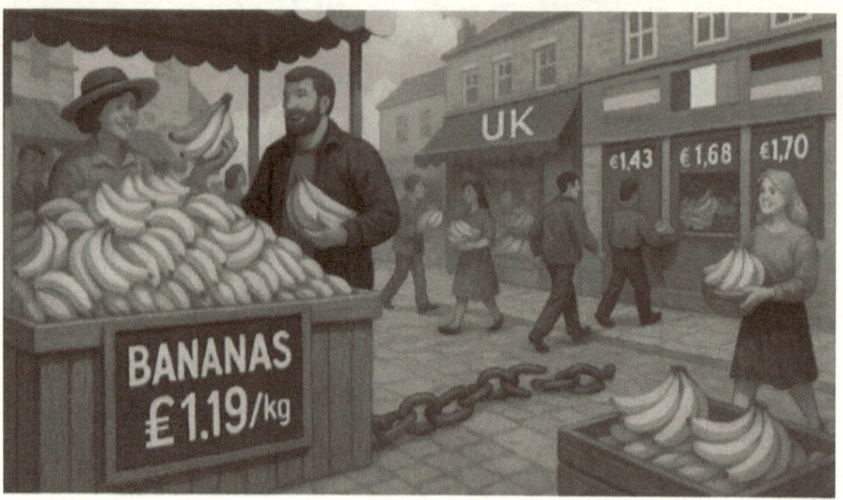

In 2019, the European Union agreed to not cut tariffs imposed on large producers of bananas, to shield the smaller producers in the French and Belgian colonial nations in sub-Saharan Africa from any increase in competition.[21] Being an EU agreement, the UK is no longer bound by this - and as part of its FTA review with the Andean Community (Peru, Colombia and Ecuador) is looking again at the banana tariffs put in place by the EU that the UK rolled over. In addition to this, banana tariff concessions have also been made to both Mexico and Peru as part of the accession negotiations to join the CPTPP.[22]

An investigation for the online news outlet loveMONEY in April 2025, found that the UK has the lowest prices for bananas in the whole of Europe, at just £1.19 per kilo on average. Compare this to Germany (£1.31), Spain (£1.43), Ireland

(£1.54), France (£1.68) and Belgium (£1.70). In 2024, the UK consumed roughly five Billion bananas – if those were purchased at Belgian prices instead of post-Brexit UK prices, then consumers would have spent over £500 Million more in 2024 on bananas for the same amount of product.[23]

These opportunities to reduce the consumer price of the UK's favourite fruit, are only able to be progressed due to the UK's departure from the EU.

9. I Have a Semillon

The UK has been able to change multiple areas of legislation around the sale and packaging of wine since it left the EU, which have both reduced the retail cost for consumers, and increased the range of products able to be sold outside of outdated measures and sizes no longer fitting consumer needs and trends.

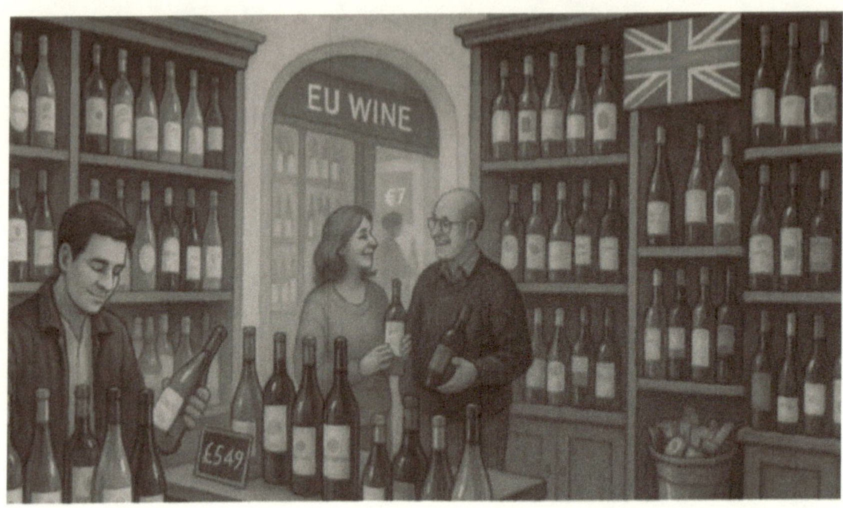

In January 2023, as part of a wider effort to reduce the volume of superfluous EU regulations from the UK statute book, the UK Government announced that it would remove the need for bottles of sparkling wine to have a foil sheath 'completely covering the stopper and all or part of the neck' of the bottle – as had been replicated from Article 57(1)(a) of Commission Delegated Regulation (EU) 2019/33.[24]

Though the foil sheath has been claimed in the past to be there from a security perspective – to ensure that the bottle had not been tampered with by people or rodents – the actual use in modern times is purely aesthetic. So, to have regulations requiring the additional cost and wastage is no longer necessary. The EU Parliament itself stated in 2020 that 'The foil does not have any other functional characteristics and is usually removed and thrown away immediately prior to consumption of the wine'.[25] The action of adding a foil sheath onto a bottle is estimated to add as much as 50p onto the retail price for the consumer – so as much as 10% of the retail price in the UK (though this of course varies with the price of the sparkling wine being purchased).

The changes to remove the legal requirement for both mushroom-shaped stoppers and foil covers on bottlenecks, came into effect on 1st January 2024. Alongside these changes, the UK government also removed restrictions that prevented the sale of a low-alcohol wine type known as Piquette; simplified labelling requirements to remove the need for an importer address to be added; and allowed wine to be sold in three other measures.[26] The Environment Secretary, Steve Barclay, was quoted as saying that 'Our departure from the EU gives us the opportunity to review and scrap outdated and burdensome rules that have been holding back our wine sector'.[27]

10. Get Them While They're Young

The Erasmus / Erasmus+ student exchange programme was heavily skewed to benefitting students from other EU member states over those from the UK and was ideologically intended to overwrite national identity with European identity. The UK Turing scheme is by every measure better for UK students and taxpayers.

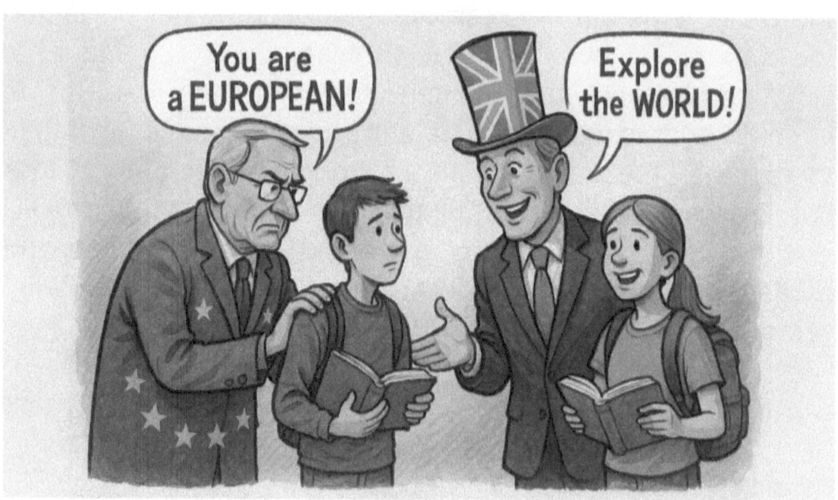

The Erasmus/Erasmus+ student exchange programme was established in 1987, and was considered a flagship EEC programme to demonstrate ways in which the EU could harmonise diverse groups, and foster within the youth of Europe a notion of shared identity of 'European Citizens' under the banner of the European Economic Community (The EEC was the predecessor to the European Union - it rebranded partially in 1993 and fully in 2009). It was part of the European Community's broader aims to push for full integration, and was seen as a key tool for using educational establishments to create a generation of students who would see themselves as citizens of 'Europe' more than citizens of their respective nations - setting the stage for 'ever closer union' in the decades to come.

As the foremost academic destination of Europe (three UK universities are in the global top ten, the EU only has six in the top 50, all ranked 26-50), the UK was one of the most attractive for EU students to apply for.[28] As such the UK's involvement in the Erasmus+ scheme was always overly in the interests of the other EU member states. At the point of exiting the EU, the UK is estimated to have hosted twice as many EU students as the number of UK students being hosted by the other 27 EU member states.[29] Why of course would this be a problem? Well as part of the Erasmus+ scheme, the host nation waived the tuition costs for the students being hosted - so if the deal was not reciprocal, then it would cost more than it would deliver. In the final year of UK participation, 2020, the UK contributed £128 Million into the Erasmus+ scheme, but it also lost an estimated £200 Million in waived tuition fees.

Post-Brexit, the UK has implemented the Turing scheme to replace the one-sided Erasmus+ scheme. This scheme focuses solely on benefiting the students of the UK and expanded its remit to also cover not only higher education, but also further education and vocational training. The Turing scheme covers overseas education in over 130 countries against the 33 offered by Erasmus+ and offers almost identical funding models - without having the larger burden and impact of waiving the tuition fees of twice as many EU students.

Ultimately the Erasmus+ scheme had to be replaced, as one of its fundamental reasons for existence was to help indoctrinate those who took part that they should consider themselves EU citizens first and UK citizens second. Thankfully this was able to be achieved with the Turing scheme, which not only replaces Erasmus+ but is better for those UK students taking part.

11. Bring Me the Horizon

The UK's post-Brexit membership of the Horizon Europe scheme has a unique ratchet clause within it, that allows the UK to claw back budget contributions if the UK doesn't get a fair share of spending from the scheme. No EU member has this ability, so the UK deal is demonstrably better.

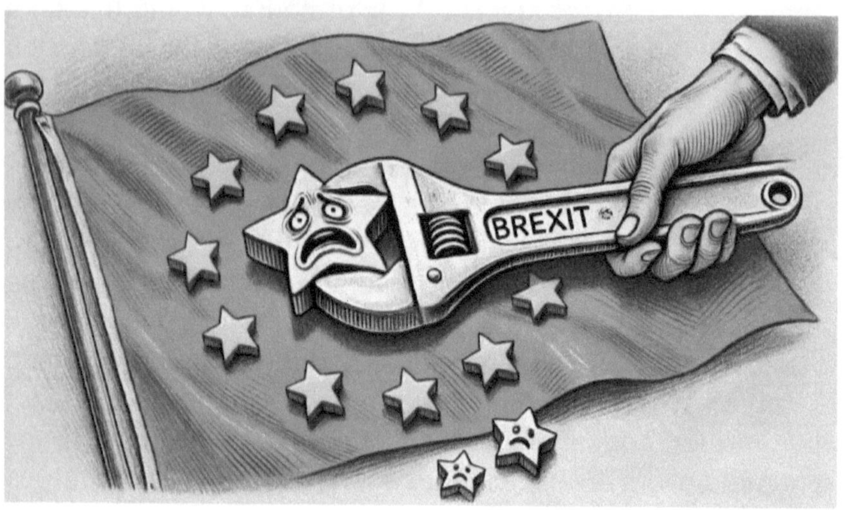

Horizon Europe is the ninth incarnation of the EUs seven-yearly research and innovation programme, which the UK actively took part in as an EU member until the UK left the EU in 2021. The terms of departure included a draft agreement to regain associated membership of these framework programmes, but this was unable to be concluded and resolved until 2023, with membership recommencing in January 2024.

The UK traditionally paid around 15% of the seven-year Horizon budget, which for the years 2021-2027 was €97 Billion. As part of the negotiations for re-entry into the EU's research framework programmes, the UK secured a condition that the UK funding would ensure a fair share of the budget being spent in the UK - and the ability to 'claw back' funding if that was found to not be the case. This unique underperformance clause allows automatic compensation if UK awards fall 16% below contributions, providing a level of financial protection not provided to EU member states.[30]

These terms are not available to EU members, who contribute without such guarantees of returns. So, the Horizon Europe terms that the UK was able to secure from a financial perspective, are better than those for EU members themselves.

12. Quads Out, Quids In

A ruling in the European Court of Justice in 2014 decided that all motor vehicles on private land would need to be covered by motor insurance, despite not being for use on public roads. This requirement was expected to increase insurance premiums by £1 Billion a year – that's an extra £50 on every single driver's car insurance.

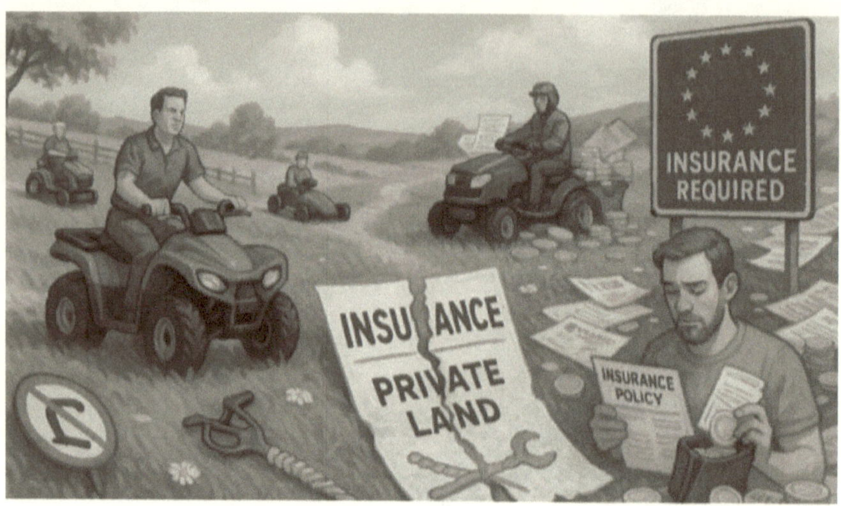

In 2014 the European Court of Justice (CJEU or ECJ) made a ruling on a Slovenian case, of a person injured by a vehicle on private land, which meant that by EU law all vehicles used on private land would need to be covered by motor vehicle insurance.[31] This ruling had wide-sweeping implications both for the insurance industry and for the public, as vehicles previously sitting well outside of motor insurance requirements would then be considered as requiring it, such as ride-on lawnmowers, quad bikes, motorsport vehicles and many other agricultural vehicles not intended for public road use.[32]

By leaving the EU, the UK Government was able to introduce primary legislation to remove the impact of this ruling from the UK statute books and return UK motor insurance laws to the way in which they were intended to operate. If left unaddressed, the ECJ ruling was projected to increase overall motor insurance annual costs by over £1 Billion a year, which would have seen consumer premiums increase by on average £50 each per year – as well as those who own motor vehicles for use on private land having to also take out an additional insurance package and the costs that that entails.[33]

When the primary legislation to remove the requirement was discussed in the House of Lords in March 2022, the Baroness Vere stated that 'if Vnuk had been implemented in full, it would have had a catastrophic impact on the motorsports industry', and that adding a motor insurance requirement to the industry would have 'brought little benefit at a very high cost' estimated at around £458 Million per year. She went on to say that this would have been 'prohibitively expensive' for the sector, effectively making most of the sector unviable. At the time of the debate in 2022, the motorsport industry in the UK turned over almost £3 Billion a year and generated full-time employment for around 38,000 people and part-time work for a further 100,000 people.[34]

In short, leaving the EU saves all British motorists around £50 a year, along with saving millions of Brits the cost of one or more additional motor insurance premiums, each and every year – and that's before calculating the increase due to inflation.

13. Less is More

Elections cost a lot of money to undertake, especially on a per voter perspective when the participation levels are very low as was the case for EU Parliament elections. Removing this additional and unnecessary level of bureaucracy saves the taxpayer in the region of £150 Million.

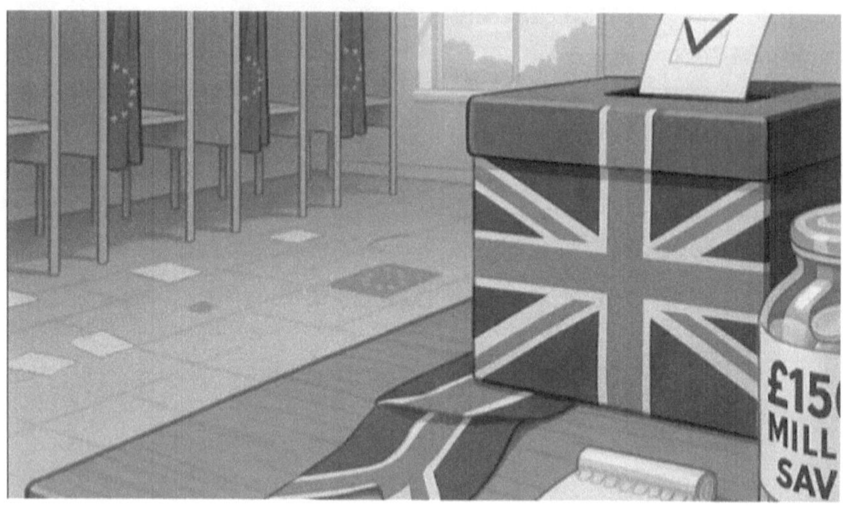

In June 2024 all EU member states undertook fresh elections for MEPs to sit in the EU Parliament. The last time this exercise was undertaken in the UK in 2019, it cost the UK taxpayer nearly £150 Million. With a supposed UK population of 66.84 Million in 2019, and the UK's allocation of 73 MEPs, that meant each single MEP represented some 900,000 people.

By leaving the EU, this additional and costly level of unnecessary bureaucracy is not only removed, but the repeated cost of running the elections every five years for those MEP positions is also removed.

Section 2

Brexit Has Returned Our Independence in Fishing, Farming, Animal Welfare and The Environment

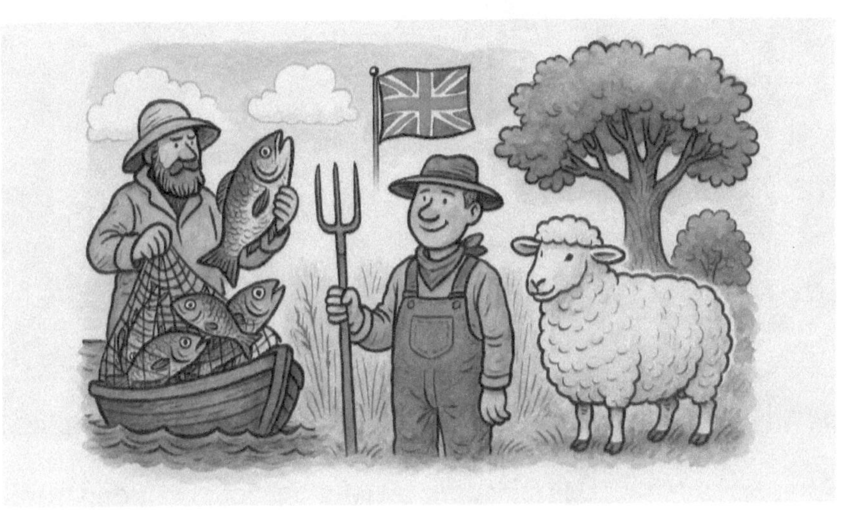

14. Huffin and Puffin

Regaining full control of both the UK statute book and the UK's territorial waters, allowed the UK and Scottish governments to implement a ban on the fishing of sandeels within the North Sea – the primary food source for beloved iconic British seabirds such as puffins, kittiwakes and razorbills.

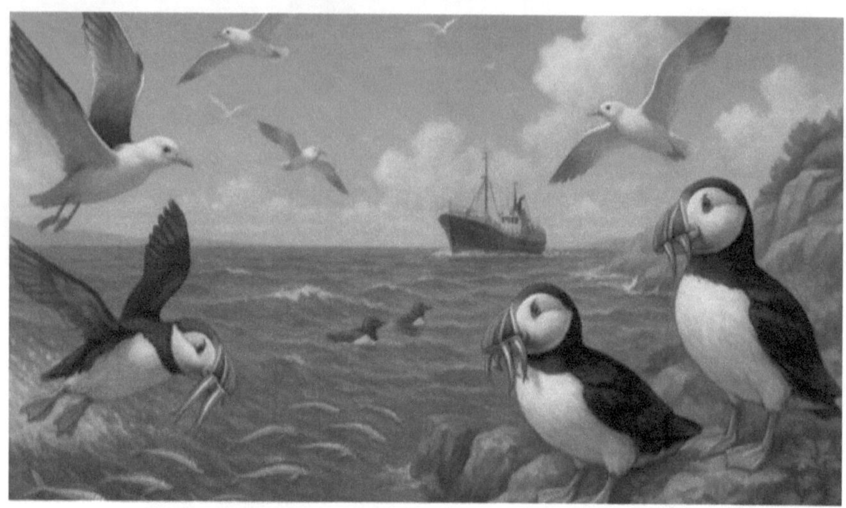

After decades of campaigning by wildlife activist groups and organisations like the Royal Society for the Protection of Birds (RSPB), the UK implemented a ban in early 2024 on the industrial fishing of sandeels in specific areas of UK waters like Dogger Bank in the North Sea.[36] This ban was to protect endangered seabirds such as puffins, kittiwakes and razorbills, for whom the sandeels are a major part of their diet (some reports state that a puffin's diet is almost wholly dependent on them). The RSPB have been campaigning for decades against the overfishing of sandeels, believing that the vastly depleted sandeel populations had directly resulted in a 'devastating knock-on effect on [seabird populations]'.[37]

The overfishing in UK waters was predominantly conducted by EU member Denmark, who caught in the region of 250,000 tonnes of sandeels in UK waters each year - the destination ultimately being the production of fish oil and fish meal.[38] As outlined in an article from Politico, 'the policies help illustrate the flexibility the UK has outside the EU on matters which would have previously been subject to lengthy negotiation under the Commons Fisheries Policy — and which Brussels and member states are outright hostile to for their own reasons.' [39]

Not only is this change only possible due to the UK regaining control of its waters through Brexit, but the changes have also resulted in the EU raising a formal dispute as it wishes the ban to be lifted, claiming that it is a breach of the EU-UK Trade and Cooperation Agreement (TCA). To quote Ariel Brunner, the director of BirdLife Europe - 'The EU's decision to challenge such a positive measure is simply shameful. The European Commission is seeking to prevent the UK from taking urgently needed action which the EU itself should have taken long ago'. [40] Irrespective of the complaint from the EU regarding the UK's actions, the power to implement such changes now lies in the hands of the UK Parliament, and not with the EU - and this power transfer is a direct and positive result of Brexit.

On 28th April 2025 the Permanent Court of Arbitration ruled predominantly in favour of the UK position – that it was legally able to put the ban in place, and that the reasoning that it provided for doing so was sound. The court also found that the EU's arguments, that ran contrary to the functioning of international law, were unfounded. The court did find that the ban in England had been put in place without due consideration for the impact on the EU as regards proportionality of the ban – but fully upheld the ban in Scottish waters and did not require the UK to reverse the ban in English waters in any way.[41] Finally, this benefit is also deserving of an award – an honourable mention if you will – as this story was the catalyst for Channel 4 News admitting to the existence of Brexit benefits. On 13th May 2025 their Chief Correspondent, Alex Thompson, wrote that the banning of sandeels was 'a remarkable example of how Brexit in practice can allow the UK government to go against EU big agribusiness when it comes to protecting the environment'.[42]

15. My Chemical Romance

Despite decades-old laws banning the testing of cosmetics on animals within the EU, contradicting laws for protecting workers from hazardous chemicals mandated animals being tested on. Leaving the EU allowed the UK to resolve this contradiction in law, and return to the outright ban on cosmetics testing on animals

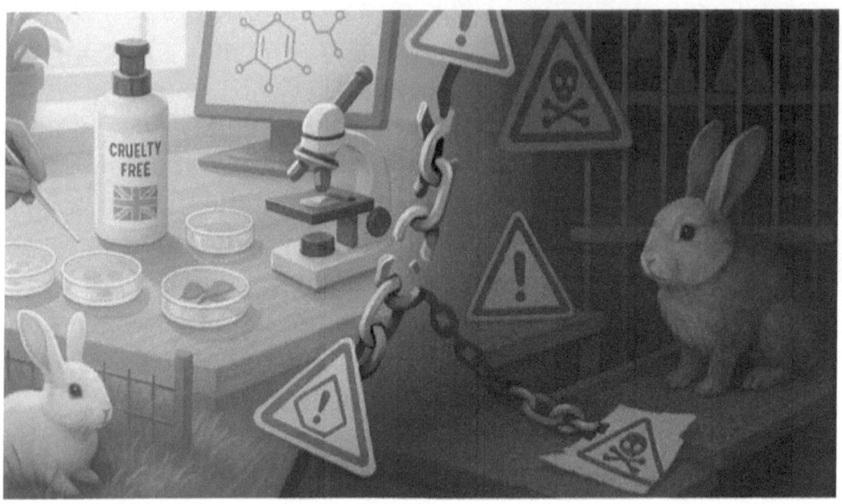

The UK, being a nation of animal lovers, has always been a global leader as regards reducing and even prohibiting the testing of cosmetics on animals, having introduced an effective ban on animal testing of cosmetics in 1998 through banning the issuing of testing licences.[43] The UK policy was in fact the forebear to the EU legislation that followed in the decades to come (2004 for finished products, 2009 for ingredients, 2013 for marketing), that the UK replicated during its withdrawal from the union. However, the EU can often be a quite bureaucratically complex place and seems to be adept at introducing legislation that contradicts and even undermines other legislation. A good example of this is the Registration, Evaluation, Authorisation and restriction of Chemicals regulations, also known as REACH 1907/2006.

REACH *requires* animal testing to determine the safety of chemicals (for example for environmental risks or worker safety) when no other non-animal alternative methodologies for testing are known to exist, even when those chemicals are specifically and solely for use in cosmetics.[44] The requirements under REACH are of higher importance to those within the animal protection legislation, with the EU courts having ruled as recently as 2023 that two cosmetic-only ingredients *had to* be tested on animals - despite the EU testing ban.[45]

The UK replicated the REACH legislation into UK law when it departed the EU, so it also replicated the contradiction. After a 2020 European Chemicals Agency (ECHA) ruling, the UK Home Office decided - without needing to do so due to Brexit - to stay aligned with the EU approach and issue guidance that animal testing would be required to stay in line with what was now the UK REACH laws. This decision when discovered by animal rights activists caused significant public backlash, and in May 2023 the UK government reversed course and diverged from EU policy to close the inconsistency loophole.[46]

As of May 2025, the UK finds itself in a stronger position as regards the prevention of animal testing on cosmetics, from all angles. The banning of testing of chemicals on animals when used solely in cosmetics, even under UK REACH, ended such testing completely within the UK. This allows for the marketing ban to also be enforced more effectively, as the previously mentioned loopholes complicated matters in this regard.

The contradictions and loopholes continue to exist to this day within the EU, with over 400 cosmetic-only chemicals currently registered under REACH - and thousands of animals having been tested on within the EU for these chemicals since 2013.[47]

16. (Don't) Bring Your Daughter to the Slaughter

Animal rights campaigners have sought for a ban on livestock being shipped across national borders purely for the purposes of fattening or slaughter. It was not possible for the UK to ban this practice from within the EU, but from the outside it has been able to not only ban the process but also prevent other countries doing so across the UK.

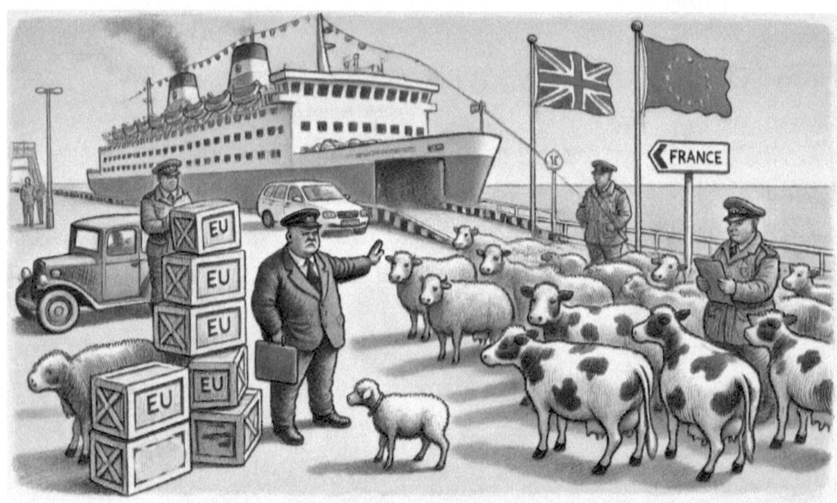

Transporting live animals over long distances for slaughter elsewhere has long been campaigned against in the UK. Better animal welfare was highlighted at the time of the EU referendum as a benefit of leaving the EU, as the EU Single Market rules prevent member states from banning live exports to other EU countries.

The Animal Welfare (Livestock Exports) Act 2024 made it an offence to export live cattle, sheep, pigs, horses, goats and wild boar from or through Great Britain (England, Scotland and Wales - Northern Ireland is treated differently due to the Windsor Framework agreement) for slaughter or fattening outside the British islands of the British Isles (so outside of the UK, the Channel Islands, and the Isle of Man). The Act also makes it an offence for Great Britain to be used as a passthrough for a journey for slaughter or fattening, which prevents the Republic of Ireland from using the UK as a land bridge for these practices.[48]

Live exports for the purposes of slaughter have been politically contentious for decades, with estimates of up to 40 Million livestock having been exported from the UK since the 1960s - which equates to nearly 14,000 animals a week.[49] Animal Rights groups such as the RSPCA and Compassion in World Farming (CWF) have been pushing for changes to rules in this area since the 1970s, being joined in recent years by other groups such as People for the Ethical Treatment of Animals (PETA) and Animal Aid.

In a rare example of the UK getting its wrists slapped for trying to breach EU rules, Thanet District Council imposed a temporary ban on live animal exports from the Port of Ramsgate in 2012, following an incident where several sheep died during transport. The council were taken to court over the ban, as it breached EU single market rules on the free movement of goods. The High Court ruling was that it was against EU law to put in place such a ban, and so the council were forced to remove it again.[50]

When the Act was passed in Parliament and received Royal Assent, the Actress Joanna Lumley - a patron of the charity CWF - was quoted as saying 'Finally, finally, finally, we can celebrate the news that live farm animals will never again be exported on long, horrendous journeys from our shores only to be fattened or slaughtered. For decades, we at Compassion in World Farming have worked tirelessly to bring this campaign to everyone's attention. We are deeply thankful to the Government for taking action at long last and to our supporters for never giving up the fight – I'm so proud to say that, together, we have banned live exports!'[51]

In May 2025, in the days prior to a long-advertised meeting between the UK and EU governments to agree a 'reset' of their relations, the RSPCA put out a statement calling on the UK government to not sacrifice hold-won animal rights battles, including the banning of livestock exports for slaughter, in the name of closer EU ties. David Bowles, the Head of Public Affairs for the RSPCA, told The Telegraph that 'the Government needs to explain to the EU that our ban on live animal exports is not on the negotiating table'.[52]

17. The Fin-al Countdown

Brexit allowed the UK to tighten domestic laws on the prevention of 'Shark Finning' – a barbaric practice where sharks are caught and de-finned, and thrown back alive to be left to die, purely for the export of shark fins into the Asia-Pacific market where they are used in alternative medicines.

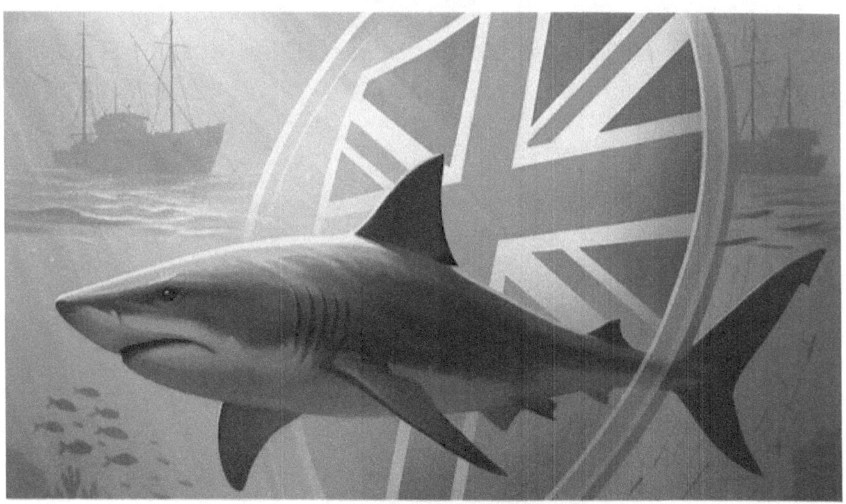

The detaching of shark fins, for its sale and use predominantly in the Asia-Pacific region, has been an unwanted but thriving industry in Europe for decades. The EU introduced a partial ban in 2003, but with the loopholes easily navigated the trade did not cease - with the four worst offenders in the EU (Spain, Portugal, France and the UK) being responsible for 13.4% of the total estimated global tonnage of shark fins collected and sold between 2000 and 2008 - with Spain identified as being by some distance the worst offender.[53]

As stated in the second reading of the Shark Fins Bill, 'A Greenpeace Unearthed report published in 2019 showed that, between January 2017 and July 2019, the UK exported 50 tonnes of shark fin to Spain' – where the fins would then be re-exported to China.[54] Leaving the EU allowed for the UK to introduce a more stringent Bill, that would see a complete ban on both the

import and export of illegally harvested shark fins – a ban that has received global praise from animal rights activists and campaign groups. Again, as stated in the second reading of the Bill, 'Clause 2 amends article one of the shark finning regulation 1185/2003, which forms part of retained EU law, to make sure that shark finning cannot take place by any vessel fishing in UK waters, or by any UK vessel fishing in non-UK waters.'
The legislation included in the Shark Fins Act 2023 gained Royal Assent on June 29th, 2023. This independent tightening of what was originally EU law, would not be possible without having left the EU.[55]

18. Skin in the Game

The EU is one of the largest producers of animal fur in the world, and Single Market rules required the UK to allow for their sale into the UK market despite overwhelming objection from British voters. This mandated position is able to be reversed and the wishes of the British people implemented, solely due to Brexit.

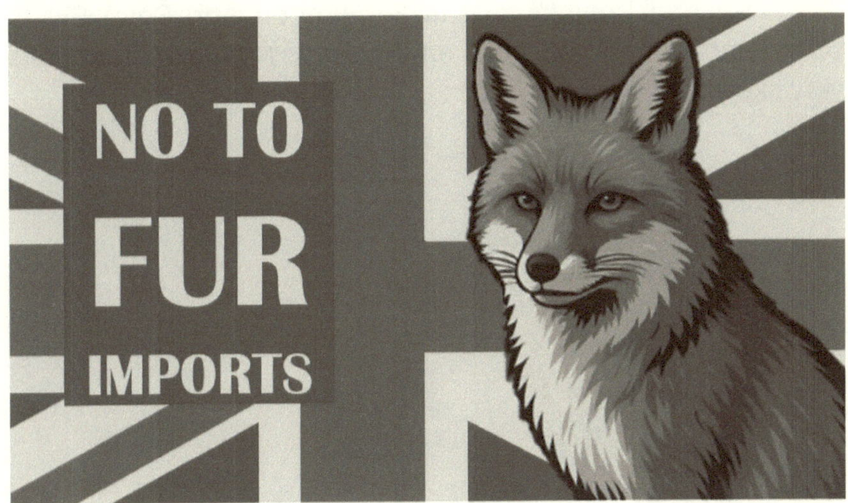

On 17th October 2024, a Private Members Bill was submitted to the House of Commons for First Reading, regarding the banning of both the importation and the sale of furs into the UK. The Bill looks to expand on existing bans on cat, dog and seal fur, to include mink, foxes, raccoon dogs, chinchillas, coyotes, and others.[56] The bill aims to end the UK's role in the global fur trade, which The Humane Society International (HSI) estimates killed approximately seven Million animals for UK imports over 2019–2023.[57]

EU Single Market rules require equal treatment regarding the sale of goods produced within an EU member state, within all other EU member states. There are multiple EU member states who still have a legal fur production industry such as Finland, Poland, Spain and Greece - and so EU Single Market rules meant that those furs had to be legally allowed to be sold in the UK, while the UK was still a member. The UK was of course able to ban the domestic production of fur and did so some two decades earlier - but it still had to allow the importation from fellow EU member states.

Alongside China, the EU continues to be one of the largest producers of fur in the world. From outside of the EU, the UK can progress with the very popular policy of banning its importation.

Second Reading of the Fur (Import and Sale) Bill is scheduled for 11th July 2025 and has cross-party support so is very likely to progress into law.

19. Plenty More Fish in the Sea

Despite a complex picture and understandable feelings of betrayal within the UK fishing community, Brexit allowed for the UK to regain control over its fishing grounds, and return much-needed increased catch quotas to UK fishermen.

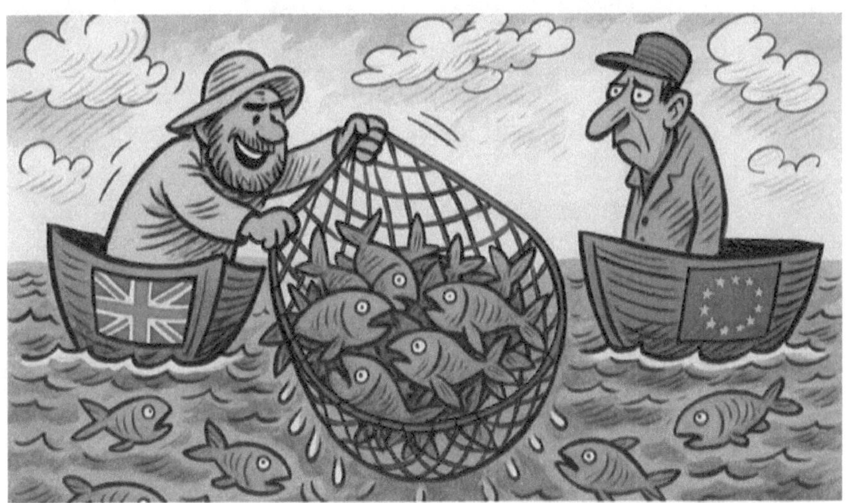

In 2021, the National Federation of Fishermen's Organisations (NFFO) published a report entitled the 'Brexit Balance Sheet', intended to go into the details of the gains and losses for the fishing industry from leaving the EU. The report states that, as things stood as regards renegotiations for access in Autumn 2021, the UK fishing fleet would suffer losses of £64.8m a year in the five years to 2026, which it summarises as a circa £300m loss of revenue over those five years. These losses would be faced primarily by the non-pelagic fishing fleet. The report does however go on to say that there are gains of £70-75m a year for the pelagic fishing fleet - which for the most observant of you is larger than the losses mentioned.[58]

This is of course a snapshot in time, in the Autumn of 2021. By the end of 2021, many of the line items within the losses half of the ledger had in fact been resolved as well – the largest of these being a 'no deal' scenario with Norway, which had been seen to equate to a £30m per year loss.[59] Overall with the improvements and resolutions on the specific line items mentioned in the losses on the report, the £64.8m a year gets reduced to just £26.8m - so with the estimated £75m per year in gains, the UK fishing industry was forecasted to be around £50m a year better off – or £250m better off over the course of the five years to 2026.

Since 2021, the UK has been engaging in annual negotiations on fishing quotas with its neighbours, as an independent coastal nation. These negotiations have seen the UK present the best interests of the nation, and secure hard-won additional quotas for UK fishermen.

In 2019, UK fishermen were able to catch – as authorised to do so by the EU – 622,000 tonnes of fish worth £987 Million to the UK economy. By 2023 through Brexit and a regaining of quota shares from the EU, this amount had increased to 719,000 tonnes and £1.10 Billion. In 2024 UK fishermen had a total allowable quota of over 750,000 tonnes.[60]

It is fair to say, as the NFFO report mentioned previously focuses heavily on, that the benefits of leaving the EU are not shared evenly across the UK fishing industry. However, it is also quite fair and accurate to point out that, as the data supports, the UK fishing industry is on the whole better off outside the EU than it was inside of it.

20. Do Sheep Dream of Electric Androids?

The UK post-Brexit implemented new laws around the recognition of animal sentience, with a stricter and more tailored application than the approach taken within the EU – the latter still catering for the many inhumane practices carried out on animals within the EU such as bullfighting and mink breeding for fur .

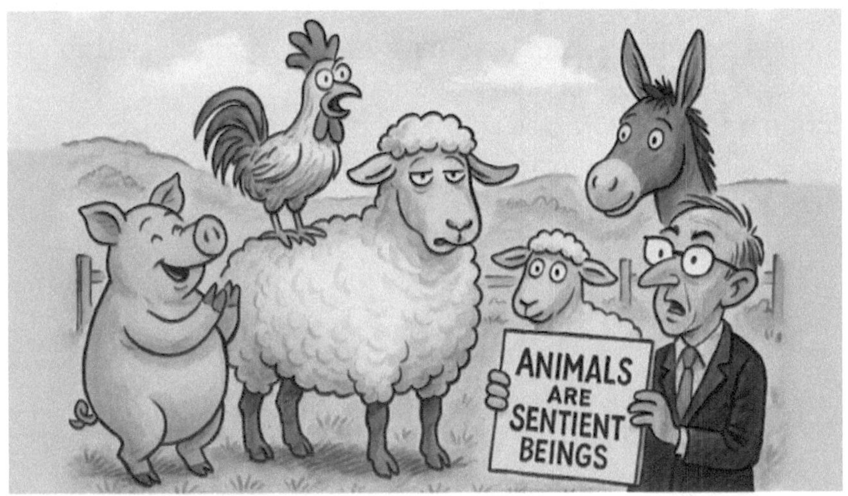

The Lisbon Treaty amended the Treaty on the Functioning of the European Union (TFEU) in 2009, recognising animals as sentient beings. Article 13 of the TFEU requires the EU and its member states to consider animal welfare when making policies regarding agriculture, fisheries transport and many other areas.

When the process of separation from the EU commenced, there were concerns that the UK government was not planning on replicating the laws relating to animal sentience into UK law. However post-departure, the UK government pushed through the Animal Welfare (Sentience) Act 2022, which formally recognised animal sentience in UK law for the first time.[61]

Both the EU and the UK now recognise animal sentience, but the UK does so with specific legislation post-Brexit, allowing for more tailored and stricter interpretations and applications. The EU's framework is broader but is often criticised for still allowing member states to maintain practices deemed inhumane by animal rights activists (such as bullfighting, breeding of mink for production of fur clothing, and traditionally produced foie gras).

Ultimately, the wish of the EU to take into consideration the cultural differences between member states has meant that around animal welfare, laws have had to be weakened to not undermine or prohibit those cultural differences that many find inhumane. The UK does not need to take these outdated cultural practices into account; and so, can implement stronger laws that deliver the desired result more effectively.

21. Poppin' a CAP in Your Ass

Leaving the EU allowed the UK to escape the almost universally hated Common Agricultural Policy (CAP), putting in place alternative methods of farming subsidy focused on good stewardship of nature and the rolling picturesque landscapes Great Britain is famous for across the world.

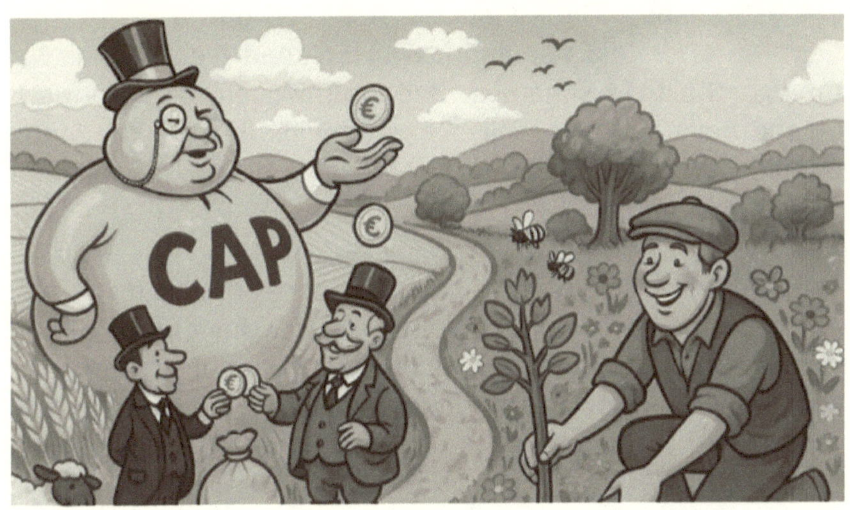

The EU's Common Agricultural Policy (CAP) has been almost universally hated in the UK for decades, with politicians of all stripes and allegiances having taken turns at taking chunks out of it over the years. In the months immediately following the vote to leave the EU in 2016, a joint statement was released from the four major nature and wildlife charities of the UK (The Wildlife Trusts, The Royal Society for the Protection of Birds RSPB, The World Wildlife Fund WWF and The National Trust) calling for the wholesale replacement of the CAP, and stating that Brexit 'provides an unprecedented opportunity to revitalise our countryside in a way that balances the needs of everyone, for generations to come'.[62] They went on to state that 'we need to replace the outdated CAP with a system that is fair to taxpayers and provides value for money'.

The CAP was always high up on the to-do list of things to replace once Brexit was completed. So, it was of surprise to no-one when the Agriculture Act 2020 sought to replace it with the Environmental Land Management Scheme (ELM) in England (as farming policy is a devolved matter so is handled slightly differently in each of the devolved nations).[63]

Brexit allowed the UK to dismantle the CAP's one-size-fits-all approach, and instead tailor UK agricultural policy to domestic needs. The Agriculture Act 2020 provided the legal framework for this transition, with England leading the way through the ELM schemes. Scotland, Wales, and Northern Ireland have pursued their own strategies, but we will focus primarily on England here as it represents the most significant departure from the CAP.

The ELM replaces the CAP's Basic Payment Scheme (BPS) with a 'public money for public goods' model. Instead of paying farmers based on land area, ELM rewards actions that deliver environmental, social, and economic benefits. It comprises three main components:

Sustainable Farming Incentive (SFI): Launched in 2022, SFI paid farmers for practices like improving soil health, reducing pesticide use, and enhancing biodiversity. Payments range from £22 per hectare for organic matter addition to £646 per hectare for maintaining species-rich grassland. By 2024, SFI included over 50 actions, such as agroforestry and robotic weeding, accessible to all farm types.

Local Nature Recovery (LNR): This scheme, a successor to Countryside Stewardship, funds targeted actions like creating habitats, planting hedgerows, or managing flood risks. It emphasises local priorities, with payments like £765 per hectare for lapwing nesting plots.

Landscape Recovery (LR): Aimed at large-scale projects, LR supports long-term restoration, such as rewilding or peatland conservation. It offers bespoke agreements for significant land-use changes, with payments like £1,242 per hectare for connecting river and floodplain habitats.

The ELM's 'public money for public goods' model is a clear win for the environment when compared to the EU CAP. By tying payments to specific actions — like creating habitats or reducing emissions — ELM ensures accountability. For instance, SFI's soil health standards have engaged thousands of farmers, with 8,000 enrolled by 2023. LR's focus on large-scale restoration, such as rewilding Exmoor, promises transformative biodiversity gains. Early data suggests ELM is increasing hedgerow coverage and pollinator populations, aligning with the UK's 25-year environment plan.

The CAP's land-based model was inherently unfair, funnelling millions to wealthy estates. Reforms since 2003 reduced some distortions, but the system remained regressive, prioritizing scale over contribution. The UK's policy is significantly fairer, redistributing support to active farmers delivering public goods.

NOTE: In March 2025, the new Labour government paused any new registrations for the SFI scheme - stating that changes to the scheme would be announced in late spring, to improve the system even further. At the time of writing, those changes have not been announced.

22. Wet Wet Wet

Single Market rules require a good legally sold in one member state, to be able to be sold in all member states. Microplastics are having a devastating effect on our natural environment, and one of the common culprits for this is wet wipes made with plastic fibres. Leaving the EU allowed the UK to ban them completely from sale.

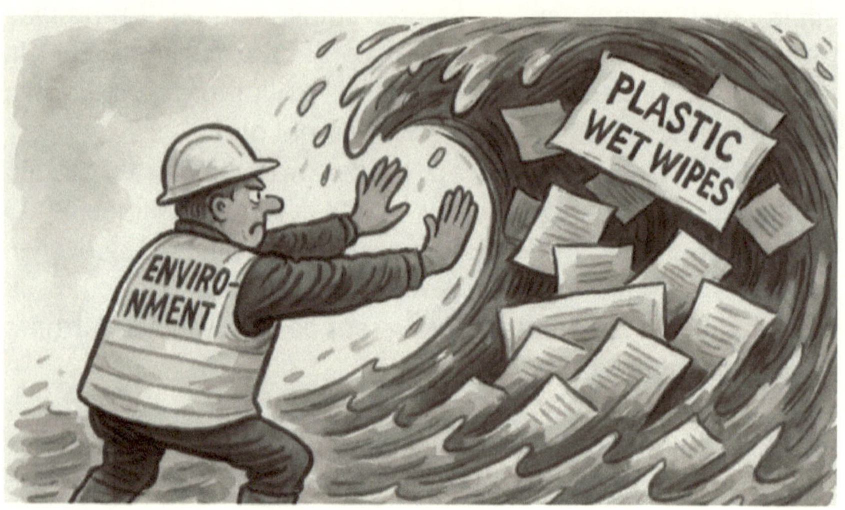

The ecological damage caused by microplastics is a very recent discovery - the word wasn't even coined until the mid-2000s, before which very little was known about the impact microplastics were having on the environment. The British public are a smart bunch when they want to be though, and by the mid-2010s there was significant public pressure on the government to act on some of the worst culprits, such as wet wipes. The problem being that the EU's Single Market rules prohibited the banning of products for sale that were legally able to be sold in other member states - and other EU member states such as Poland were significant producers of wet wipes that used plastic fibres.

Two consultations were held post-Brexit, in 2021 and 2023, around the potential banning of wet wipes that included plastic fibres. These consultations showed an almost unanimous support for the ban, with 95% and 96% support respectively. Data released in 2021 showed that 11 Billion wet wipes were estimated to be sold and used in the UK each year, with 90% of those used containing some form of plastic.[64]

The UK government passed legislation in April 2024 to ban wet wipes that included plastic, and at the time of writing the UK is one year into the 18-month transition period allowed for UK businesses to move away from their use.[65] Leaving the EU has allowed the UK to address this issue head-on and is leading the charge yet again as it often does. On announcing the new legislation, the Marine Conservation Society commented that 'the announcement to ban plastic in single use wet wipes from governments across the UK today on Earth Day is fantastic news for UK beaches. Our volunteers found over 21,000 wet wipes on UK beaches in 2023 with some hotspot beaches recording thousands in a single 100m stretch.'

23. Honk Honk

The UK banned the production of traditionally-made foie gras in 2006, but was unable to ban the import and sale of the product despite the widespread feeling amongst the British public, due to EU Single Market rules – the current government has pledged to rectify this post-Brexit, now it has the ability to do so.

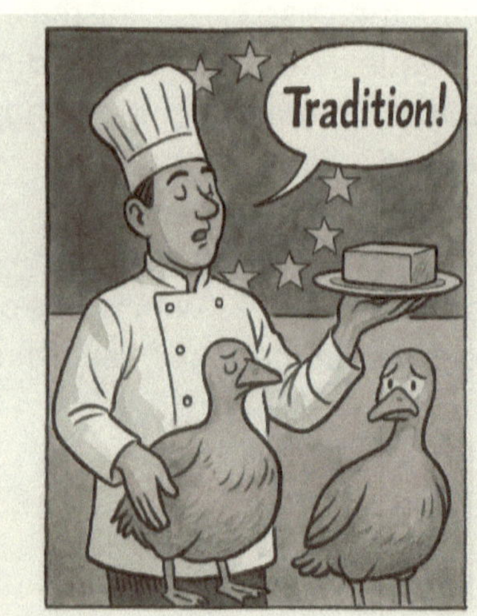

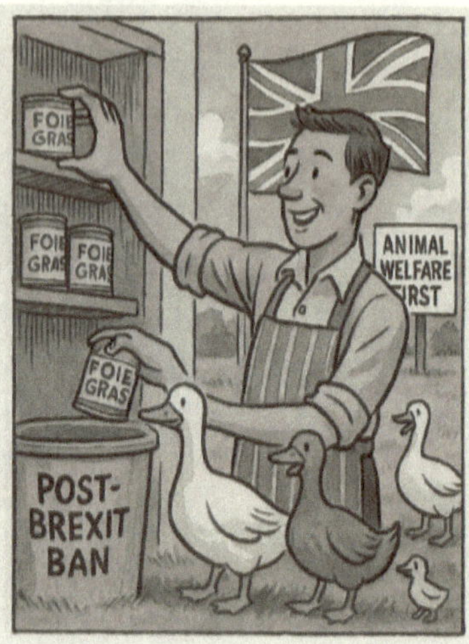

In 2006 the UK, through the Animal Welfare Act, banned the domestic production of traditionally-made *foie gras* - where a process called gavage is used to force-feed ducks or geese to swell their livers to a wholly unnatural size, thought to cause significant physical and psychological distress to the birds in the process.[66] The ban was welcomed by the general public, the UK being a nation of animal lovers, but the ban was unable to prevent the sale of imported foie gras produced through the same methods.

Despite having laws within the EU to recognise animal sentience and to prevent animal cruelty, there are exceptions allowed for certain member states to continue production that would contravene those rules, where there is a cultural tradition or practice predating the EU's rules. This is the case with France, who produces nearly 85% of the world's traditionally made foie gras.[67] The combination of this ability to contravene animal welfare concerns on the grounds of traditional practices, coupled with the EU principle of mutual recognition (where a product able to be legally sold in one member state must be allowed to be sold in all member states), ensured that a product banned from production in the UK would at the same time have to be legally stocked on British shelves if it was made in another EU member state such as France.

Public sentiment during and after EU departure has overwhelmingly supported the banning of this product from UK shelves once and for all, with a YouGov survey in 2024 showing 85% of respondents favouring an import ban.[69] It is estimated that the reduction of sale stemming from a UK ban would result in over 250,000 birds being spared on an annual basis.[69] The current Labour government committed to bringing in a ban during the next Parliament - a ban that would not be possible, were the UK to still be a member of the EU.

24. Hush Puppies

Animal breeding and smuggling is rife in the EU, with an estimated 79% of dogs for sale in the EU being unable to be traced back to a legal source. Preventing this vile Billion-Euro industry required changes to legislation that sat with the EU until Brexit, so this problem can now be halted at the English Channel.

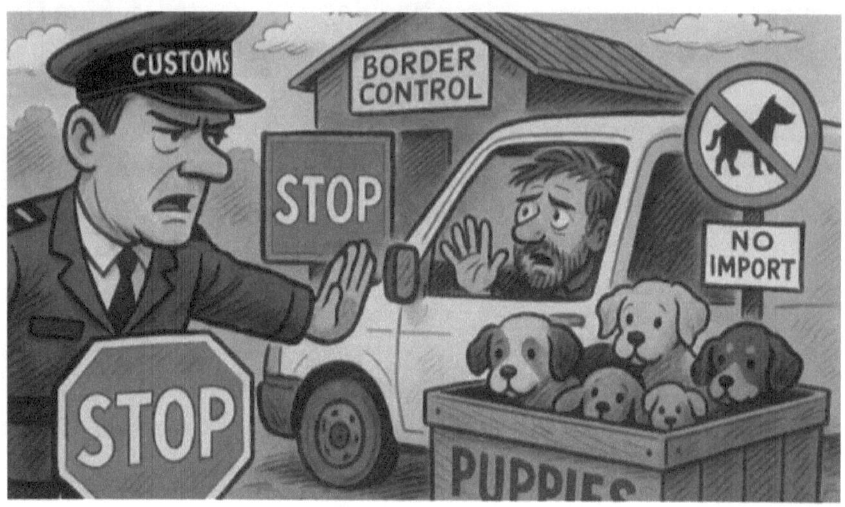

The breeding and smuggling of pets within the EU, especially dogs, is a Billion-Euro industry that sees intensive breeding of popular breeds in inhumane conditions to meet the high consumer demand. A report from the charity Four Paws found that an estimated 79% of dogs for sale in the EU cannot be traced back to verified or legal sources.[70]

The prevention of this cruel trade requires stronger laws at the EU level for member states, as the legislation that would require change sits within the area of competence that members sacrifice to be controlled centrally when they become members. However, being outside of the EU means that the UK can now make those changes recommended by animal welfare charities like Four Paws.

In the former Conservative Government in 2024, a Bill was submitted and partially progressed to do exactly that. Unfortunately, the timing of the election meant that this Bill did not progress into law. The Labour Party however did commit within their manifesto to support such a Bill if they were to win, and following their victory have supported a Liberal Democrat Private Members Bill which does exactly that. The progression of the Bill through second Reading was a rare example of unison with the three major UK political parties, with a round of applause even taking place.

Again – the ability for the UK to make such changes, supported by even the very Pro-EU Liberal Democrats, required departure from the EU. At the time of writing, the Animal Welfare (Import of Dogs, Cats and Ferrets) Bill was at the Committee Stage in the House of Commons.[71]

Section 3

Brexit Means Better Trade

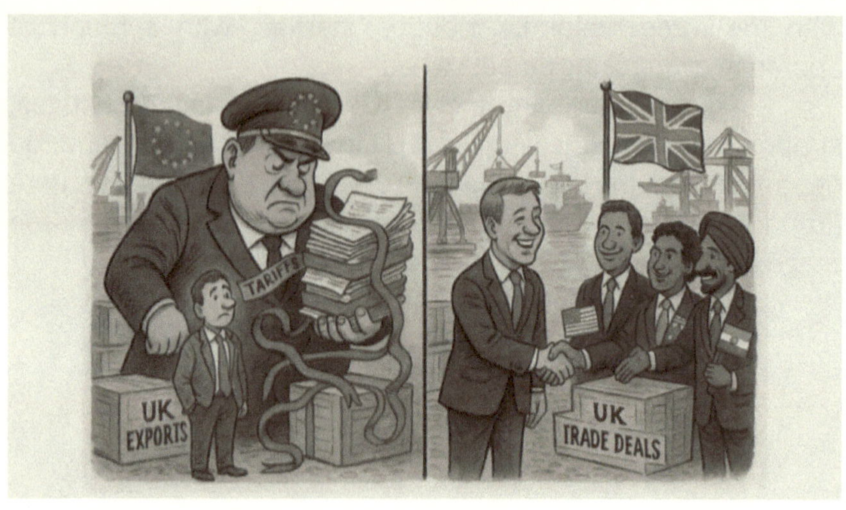

25. Harder, Better, Faster, Stronger

Trying to make a trade deal that suits 28 different economies is like trying to order a pizza that 28 different people will like. The order takes ten times longer to place, and the outcome is so bland that no one is happy with it. The UK can strike trade deals quicker that fit better with the UK economy, all on its own.

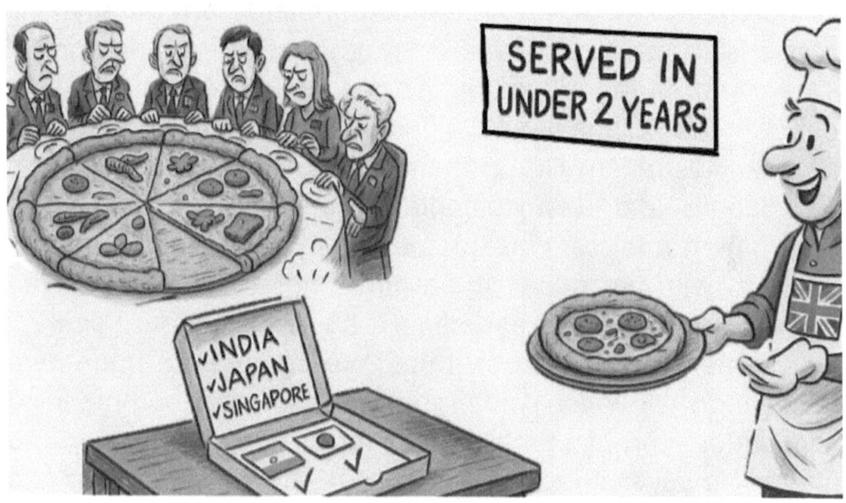

Since the formal departure of the UK from the EU in February 2020, the UK has undertaken numerous trade agreement negotiations with global partners. In the case of Australia and New Zealand, the intention was to secure entirely new trade agreements that EU membership did not provide an alternative for. However, the UK also undertook negotiations with the aim to improve on the deals that it had already secured continuity on, or was yet to secure continuity of, with nations who had an existing trade agreement with the EU.

In the case of Japan, the EU JEEPA agreement was used as a baseline, with the more comprehensive UK CEPA agreement the result of those negotiations. In the case of Singapore, minor improvements were able to be made in the continuity agreement, with then further improvements made since, targeting the digital economy.

As of May 2024, when the general election was announced, negotiations on improving EU continuity agreements were underway with Mexico, Israel, Turkey, Switzerland and South Korea. Negotiations for completely new agreements were also underway with India, the six-nation Gulf Cooperation Council or GCC, The Maldives and with Greenland. Just one year later in May 2025, the UK and India announced that they had concluded negotiations on a full and comprehensive FTA, one more comprehensive than anything previously agreed by India with any other country in the world.[72]

At the time of writing, the negotiations for a trade deal between the EU and Australia had been postponed indefinitely by the Australian Government, over what it saw as an unwelcome and unsustainable EU negotiating position. A government minister was quoted as saying at the time that 'I think it will be quite some time before any Australian government, or any EU leadership is able to negotiate a deal'.[73]

The average time for the EU to complete a trade deal negotiation – by which I mean going from formally commencing negotiations through to the agreed terms of a deal coming into effect – is seven to ten years. The UK average, including the completely new agreements and the continuity agreements, is less than two years. The global average for bilateral trade agreements is 18 months to three years.

Amendments made in the Free Trade Agreement with Japan:
- Reduced tariffs and Improved customs provisions
- Streamlined access for UK financial services
- More liberal Rules of Origin (RoO)
- Tenfold increase in Geographical Indicators (GIs)
- Improved provisions on tackling IP infringement
- Improved access for digital and data services
- Improved business VISAs (Visitor International Stay Agreement)
- Improved VISAs for families of UK workers
- Whole new chapter on Women & Equality

Amendments made in the Free Trade Agreement with Singapore:
- Rules of Origin and cumulation - allowing goods which include EU components, or some processing within the EU, to be considered as having taken place in the UK or Singapore when meeting Rules of Origin for exports
- QFB Location allowances - the deal goes further than the EU agreement on allowances for how many UK bank branches can operate within Singapore, from 25 locations to 35. This affects the two UK banks who meet the criteria for Qualifying Full Bank (QFB), being HSBC and Standard Chartered
- Digital Economy Agreement – incorporation of seven separate bilateral agreements into the original FTA, which are:
    - The Core Digital Economy Agreement
    - The UK-Singapore FinTech Bridge
    - The Digital Customs Agreement
    - The Cybersecurity Agreement
    - The Digital Identities Agreement
    - The Electronic Trade Documents Agreement
    - The Electronic Invoicing Agreement

26. How Low Can You Go?

The UK after Brexit took the opportunity to simplify its applied tariff regime – the tariffs that fellow WTO members without a trade deal need to be charged for their exports – as well as removing many so-called nuisance tariffs, where the effort to collect the tariff costs more than the tariff itself, making the whole effort pointless.

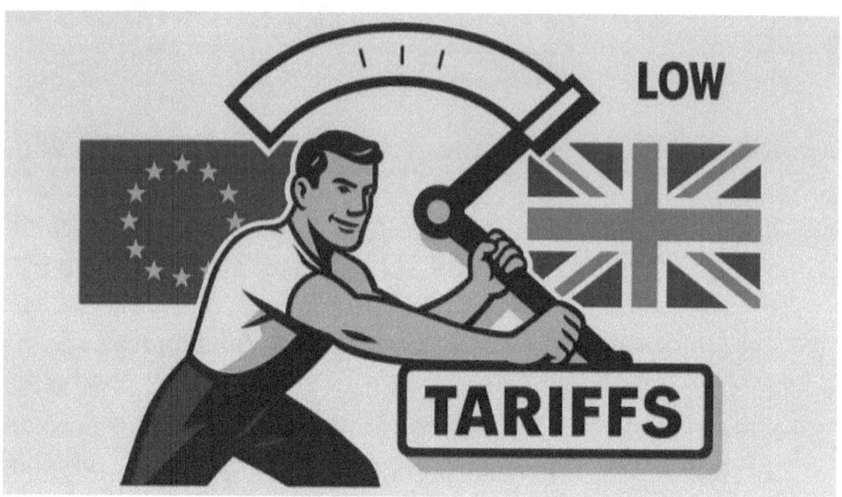

After leaving the EU, the UK was able to retake its existing independent seat at the World Trade Organization (WTO) - but this requirement also came with obligations to declare what bound and applied tariffs the UK would offer fellow WTO members within its independent trade schedule.[74] Bound tariffs are the upper limit for what a WTO member would ever charge for a given item, and applied tariffs are those currently being applied, where they differ from the bound tariffs.

The UK took the opportunity to remove hundreds of so-called nuisance tariffs, as well as tariffs intended to protect industries of the EU, that the UK had no need to protect. The effect of this tariff liberalisation was to increase the volume of product lines that were completely tariff free, from 27% in the EU Common External Tariff (CET) to over 47% in the new UK

Global Tariff (UKGT) – making goods cheaper than they otherwise would have been for the UK consumer. This amounted to over 2,000 product lines having tariffs removed completely.[75]

Product categories that saw the most tariff removal included 'Articles of Stone & Plaster' (around 45% of tariff lines eliminated); 'Machines and Mechanical Appliances' (around 35%); 'Leather and Leather Goods' (around 25%); and 'Wood and Articles of Wood' (around 25%).

To quote the former Minister of State at the Department for Business and Trade, Nigel Huddleston: 'I will not apologise for the fact that when we left the EU, we got rid of hundreds of useless tariffs that were doing nothing other than pushing up prices for British consumers. We liberalised tariffs on environmental goods, and we liberalised tariffs on goods that we generally do not produce in the UK, thus massively reducing the total number of tariffs faced by British consumers. That is a good thing, throughout the UK'.[76]

As confirmed by the HM Revenue & Customs Policy paper on the integrated tariff schedule published in January 2021, 'If we had retained CET tariff levels, about 86% of the UK's imports would come in tariff free, compared to approximately 91% under the UKGT (subject to satisfying rules of origin).' The paper also provided concrete examples of household goods that would be directly affected by the change, such as:

- Fridges (from between 1.9% - 2.5%, to 0%)
- Freezers (from 2.2% to 0%)
- Cocoa powder (from 8% to 0%)
- Dried bakers' yeast (from 12% to 0%)

27. Common People

The Commonwealth has a population of over 2.5 Billion people across 56 countries, spanning every continent on the globe – and being a part of the EU made the UK's relationship with the Commonwealth more difficult. From outside of the EU, the UK can regain the links that it had once had to sever, and reap the benefits from doing so .

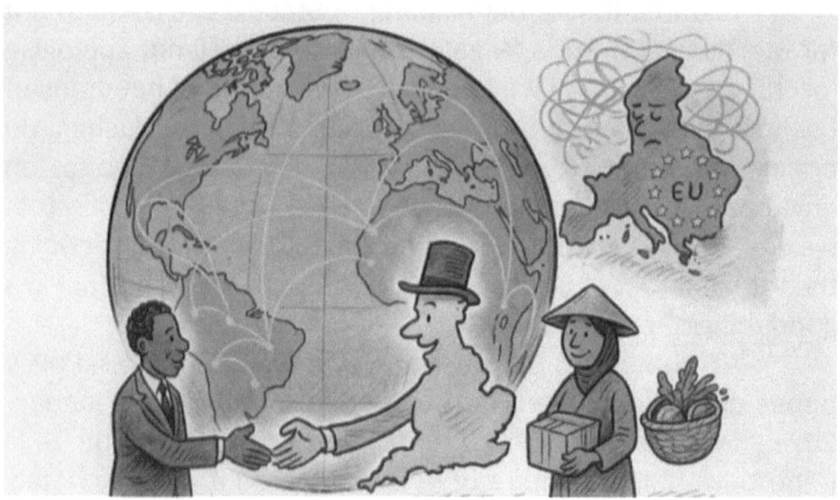

In a television interview on the occasion of his 80th birthday in 1963, former Labour Prime Minister Lord Clement Attlee was asked why he opposed the UK joining what was then called the EEC Common Market – he replied that 'It is a very limited alliance, purely European, and it really I think breaks the unity of the Commonwealth'. He went on to say that to his mind 'The Commonwealth is immensely important, because it is multi-racial'.[77]

The Commonwealth is of course multi-racial and spans every populated continent of the world. But we do not need to look solely at diversity to see the benefit of the Commonwealth in action – and trade is a wonderful example. There is a very real and demonstrable trade premium that exists between Commonwealth members and is thought to provide an average of 21% lower costs to trade. This is due to the similar legal and administrative systems, the shared use of the English language, the shared history, and the existence of large diasporas in each other's countries.[78]

When the UK joined the Common Market in 1973, this 'Commonwealth Advantage' was severed – in some cases quite catastrophically. One only need look at the impact on New Zealand, and their need to completely reimagine their global trade outlook, to see how that decision damaged relationships with the UK's closest allies and families.

On leaving the EU and retaking its independent seat at the World Trade Organization (WTO), the UK undertook a review of its baseline tariffs that it would offer to all 165 WTO members in the absence of any bilateral FTA – and the outcome was the United Kingdom Global Tariff (UKGT). This refined and simplified applied tariff regime removed a whole host of so-called 'nuisance tariffs' lower than 2.5%, where the hassle of collecting the tariff is more effort than it is worth. The UKGT also introduced tariff bandings, in a further simplification, and removed tariffs on products that the UK does not produce but the EU does. These changes are not only good for the UK, but also for trade with the wider Commonwealth – as explained by Nigeria's President Buhari: 'Already [the UKGT] has reduced, removed or simplified tax on thousands of imported goods, an important step in reconfiguring Commonwealth trade'.[79]

The value of UK exports to the Commonwealth increased by 23% year-on-year in 2022 to over £90 Billion, while the value of imports from the Commonwealth increased by 30% to over £74 Billion. The Commonwealth accounted for over 9% of total UK trade in 2023, and 10% of the UKs exports.[80]

Lord Attlee wrapped up his response on the Common Market versus the Commonwealth with this thought, that 'I might want the closest of relations [with the Common Market], but it is quite another thing to submit entirely to what I would consider to be very largely a dictatorship of civil servants'.

28. Epic Berne

Since 2019, EU members have been unable to trade in Swiss equities due to a breakdown in the EU-Swiss relationship and a ban having been put in place. Outside of the EU, the UK was able to return this trading, which is worth about £1.6 Billion a day, which means Billions a year in additional HMRC revenue.

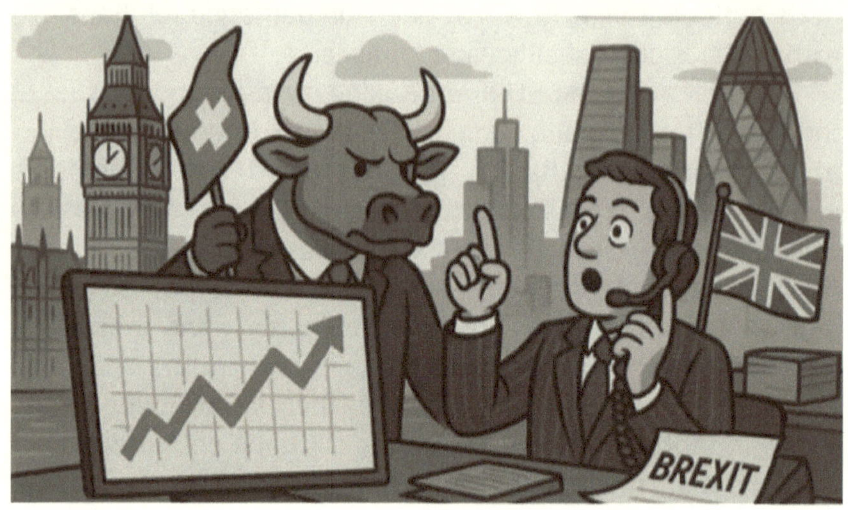

In early July 2019, Swiss regulators introduced a ban on EU exchanges being able to trade in Swiss equities, following a collapse in negotiations with the EU and the resultant loss of equivalence status for the Swiss stock market – after the European Commission allowed the time-limited status to lapse.[81] In a statement on 25 June 2019, the London Stock Exchange (LSE) wrote 'In the event that the EU equivalence decision for Swiss trading venues is not extended beyond its current expiration date of 30 June 2019, it is likely the Swiss authorities will remove the recognition that allows EU trading venues to offer trading in the Swiss equity securities'. The LSE went on to say that, due to their legal inability to trade in Swiss securities, that they would 'halt trading in 254 equity securities (SHRS) issued by Swiss companies'.[82]

Fast-forward two years to February of 2021, and the UK now being outside of the EU regained the ability to trade in Swiss stocks on the London markets. Again, the London Stock Exchange put out a statement, this time with a more positive tone. 'The Exchange is now recognised as a foreign trading venue pursuant to the Federal Council Ordinance of 30 November 2018, therefore, the trading of 204 Swiss equity securities will be reinstated for on Exchange trading with effect from the start of business on Thursday 4th February 2021'.[83]

Before the ban was put in place in 2019, London platforms handled around 1.2 Billion euros daily in Swiss shares which with necessary fees would net around £8 Million per day to HMRC. Over the course of the year that equates to around £2 Billion that EU membership took away from the UK coffers in 2019 – and Brexit was able to return them. This is without mentioning the additional taxes generated from the resulting share dividends and capital gains.[84]

In December 2023, the UK and Switzerland signed The Berne Agreement - a Mutual Recognition Agreement (MRA) in Financial Services. In the UK government press release, it states that the MRA 'provides stability for UK businesses supplying financial services to clients in Switzerland and supports unprecedented new market access secured through the agreement. It will also reduce regulatory barriers for the sectors it covers, making doing business with Switzerland easier than ever before'. This agreement is currently going through the processes of ratification in both countries and is expected to come into place in January 2026 (if not earlier).[85]

Note: It was announced in late-January 2025, that following a thawing of relations between the EU and Switzerland, that the Swiss regulators would remove the ban on EU exchanges being able to trade in Swiss equities. This removal took place in May 2025, so the UK has had four years of access (and tax revenue) that the EU was unable to take advantage of. However, the terms of the Berne Agreement once ratified and brought into effect will still see the UK having greater access than EU markets.[86]

29. Competency? What Competency?

Modern comprehensive trade agreements often cover areas of policy that do not (yet) sit within the remit of the EU to be able to negotiate and agree to - meaning that EU member states themselves also have to sign them off, causing years of delays and ultimately a limited scope of ambition during negotiations.

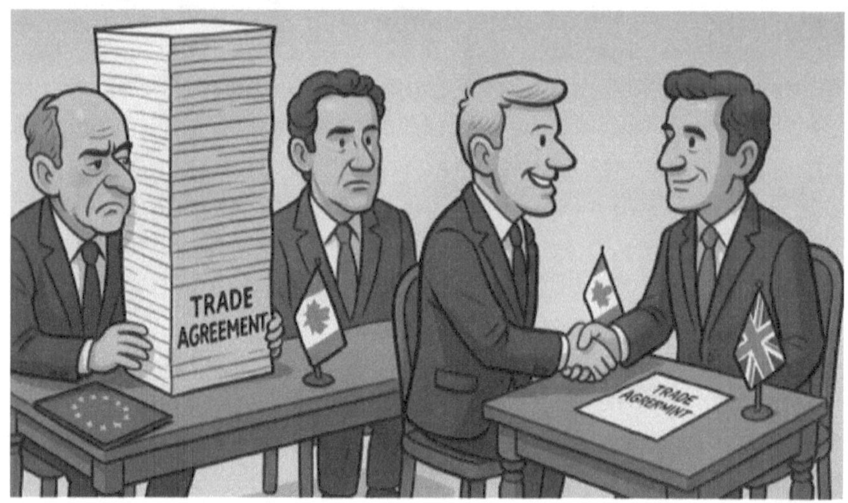

As an EU member, a member state sacrifices control of a whole swathe of legislative competency, to be controlled centrally by the EU themselves. One of these areas, as has been spoken about multiple times in other benefits, is international trade. The growing trend within international trade agreements, however, is for them to be more comprehensive and wide-reaching than would fall into this narrower scope of EU competency - which results in what the EU calls 'mixed competency agreements'.

A mixed competency agreement is essentially an international agreement where the EU cannot agree to all the terms themselves - as some of the terms still sit within the competency of the member state themselves. The EU-Canada FTA, also known as the Comprehensive Economic and Trade Agreement (CETA), is an example of such an agreement.

The parts of the agreement where the EU has sole competency over have been provisionally applied since 2017. However, as of August 2024, only 17 of the 27 member states have ratified the agreement - meaning that despite having been negotiated and agreed over eight years ago, it is *still* not fully implemented.[87]

As a country outside of the EU, the UK is fully in control of the ability to agree and sign international agreements and holds the sole competency for ratification of agreements that it wishes to make. The UK-Canada Trade Continuity Agreement (TCA) replaced CETA when the UK left the EU - it was signed in December 2020 and came fully into effect five months later in April 2021.[88]

In April 2018, Canadian Prime Minister Justin Trudeau was asked about the trading relationship between the UK and Canada following the vote to leave the EU, and his thoughts on future negotiations for an FTA. He replied that Canada would be interested in opening negotiations 'the day after Brexit', and that the UK and Canada would be able to agree 'an even better or larger or more impactful' deal bilaterally than agreed with the EU. He went on to say that 'it should be fairly easy for all of us to get to an improved approach on trade between Canada and the UK'.[89]

30. Through the Barricades

Since its establishment as part of the process of leaving the EU, the Department of International Trade has been able to build up a database of non-tariff barriers to UK exports across the world, and has been systematically working to remove them – an effort worth billions a year to the UK economy.

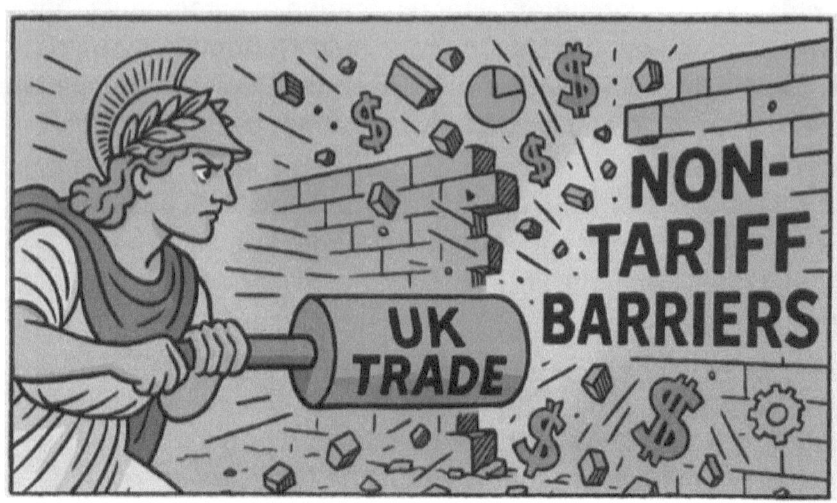

In February 2019, in advance of the UK's impending departure from the European Union, the newly formed Department for International Trade (DIT) - a department formerly surplus to requirements as its responsibilities sat in Brussels and not Westminster - established the Digital Market Access Service (DMAS). This service would allow the department to collate a list of non-tariff barriers that UK businesses were facing, that the government would have a greater capacity to resolve once EU departure was completed.[90]

The DMAS was, as the International Trade team explained it, to record Market Access Barriers (MABs) of a 'legal, regulatory or administrative nature imposed by another government or regulator that was seen to be impeding a UK business exporting or investing overseas'. This way the team at DIT would be able to prioritise a hit list to attempt to resolve, increasing opportunity around the world for UK businesses and investors.

In the first year of operation, over 1,000 trade barriers were reported to DIT, and added to the DMAS. A further 680 were added in the financial year 2020/21. In the first year of the DMAS being used, 181 barriers to trade had been addressed and either partially or fully resolved by DIT, with a further 217 in the following year. That is nearly 400 trade barriers able to be removed in full or in part within two years, that would have otherwise remained in place and impeded UK export and investment opportunities.[91]

The removal of many of these barriers would not have been possible from within the EU and its Customs Union, as the responsibility for negotiating removal of barriers to international trade sat squarely with the EU. As the Department for International Trade stated themselves - 'The UK gained greater freedom to remove trade barriers, along with the ability to negotiate its own Free Trade Agreements (FTAs), when it left the European Union.'[92]

Some examples of barriers that were able to be removed, through the departure from the EU and the creation of the DMAS - as provided by DIT:

- Removing animal testing requirements for the export and sale of UK beauty products in China, opening up a market worth £500m and helping brands that specifically avoid such testing like Unilever's REN to export to China for the first time
- Overcoming bureaucratic issues to allow the export of pet supplements to India worth £1.4m to Lancashire-based VetPlus over five years
- A simplification in the Indonesian cosmetics certification process
- Helping poultry exporters in the UK such as Moy Park remove processes in Mongolia that were preventing them supplying KFC in that region

In response to a written question in March of 2023 the now renamed Department for Business and Trade (DBT) revealed that, in the year ending March 2022, its team had been able to resolve 192 barriers to trade in 79 countries - barriers that had been highlighted to them as a priority by UK businesses through the 'report a trade barrier' service of the DMAS. Of those 192, 45 of them were called out specifically as having significant value to UK businesses – estimated to be worth £5 Billion over a five-year period. That would mean an additional £1 Billion per year of extra revenue for UK businesses, just from these 45 trade barrier removals, due to having left the EU.[93] In the financial year ending March 2023, in the Latin-American (LATAM) region alone, the UK was able to remove 34 non-tariff trade barriers to UK exporters – with 24 of these having a combined forecasted worth of £1.3 Billion to the UK economy.[94]

31. In It for the Long Haul

Having left the EU, the UK was able to implement the positive outcomes of a trial using longer trucks for domestic haulage, which resulted in reduced costs for hauliers and reduced carbon emissions as well – this change was not possible if the UK remained in the EU.

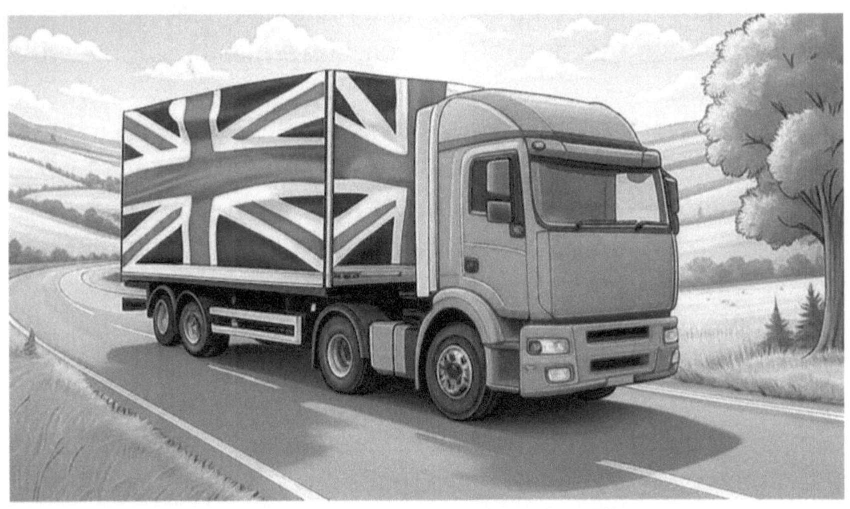

In May 2023, the UK Government introduced new legislation to allow longer lorries on British roads from later that same month, following an 11-year trial to ensure they could be used safely on UK roads. With the legislation changes now in place, hauliers can use longer semi-trailer (LST) combinations up to 18.55 metres – 2.05 metres longer than the standard size and previous legal limit. This extra length enables them to move the same volume of goods using 8% fewer journeys than with the previous maximum length – generating an estimated £1.4 Billion in economic benefits and taking one standard-size trailer off the road for every 12 trips. Evidence also showed that LSTs were involved in around 61% fewer personal injury collisions than conventional lorries.

Vehicles using LSTs are subject to the same 44 tonne weight limit as those using standard trailers, and the new vehicles are expected to cause less wear on the roads than conventional lorries due to the type of steering axle used.

With more than 300 companies in the UK having already taken part in the trial, and almost 3,000 on the road, some of the biggest brands including Greggs, Morrisons, Stobart, Royal Mail, and Argos, will be rolling out the longer semi-trailers. On the changes and their participation on the trial, the Supply Chain Director at Greggs stated that the move to LSTs allowed the company to reduce their annual haulage travel by over half a million kilometres, and reduced carbon emissions by over 400 tonnes.

The average CO2 reduction across the lifetime of the trial is similar to the amount of CO2 captured by roughly 11,600 acres of forest per year, while the savings in NOx emissions averages to the entire annual NOx emissions of around 2,000 diesel cars per year.[95]

Within the final impact assessment from the Department for Transport, to conclude the trial and allow LSTs to enter into general circulation, it states quite clearly that though EU law allowed the trial to take place it would not allow the change to become permanent. It states that 'Council Directive 96/53/EC places constraints on the size of vehicles that EU Member States may permit in national or international traffic.' It goes on to state that 'the UK now has the clear freedom to changes these rules for domestic transport outside trial conditions.' The UK would not have been able to bring in this win-win change in regulations without having left the EU.[96]

32. Feed the World

The UK's Developing Countries Trading Scheme (DCTS) - which has the UK providing aid through trade with 65 developing nations across the globe - goes further than the EU's equivalent GSP+ and EBA schemes. This was simply not possible to do from within the EU, as this was fully within their remit and control.

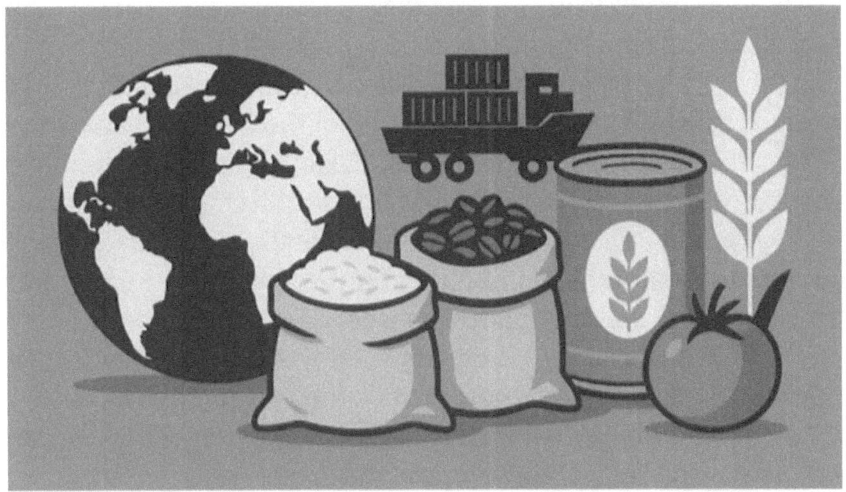

As an EU member, the UK's trading relationship with developing nations was governed by the EU's Generalised Scheme of Preferences (GSP). Established in 1971, the GSP provided preferential market access to the EU (then EEC) for developing countries through reduced or zero tariffs - with the noble intent of providing aid to these poorer nations through access to trade with the much richer EU consumer.[97] When the UK left the EU, it essentially made a carbon copy of the EU GSP, even calling the UK scheme the same name - the UK Generalised Scheme of Preferences (UK GSP). This carbon copy was introduced as a stop gap measure to ensure continuity, whilst a replacement UK scheme was designed.

Fast forward to the Spring of 2023, when the UK brought into effect the Developing Countries Trading Scheme (DCTS) - a scheme designed to be simpler, more generous, and more aligned with the needs of both the developing countries themselves and the UK economy. The transitional GSP, while effective, was a legacy of EU policy and did not fully reflect UK priorities. The UK government recognised that an independent scheme could address specific challenges faced by developing countries, such as complex rules of origin or restrictive conditions, while tailoring benefits to UK market needs.[98]

At a high level, the concept and motivations of the DCTS are fundamentally the same as the EU GSP. However, it is in the re-crafting of the agreement 50 years after the GSP was conceived, as well as it being focused on the aims of just the UK and not those of the wider 27 nations of the EU, that allows the differentiation to add value. The DCTS was developed through a meticulous process involving public consultation, stakeholder engagement, and analysis of global best practices. The UK government launched a consultation from July to September 2021, seeking input from businesses, civil society, developing country governments, and other stakeholders. The DCTS applies to 65 countries, categorised into three tiers based on their economic vulnerability and development status, as defined by the United Nations and the World Bank:

Comprehensive Preferences (CP): For Least Developed Countries (LDCs), offering duty-free, quota-free access on all goods except arms and ammunition.
Enhanced Preferences (EP): For low-income countries (LICs) and lower-middle-income countries (LMICs) deemed economically vulnerable due to limited export diversification. This tier provides duty-free access on 85% of eligible goods.
Standard Preferences (SP): For other LICs and LMICs, offering reduced tariffs on a range of goods.
This tiered structure ensures that the most vulnerable countries receive the greatest benefits, while still supporting broader trade with other developing nations. Notably, countries classified as upper-middle-income for three consecutive years

or those with a free trade agreement (FTA) with the UK are excluded, focusing the scheme on those most in need.

The DCTS significantly lowers or eliminates tariffs on thousands of products. For LDCs, nearly all goods enter duty-free, while EP and SP countries benefit from zero or reduced tariffs on a substantial portion of their exports. The scheme simplifies the tariff schedule by removing 'nuisance tariffs' (those below 2%) and some seasonal tariffs, making trade more predictable and cost-effective.[99]

But how, I hear you ask, does the UK DCTS differ from its EU GSP predecessor?

Expanded Cumulation: LDCs can cumulate inputs from other DCTS countries, Economic Partnership Agreement (EPA) countries, the UK, the EU, Norway, and Switzerland. This means, for example, an Ethiopian exporter can use Kenyan materials and still qualify for duty-free access to the UK, provided the materials meet specific conditions.

Conditions and Suspensions: Unlike the EU GSP, which required countries to ratify 27 international conventions for enhanced preferences (GSP+), the DCTS simplifies conditions. The UK rejected this approach due to insufficient evidence that it drove meaningful change and to reduce complexity. Instead, the DCTS retains the power to suspend preferences for serious violations of human rights, labour rights, anti-corruption, climate change, or environmental conventions, with an expanded list of relevant treaties. This allows flexibility while maintaining ethical standards.

Goods Graduation: To prevent highly competitive products from dominating preferences, the DCTS uses a goods graduation mechanism. Unlike the EU GSP, which graduated products based on broader Harmonised System (HS) sections, the DCTS assesses graduation at the HS chapter level, making it more targeted. For instance, India and Indonesia face suspensions on certain goods due to their export competitiveness, ensuring preferences benefit fewer dominant exporters.

Generosity: The DCTS offers duty-free access on 85% of goods for EP countries (compared to 66% for GSP+ in the EU) and simplifies Rules of Origin (RoO), with a lower average restrictiveness score (2.50 vs. 3.59 for the EU GSP).

So, to summarise - the DCTS is a simplified and more targeted implementation of its ancestor the EU GSP, which is better for those countries who benefit from it and better for the UK as well. It lowers tariffs to provide aid through trade with 65 developing nations across the world, and gives UK consumers access to goods at a lower price.

33. Ill Customs are Seldom Forgotten

The UK has rolled out an Advance Valuation Ruling Service (AVRS), giving importers legal certainty that their chosen customs valuation method is correct, and 'reducing their administrative burden'. This would not be possible for the UK to implement independently, from inside the EU Customs Union.

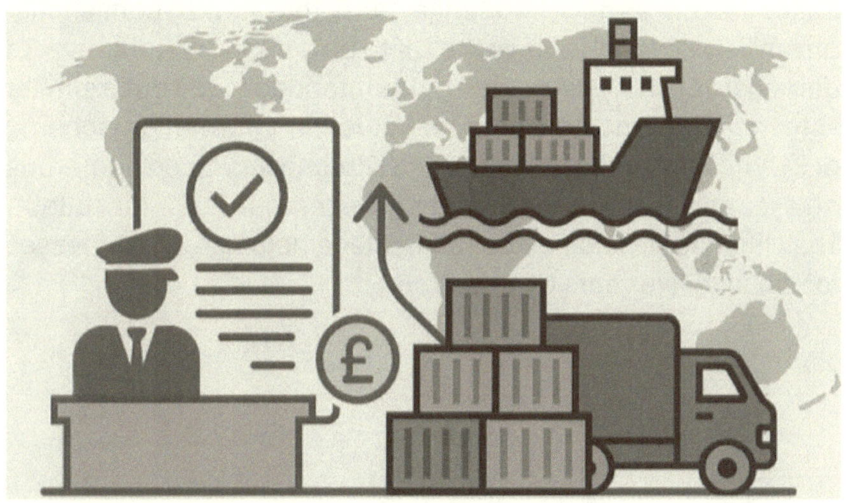

Legislation was introduced as part of the Spring Finance Bill 2023, to allow businesses to request a judgement in advance on the import cost of a particular good – a service known as an Advance Valuation Ruling (AVR or AVRS). This service allows businesses to receive a legally binding judgement on the tariff classification of a given type of goods that they wish to import, and so alongside it a known cost for importation that they can rely upon as being accurate. The AVR lasts for three years, so provides businesses with peace of mind that they are fully aware of the costs at the border for their importation, before they begin importing.[100]

As the UK government outlined in its introduction to AVRS publication, the UK did not previously offer this service as an EU member, 'because customs valuation rulings were not provided for in the EU'.[101] This implementation was also one of the changes required to accede to the Indo-Pacific trade agreement known as the Comprehensive and Progressive agreement for Trans-Pacific Partnership (CPTPP).

Since the rollout of the AVRS, its access has been expanded from the original scope, it has supported UK FTA compliance, and it has aligned the UK with global customs practices. The AVRS supports the Brexiteer argument that leaving the EU would allow the UK to innovate and implement policy faster, as independence from the slower consensus-driven EU approach allows the UK to be nimble and adaptive. To demonstrate this point - the EU has intended to roll out a similar scheme (The Binding Customs Valuation Information scheme or BCVI) for a number of years. The scheme has faced numerous delays, and is currently targeting December 2027 for rollout. The UK scheme will have been in place helping UK businesses for close to five years by that time.

34. Perfect 10

In April 2025 the newly elected Trump administration in the United States announced that they would be levying tariffs on trade based on their perceived trade imbalances and unfair practices with their trade partners. The UK was able to be treated independently and better, by not being bundled with the rest of the EU.

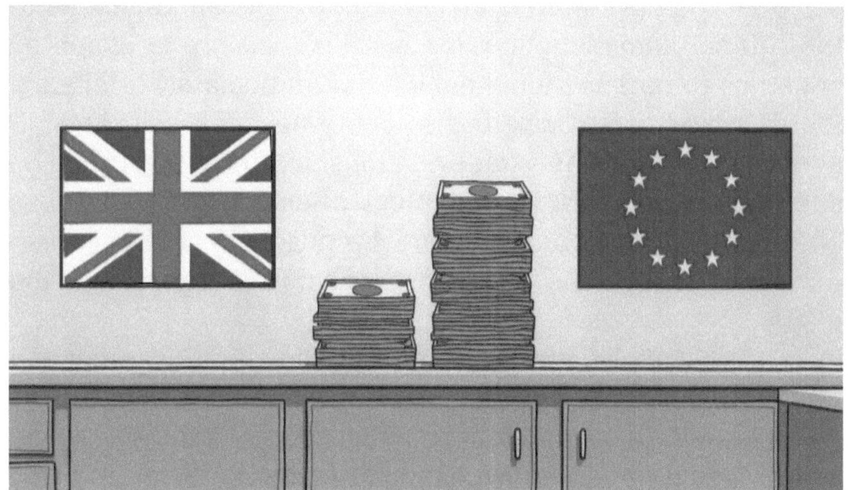

In April 2025, the US Administration under President Trump announced that they were to levy a new import tariff policy, based on two factors:

- A new global minimum applied tariff of 10% on all goods imports
- A per country tariff, over the 10%, based on the balance of bilateral trade

Each country or trading bloc received its own analysis of trade balance from the Office of the US Trade Representative (USTR), and with it an allocated new baseline tariff to be levied on all imports from that country or bloc.[102]

The EU was seen to have an unfair balance of trade, exporting 40% more to the US than it imported from them. This resulted in a calculation that all imported goods from the EU should receive a 20% tariff applied to them. The UK however has an almost perfectly balanced level of trade with the US (imports as much as it exports) and so was given the new global minimum applied tariff of 10%.

Were the UK to still be in the EU at the time of this calculation, the UK-US balance of trade would have been completely ignored, as the UK would have been included in the wider EU calculation - and so the UK would have also been subject to the same 20% tariff level as the rest of the EU.

In the days immediately following this announcement, the Trump administration made the decision to grant all countries or trading blocs that did not immediately retaliate a 90-day grace period where they could negotiate with the US administration for a new trade relationship. The UK again had no such metaphorical Sword of Damocles hanging over it - and was already at the 'front of the queue' for negotiating an improved trade relationship. The EU was not even considered to be in the queue.[103]

In May 2025, just two days after the announcement of a full and comprehensive FTA with India, the Trump Administration confirmed that the first country to have reached a new trading agreement with them was the UK. Far from being at the 'back of the queue' as had been suggested by former US President Barack Obama in 2016, the UK was quite literally at the front of the queue.[104]

The ability of the UK to be judged on its own individual merits, for the UK-US relationship to be considered independently, and the UK to be able to move more rapidly in an increasingly volatile global landscape, is solely down to the UK having voted to leave the EU in 2016. Or to put it another way, I could quote an article from Bloomberg remarking on the agreement - 'Brexit means the UK has been able to be more nimble than the trading bloc it left five years ago. The EU…has so far made little progress, and the bloc expects many of Trump's taxes to stay'.[105]

Reciprocal Tariffs

Country	Tariffs Charged to the U.S.A. Including Currency Manipulation and Trade Barriers	U.S.A. Discounted Reciprocal Tariffs
China	67%	34%
European Union	39%	20%
Vietnam	90%	46%
Taiwan	64%	32%
Japan	46%	24%
India	52%	26%
South Korea	50%	25%
Thailand	72%	36%
Switzerland	61%	31%
Indonesia	64%	32%
Malaysia	47%	24%
Cambodia	97%	49%
United Kingdom	10%	10%
South Africa	60%	30%
Brazil	10%	10%
Bangladesh	74%	37%
Singapore	10%	10%
Israel	33%	17%
Philippines	34%	17%
Chile	10%	10%
Australia	10%	10%
Pakistan	58%	29%
Turkey	10%	10%
Sri Lanka	88%	44%
Colombia	10%	10%

35. Time to Make the Chimichangas

In March 2018 the EU forced a rollout of 'Double Volume Caps', as part of their MiFID II financial services regulations, limiting the volume of equity trading in off-market venues, hurting UK markets more than any other member. Outside of the EU, the FCA was able to stop applying these volume caps, reversing the damage.

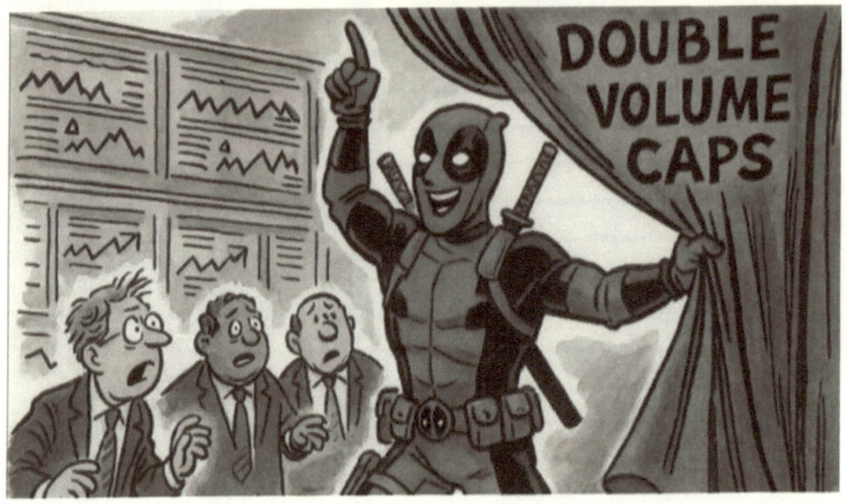

Dark Pools are not as the name may suggest Deadpool's support act from the Marvel Cinematic Universe - they are private venues run by banks, exchanges or independent operators where transactions are cheaper, anonymous and only disclosed after a trade, unlike on open markets. MiFID II limited dark-pool trades to just 4% of the total traded volume in an equity on any single trading venue over a rolling 12-month period and a maximum of 8% of total traded volume in an equity across all dark pool trading venues. If these traded volume limits are reached, then dark-pool trading in that equity is suspended.

These limits hurt the UK markets more than any other EU market as there are more large investment funds based in the UK that need to trade in large volumes. When the caps started in March 2018, 800 equities breached the limits in the first quarter of trading including 85 of the FTSE100 companies, which hit the 8% cap. This was detrimental to the market as it restricted one of the most effective methods of trading large blocks of shares. The main effect of this ill thought through EU Regulation was to drive large-volume trading to other off-market trading methods such as systematic internalisers and periodic auctions.

The FCA stopped applying Volume Caps to UK equities in Dec 2020 and then to all equities traded in the UK in March 2021.[106] This was formalised in the Financial Services Bill in July 2022.[107]

The EU still has Double Volume Caps; at the moment in the EU dark-pool trading has been suspended for 196 equities for all EU dark-pool trading venues having hit the 8% limit, while 35 equities have been suspended on an individual trading venue having hit the 4% limit.

36. Digital Killed the Analog Star

Leaving the EU has allowed the UK to develop fully digitised international trade solutions with like-minded partners in the CPTPP such as Singapore, culminating in the world first accomplishment in September 2023. These changes will make trading cheaper, easier and more secure for UK businesses.

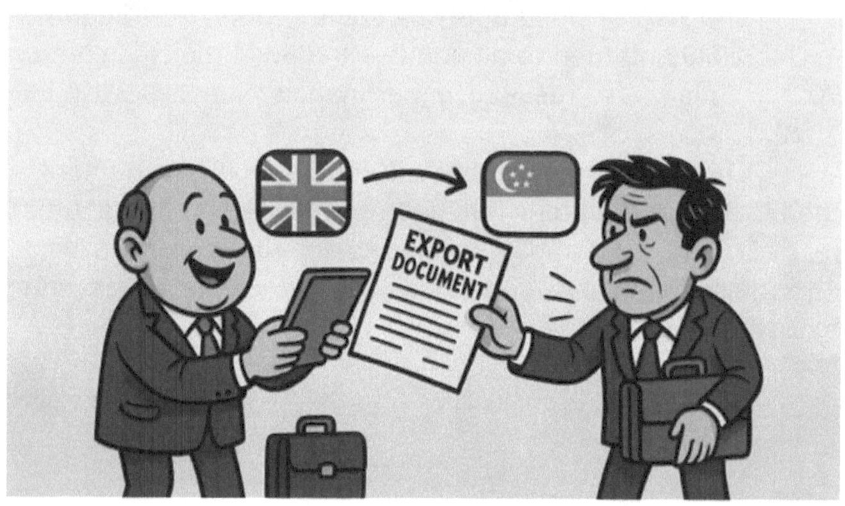

Leaving the EU has allowed the UK to develop fully digitised international trade solutions with like-minded partners in the CPTPP such as Singapore, culminating in a world first accomplishment of a fully digital end-to-end goods shipment in September 2023.

As reported by The Straits Times at the time of the milestone world-first shipment, The United Nations Conference on Trade and Development (UNCTAD) estimates that the typical customs transaction around the world takes on average 40 different physical documents to be generated. This shipment took zero, completing all formalities 'fuss-free and entirely online'.[108]

This world first was able to be completed between the UK and Singapore due to the comprehensive terms agreed between the two countries within the UK-Singapore Digital

Economy Agreement - which was an expansion of the continuation trade agreement that the UK replicated from the EU when it departed in 2021.

Members of the EU delegate all international trade agreements to the EU, as is necessary as part of a customs union. So, this world-first capability was only possible to complete thanks to having left the EU.[109]

37. Rotterdam or Anywhere, Liverpool or Rome

Companies like Mazda are now shipping directly to the UK instead of to a central hub in The Netherlands to be reshipped later from there - and in the process providing more jobs to UK citizens, reduced lead times, more choice, higher reliability and better service to their customers.

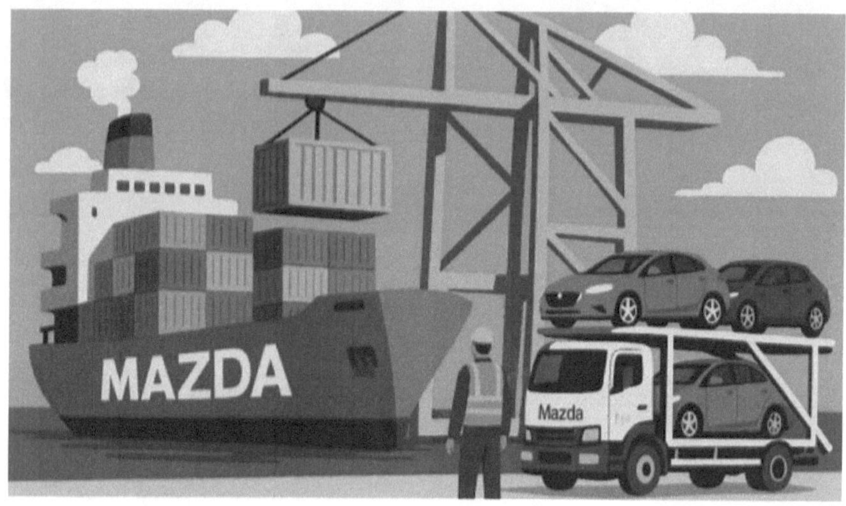

The Rotterdam Effect is a well-known concept in EU trade discussions, and relates to how trade between fellow EU members can be incorrectly overestimated, due to the volume of shipments by sea that first arrive into the EU at either Rotterdam or Antwerp to then be redistributed from that central hub.[110] What is not as commonly discussed, is the effect this centralisation has on the products being imported, and the location of many of the jobs required in shipping and logistics.

Companies like Mazda, who routinely import goods manufactured overseas for sale in the UK, have been moving away from importing to Rotterdam first as a central hub - as it no longer favours their business model and profit margins to do so.

Mazda, like many companies, are now shipping direct to the UK - which in doing so provides more jobs in the UK in

99

shipping and logistics. It also provides reduced lead times, more choice, higher reliability and better service.[111]

As stated by Mazda regarding the change: 'The new shipping logistics route streamlines UK deliveries...and removes the risk of delays caused by Europe to UK transit issues' (read: delays caused by the all too frequent workers strikes at the French borders).[112]

The digitalisation of paperwork within international trade allows for higher profits, lower costs, faster processing and a more productive workforce. All of this is unlocked by the Electronic Trade Documents Act, which would be impossible for the UK to have even explored let alone rolled out without having left the EU.

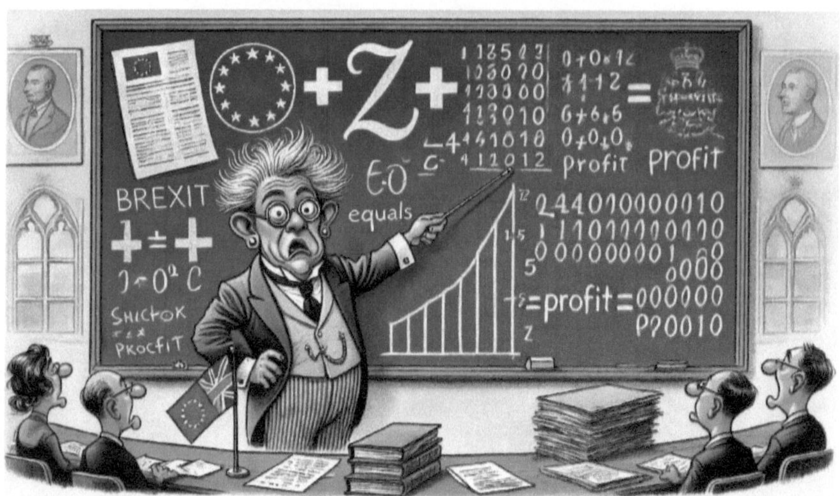

It is a common cliché in UK politics that every new Bill or agreement is at some point touted as being groundbreaking or even landmark in its nature. When we consider the Electronic Trade Documents Act (ETDA) however, it is fair to say that this change in UK law is indeed groundbreaking.[113]

The Act addresses the necessary move into the modern age, in what is a complex area heavily burdened with the use of paper. The Act grants electronic versions of trade documents such as bills of lading and exchange, the same legal status as their paper equivalents under English law. The reason why this is so important is that English law is the basis for 80% of trade documents used across the world - so a change in English law in this regard quite literally has an effect across the globe. The benefits of this move are quite easy to understand, but to go into more detail on a few areas:

Cost Savings: The UK Government estimated that the move to electronic trade documents would generate over £1.14 Billion in net benefits to UK businesses over ten years, by reducing the costs of producing handling and couriering paper documents. An example would be the processing of a digital bill of lading, which can take in the region of ten minutes compared to seven days for the paper version.
Efficiency: Digital documents allow for faster transactions, able to be transferred in seconds to all corners of the globe as opposed to days or even weeks. Real-time access to documents improves on supply chain visibility and cash flow, benefiting small and medium-sized businesses.
Security: Using secure electronic document systems, such as those on the blockchain, vastly reduces the risk of fraud, loss or unauthorised alteration.

Environmental: The global container shipping industry, just one part of the global trading system, generates literally billions of pages of paper documents every single year. Digitalisation cuts down paper use and the emissions used to create, print, courier, store and destroy it.

To give an actual case study of the savings available to UK businesses – CueTheBBQ, a company who specialise in the import of wood and charcoal from trees not grown in the UK, estimated in 2024 that they saved in the region of $200 per container – and were in receipt of 10-12 containers a week. So the implementation of this Act was quite literally saving their business thousands of dollars a month in administrative costs.[114] The UK branch of the International Chamber of Commerce (ICC) called the ETDA a 'missing piece in the jigsaw' for digitalising trade, and echoed the government's projections that it would save UK businesses in the region of £1.1 Billion over the course of the next decade.

Chris Southworth, the Secretary General of ICC UK wrote in December 2024 that the ETDA 'enabled 80% of bills of lading and 60% of trade finance, marine insurance, shipping and commodity transactions to be digitalised worldwide'. He added that UK companies leveraging the benefits of the ETDA were seeing as much as a 15% increase in business profitability alongside an 80% reduction in transaction costs and cross-border shipping times.[115]

The UK as an EU member was not able to unilaterally explore innovation in this area, as the trade documentation used within the EU Single Market and Customs Union was the responsibility of the EU itself and had to be uniform across all member states.

39. Liberalisation, Across the Nation

Leaving the EU allowed the UK to sit outside of the EU Customs Union and Single Market rules, which artificially cushion Intra-EU trade against competition outside of the EU with its high walls. From outside the EU, the UK actually has fewer net barriers to trade in place than it did as an EU member state.

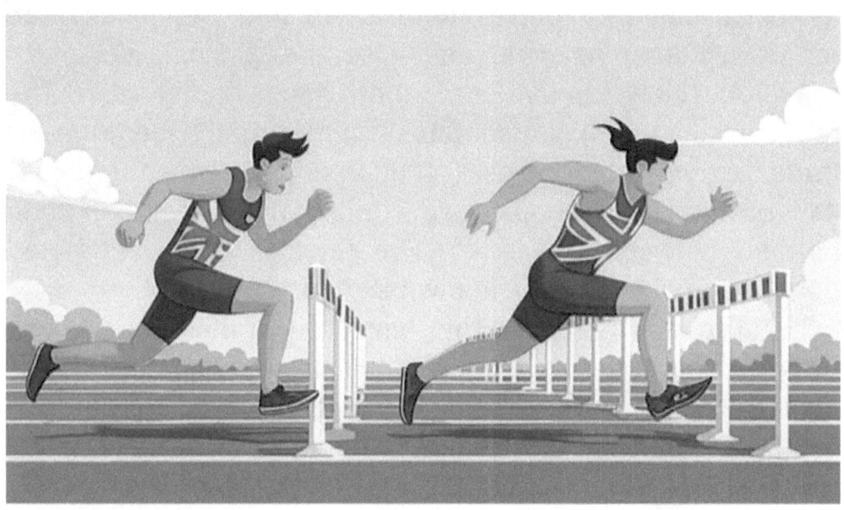

As a member of the EU, and as an extension of that the EU Customs Union, trade barriers and the lack thereof were essentially a centralised matter for the EU to control and oversee. By leaving the EU, the control (the 'sovereignty') over such matters was returned to the UK government, allowing a different approach to be taken as regards trade protectionism.

Every two years, the Tholos Foundation publishes its 'Trade Barrier Index' (TBI) report, which compares countries across the globe against how protectionist their trade policies are, or how 'free' their global trade approach is. The report in 2021 looked at a recently departed post-EU UK and concluded that the UK had taken a less protectionist stance – that the very act of leaving the EU had reduced trade barriers between the UK and the rest of the world.[116]

To quote the Tholos TBI 2021: 'One of the most newsworthy insights of the 2021 TBI is the remarkable progress of the United Kingdom in lowering its own trade barriers after Brexit. Once the UK exited the EU's common external tariff at the beginning of 2020, it embarked on one of the world's most ambitious efforts at unilateral trade liberalisation.'

The European Department of the International Monetary Fund (IMF) released a report in December 2024 entitled 'Europe's Choice: Policies for Growth and Resilience'. The report was damning on the efficacy of the EU Single Market for the removal of trade barriers for both goods and services. The report states that their estimates 'suggest that these [Intra-EU trade barriers] might be as high as a tariff equivalent of about 44% on average for goods trade – three times higher than trade barriers between US states. For services these estimated barriers are even steeper, equivalent to a 110% tariff'.[117]

The entire premise that being an EU member reduces trade barriers sufficient to warrant the high cost and the barriers being raised against non-EU trade, has been completely eroded by the outcome of Brexit and the trade data that has followed.

40. A Stay of (Tariff) Execution

From outside of the EU, the UK has been able to offer UK businesses the opportunity to petition the government to remove tariffs on a given type of product for a limited period of time, which the government then reviews and if approved looks to implement - as it did in April 2024 with over 120 tariff lines.

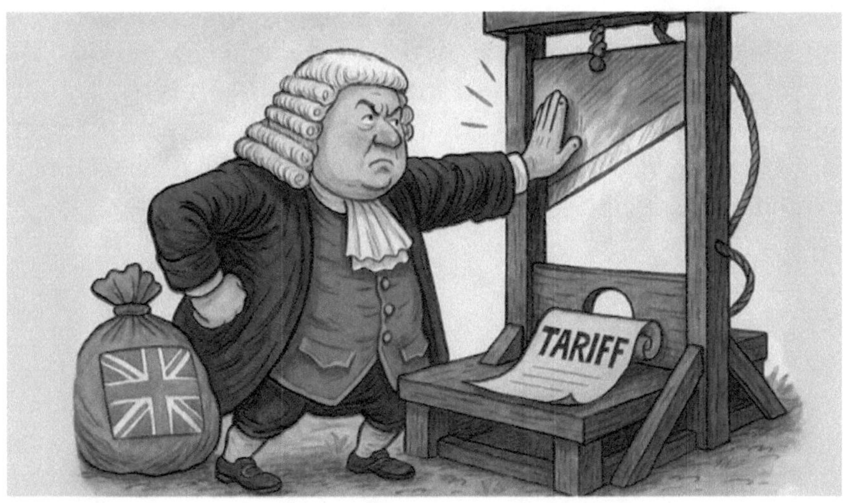

With the UK now firmly outside of the EU Customs Union (at least at the time of writing), the UK government has been able to offer UK businesses the opportunity to petition the government to remove tariffs on a given type of product for a limited period of time, which the government then reviews and if approved looks to implement – as it did in April 2024 with over 120 tariff lines.[118]

Import tariffs on goods including flowers, fruit juices and chemicals were suspended for two years on 11 April 2024 and so will remain as such until June 2026, according to the Department for Business and Trade. UK importers of more than 120 products from all countries could benefit from the temporary withdrawal of duties. The affected products – primarily used as inputs in domestic production – include juices, preparations and starches, and non-agricultural goods such as ceramics, car parts and leather. The measures are aimed at helping make the UK's small and medium-sized enterprises (SMEs) more globally competitive.[119]

This would simply not be possible from within the EU, as tariff lines within the EU Customs Union must be the same for all member states.

In April 2025 the newly elected Labour government continued with the now annual scheme, removing tariffs completely on 89 goods for a period of two years – with forecasted savings of £34 Million over the two-year period. The list of goods included mixed fruit juices; dried raisins; ground peppers of numerous varieties; shelled pinenuts; frozen whiteleg shrimp; coconut oils; certain types of plywood; and certain types of uncooked pasta.[120]

41. Oh (Antipodean) Brother, Where Art Thou?

From 31ˢᵗ March 2024, due to the terms of the UK-Australia Free Trade Agreement, all artwork re-sold in Australia made by British artists will see 5% of the resale price paid to the artist (where the resale value is over AUS$1,000). This would not be possible without the UK-Australia FTA, which in turn would not be possible without having left the EU.

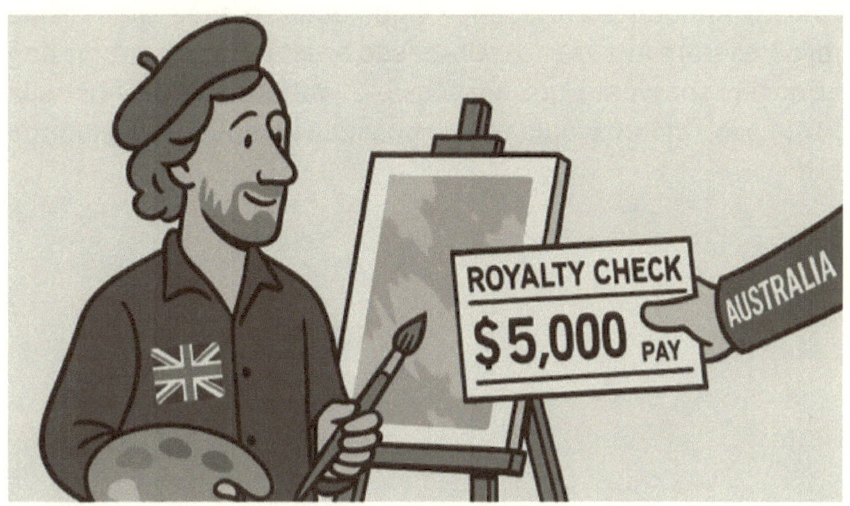

Since March 31st 2024, due to the terms of the UK-Australia Free Trade Agreement, all artwork re-sold in Australia made by British artists now sees 5% of the resale price paid to the artist (where the resale value is over AUS$1,000). Under this agreement, UK artists will now be entitled to claim resale royalties each time their artwork is resold in the Australian professional art market.[121]

The Artist's Resale Right (ARR) serves as a crucial income source for emerging artists, with a vast majority utilising these royalties for living expenses and art materials. On average, artists earn £5,000 annually from ARR, highlighting its importance in sustaining their artistic endeavours.

Under the new legislation enacted by the Australian parliament, UK artists will receive resale royalties equivalent to

5% of the sale price for artworks sold commercially for AUS$1,000 or more. This reciprocal agreement replaces the previous scenario where British artists did not receive any royalties from Australian sales. Starting 1st April 2024, ARR royalties in the UK will be calculated in pounds instead of euros, a post-Brexit adjustment aimed at better reflecting the UK market and reducing costs for businesses processing royalty payments.

In May 2025, the Design and Artists Copyright Society (DACS) announced that they had received their first resale royalties from Australia for UK-based artists.[122] The commission arrangement would not be possible without the UK-Australia FTA, which in turn would not be possible without having left the EU.

Section 4

Brexit Means We Run Our Own Country Again

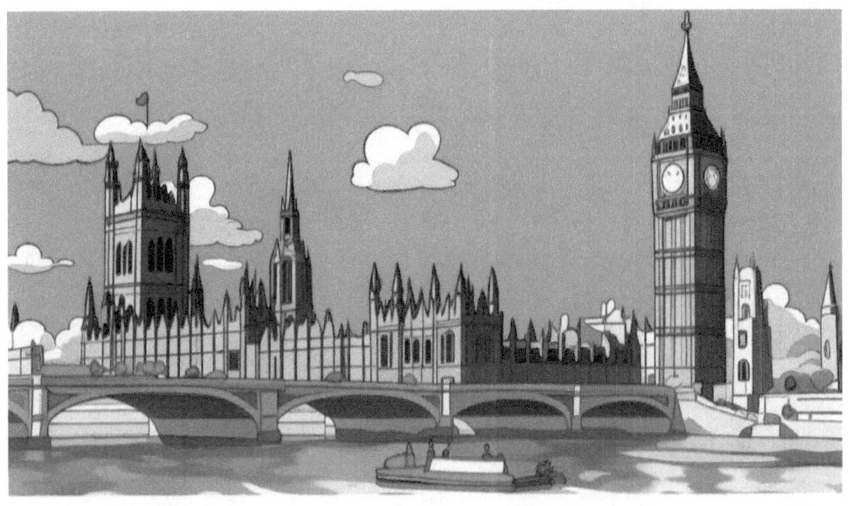

42. Some Are More Equal Than Others

The UK had the single worst ratio of MEPs to citizens in the entire EU Parliament, with each MEP representing nearly one million people - this compares to smaller nations like Malta, where each MEP represented only 84,000 people. This means that Maltese citizens had over ten times the representation in Parliament than UK citizens did.

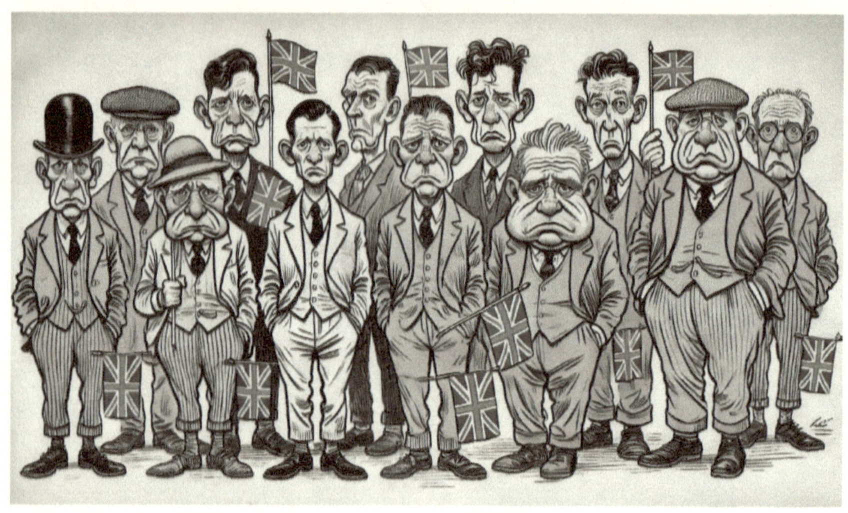

Estimates of the amount of UK laws controlled or influenced by the EU vary wildly depending on how they are calculated (and by whom), but efforts by The House of Commons Library in 2010 placed the figure at somewhere between 15-50%.[123]

Despite the difficulty in pinning down a more robust estimate, FullFact have made the observation that 'In agriculture, fisheries, external trade, and the environment, it's fair to say that EU legislation and policy is indeed the main driver of UK law and policy.'[124]

The EU allocates MEP seats based on the populations of each member state but gives a higher proportion per capita to the smaller member states than to the larger states. For the UK in 2019, there were 73 MEPs - that's the equivalent of one MEP for every 915,500 people, and the highest in the EU. For Malta, the smallest EU member state, they had one MEP for every 84,000 people - which means that Maltese citizens through their MEP effectively had over ten times the say in EU laws as UK citizens did.[125]

In the UK Parliament, MPs represent approximately 90,000 people and constituency sizes are routinely adjusted to ensure they remain balanced. So for those areas where EU legislation is the main driver of UK law, the UK voters are now back in control of the policies which affect them, and have over ten times the level of say in those policies in terms of constituency representation, compared to the representation given in the EU Parliament.

Country Name	Population in 2019	MEPs in 2019	Population per MEP in 2019
Malta	504,000	6	84,000
Luxembourg	620,000	6	103,333
Republic of Cyprus	1,229,000	6	204,833
Estonia	1,327,000	6	221,167
Latvia	1,914,000	8	239,250
Lithuania	2,794,000	11	254,000
Slovenia	2,088,000	8	261,000
Croatia	4,065,000	11	369,545
Bulgaria	6,976,000	17	410,353
Slovakia	5,454,000	13	419,538
Finland	5,522,000	13	424,769
Denmark	5,814,000	13	447,231
Ireland	4,934,000	11	448,545
Hungary	9,771,000	21	465,286
Austria	8,800,000	18	488,889
Portugal	10,290,000	21	490,000
Czech Republic	10,670,000	21	508,095
Greece	10,720,000	21	510,476
Sweden	10,280,000	20	514,000
Belgium	11,490,000	20	574,500
Romania	19,370,000	32	605,313
Netherlands	17,340,000	26	666,923
Poland	37,970,000	51	744,510
Italy	59,730,000	73	818,219
Germany	83,090,000	96	865,521
Spain	47,130,000	54	872,778
France	67,390,000	74	910,676
United Kingdom	66,840,000	73	915,616

Fig 1: Population per MEP, all EU member states, 2019

43. Rise of the Machines, Interrupted

The EU has mandated that all new cars sold in all member states must come fitted and enabled with driver-assist technology as standard – technology that is still in its infancy and has been found with some brands to be 'more of a hindrance' and in some cases 'borderline dangerous'. The UK can choose differently.

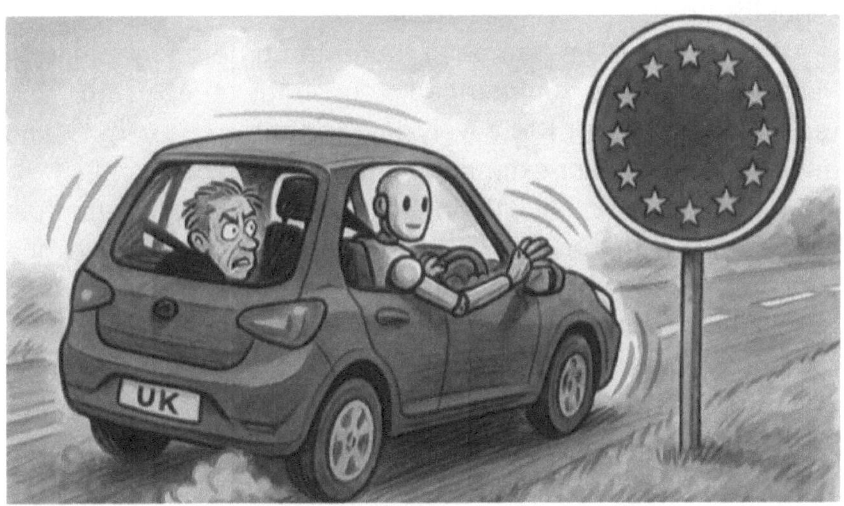

EU Regulation 2019/2144, known as the 'New Vehicle General Safety Regulation' or GSR2 for short, brought in mandatory automated vehicle driver assistance tools for all new cars, rolling out in three phases - phase one in July 2022, phase two in July 2024, and phase three in July 2026.[126]

These regulations stipulate that not only must all new motor vehicles sold in the EU be fitted with these features by default, but they must also be enabled by default - with them all re-enabling themselves on each engine restart, even if the driver manually disables them. All of these features have their inherent flaws, as they introduce an overriding of the driver by autonomous systems - but one in particular is well known and reported to have significant inherent dangers and can itself be the cause of accidents.

Emergency Lane Keeping Systems, or ELKS, use front-mounted cameras to detect road markings - and then decide in real time whether or not the driver is using the correct lane or unintentionally veering out of lane. Should the system believe that the driver is unintentionally drifting out of their intended lane of traffic, the vehicle will first try to draw attention to this through haptic feedback (steering wheel vibration and/or alerts), but will then intervene directly and alter the steering direction of the vehicle to return to where it believes the car *should* be.

The ELKS system has been found in numerous models to have concerning unintended consequences, with the technology itself being relatively new and still prone to mistaken decision-making. For example, testing in July 2024 on the new MG 4 conducted by Which? magazine, found multiple occasions where the ELKS system pulled the car onto the wrong side of the road - and in one case into oncoming traffic. Which? have since received multiple complaints from MG owners, reporting similar incidents.[127] The editor of Auto Express goes one further, and commends the Renault Megane in September 2024 for having an easy to reach physical button for turning the feature off, as he finds the technology to be 'more of a hindrance' and 'even borderline dangerous'.[128] There are also quite valid concerns from other road users, with automated systems needing to make priority calls over whether the car should cross a white line, or avoid a near pass or potential collision - as was discussed in an article in Bike Radar magazine, and confirmed with an interview with the team at Volvo.[129]

The ELKS system is mandated as part of Phase two, and so is already a mandatory feature of all new vehicles sold in the EU. These features are also being included in many new vehicles sold in the UK as standard, but the difference is that there is no law requiring them to be used, nor are they required to be enabled by default. UK drivers have the choice to remain in full control of their vehicles, and to not be forced to trust vehicle steering into the hands of knowingly flawed automated systems.

Phase three of the GSR2 rollout mandates driver-facing cameras to be installed in the dash, to continuously monitor the driver and track eye movements for signs of fatigue. If the idea of the government requiring your car to be filming your face continuously does not fill you with dread and concern for government overreach, then I am not sure what would.

The UK is outside of the remit of EU laws (or at least most of it is, Northern Ireland being the exception), and so can happily ignore these mandatory inclusions - or even insist that UK car retailers disable them by default. The UK would not have the ability to do so, if it was still a member of the EU.

44. (No Longer) Arrested Development

As covered by The Spectator in 2023, a partnership on cancer treatment R&D between the UK govt and BioNTech was and is only possible due to the post-Brexit regulatory environment that we have been able to put in place - which is just one of the many benefits in medicinal research and treatment with thanks to Brexit.

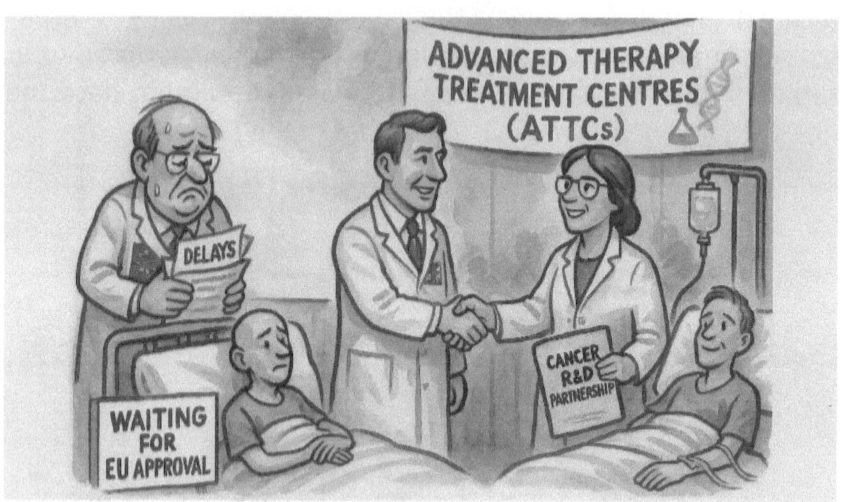

Leaving the European Union (EU) has led to significant changes in the UK's regulatory environment for medicines, offering several advantages and fostering new partnerships with drug manufacturers. The enhanced regulatory autonomy has allowed the UK to introduce mechanisms like the Advanced Therapy Treatment Centres (ATTCs), to expedite the approval process for new drugs. This means quicker patient access to innovative treatments, faster than the EU due to the removal of bureaucratic layers.

As a further example of this, as covered by The FT and The Spectator in early 2023 - a partnership on cancer treatment R&D between the UK government and BioNTech is only possible due to the post-Brexit regulatory environment that we have been able to foster and develop.[130] The Spectator article lays out two ways in which the BioNTech agreement demonstrates Brexit benefits:

> 1. It allowed the UK to create a more flexible, simpler regulatory structure, and one that is better suited to our needs, and avoids the 'if in doubt ban it' bureaucracy that dominates the rest of Europe.
>
> 2. The UK can use it to become a laboratory for advanced science and technology, even more than it already was. Life sciences are the most obvious example of that, partly because the UK was already strong in that industry.

The founder of BioNTech, Ozlem Tureci, told the BBC that 'we have seen in the Covid-19 pandemic with the fast approval of vaccines in the UK, that the [post-Brexit] regulatory authority is exceptional. And then there is the genomic-analysis capabilities. The UK is one of the leading nations in that regard.'

In October 2020 the UK Government announced that it would participate in two international medical research schemes, called 'Project Orbis' and 'Access Consortium', from 1st January 2021 – the earliest the UK would be able to participate due to the need to be fully outside the EU to do so. These two schemes looked to leverage multiple regulatory authority processes in multiple countries, to fast-track life-saving new treatments primarily for cancer. Multiple new treatments have now been made available in the UK through these schemes, quicker than they otherwise would have been if the UK had still been in the EU.[131]

45. Running Up That Bill

Since Brexit, the UK government has been able to better respond to public demand and public need, removing VAT on multiple goods like women's sanitary products; children's car seats; and green energy items like solar panels, insulation and heat pumps – reducing consumer bills and helping change public behaviour for the better.

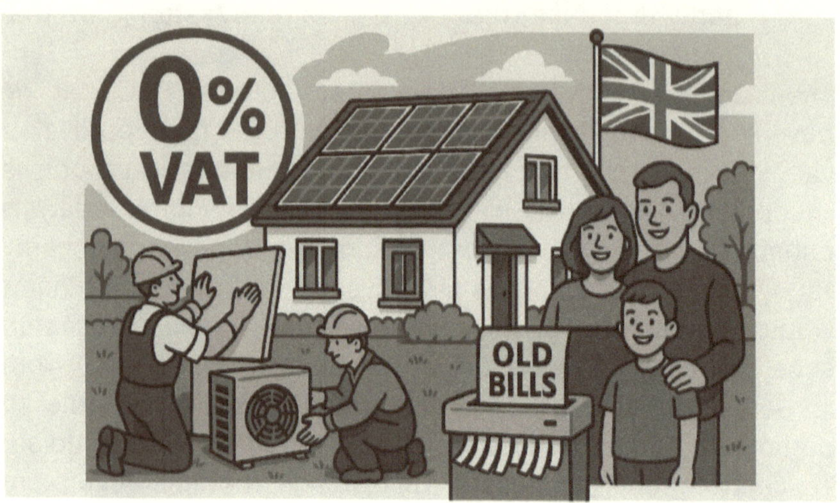

Following the UK's departure from the EU, the British government introduced several policies where VAT has been either reduced or removed completely – either to correct what is seen in the UK to be a historical oversight and mis-categorisation, or to encourage the uptake of a particular type of product with an overarching aim to change public behaviour for the common good. Below are just some of the many examples of such changes:

- In January 2021, VAT was removed from women's sanitary products[132]
- In March 2022, VAT was removed from green energy purchases such as solar panels, insulation and heat pumps until 2027[133]

- In January 2024, the categorisation of women's sanitary products mentioned above was expanded to include period underwear, following a successful public petition on the matter[134]

Though EU member states can determine their own rates of VAT to be charged within their countries, there are minimums in place that member states cannot go below without prior approval and an EU-wide agreement for the same treatment. The EU VAT Directive requires member states to apply a standard rate of at least 15% VAT on most goods and services, with a smaller group of limited exceptions being allowed a lower minimum rate of 5%.[135]

The changes that the UK has made to VAT since leaving the EU would not have been possible to make unilaterally without Brexit.

46. I've Got the Power(s)

With the return of sovereignty to the UK for multiple areas of government policy and UK Law, the ability to petition your representative - and to vote to remove them should they prove to be ineffective or negligent in the areas you care about - has not been as possible as it is now since the 1970s.

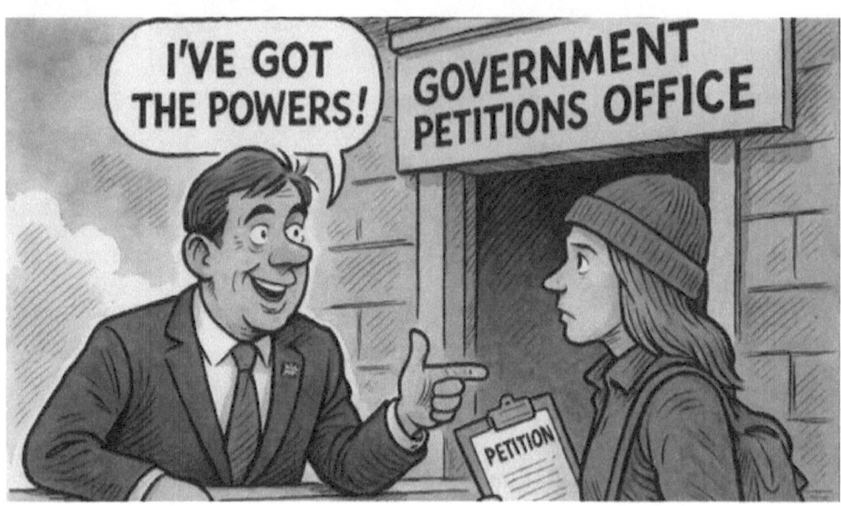

The UK Parliament has a long-standing tradition of encouraging and allowing the general public to petition it for change, dating all the way back to the 1600s. The processes involved in this have of course evolved over the centuries, but the general principle of being able to petition the Government to enact change has remained broadly the same.

As a member of the EU, the laws of the EU took primacy over UK laws – and so the decisions of the EU Courts and EU Parliament also took primacy over the UK Courts and Parliament.

Members of the public continued to submit petitions to the government during this time, but many were unable to even be addressed by the UK Parliament – as the topics in question were outside of the remit of the UK Government, but in fact sat with the EU. The general public were mostly unaware of how they were, to coin a phrase, 'barking up the wrong tree'.

Outside of the EU, those who wish to petition their government to enact change can again do so, in the knowledge that they are in fact contacting those with the power to make such changes. In other words, the British public are now talking to the organ grinder, not the monkey.

A few examples of such petitions, that the UK government were legally unable to respond to whilst still an EU member:

Petition 41492, November 2012: 'Stop mass immigration from Bulgarians and Romanians in 2014, when EU restrictions on immigration are relaxed'.

The government response to this petition states that 'continuing the controls beyond the end of this year is not possible because of the terms of the accession treaties...under which these two countries joined the EU'.[136]

Petition 29349, February 2012: 'Return VAT on Air Ambulance fuel payments'[137]

Petition 64331, April 2014: 'End non-stun slaughter to promote animal welfare'[138]

Petition 107516, September 2015: 'Stop all immigration and close the UK borders until ISIS is defeated'[139]

47. Cellophane, Mr Cellophane

A ECJ ruling in 2022 has resulted in member states having to shut down open registers of corporate ownership, reducing transparency and increasing the risk of corruption - as the UK is outside of the EU and the ECJ, it can happily continue with the pre-existing more transparent approach.

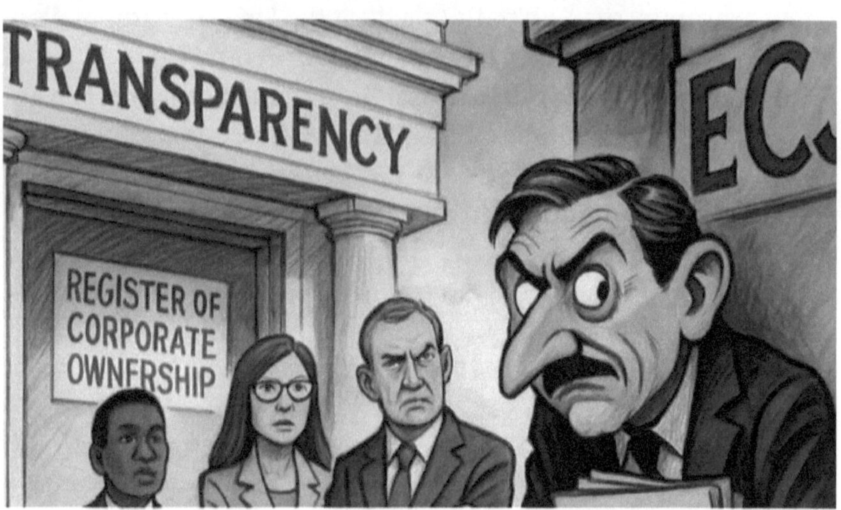

A ruling in 2022 by the Court of Justice of the European Union (CJEU or ECJ), declared that EU legislation around the ownership of companies within the EU was invalid and as such illegal.[140] The legislation had been in place since 2017 and had required all EU member states, including the UK at that time, to maintain central registers containing information on the 'beneficial owners' of legal entities (companies) established within their jurisdiction.

In this context, the term 'beneficial owner' is interpreted quite broadly - as it includes not only the people who hold a significant share in the company, but also those who have significant influence in the decision making.

As the UK had already left the EU when the ECJ made the ruling, the UK was under no obligation at all to take the ruling into consideration – and as such completely ignored it. In fact, the UK has since doubled down and taken the intent of better transparency even further with the Economic Crime and Corporate Transparency Act of 2023 (ECCTA).[141]

In the words of Macfarlanes LLP, 'The CJEU's decision now means that beneficial ownership information will be more publicly available and easily accessible in the UK than in the EU.'[142]

48. School's Out for Starmer

In summer 2024 Labour announced it would remove the VAT exemption for all UK independent schools - this would not be possible without Brexit, as EU law states educational establishments must be exempt from VAT, and other member states have been prosecuted in the past for attempting to implement the same policy.

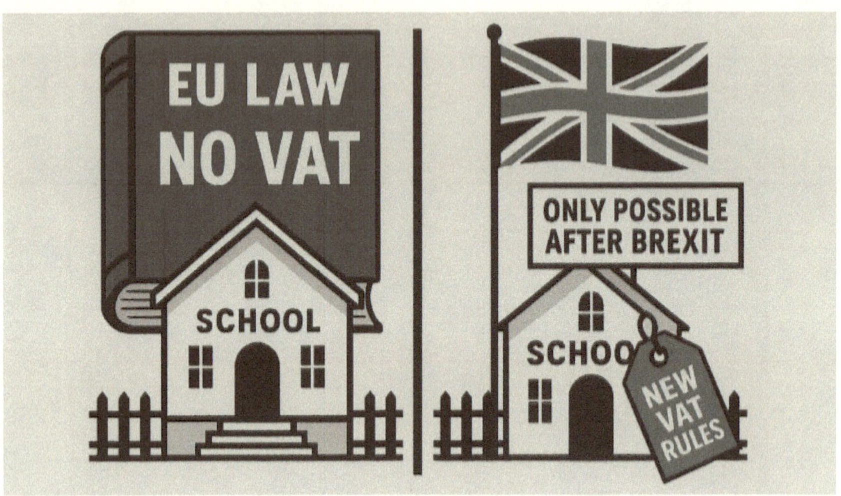

In the run-up to the general election campaign of Summer 2024, the Labour Party announced it would remove the VAT exemption for all independent / 'private' schools in the UK.[143] Since securing their election win, the now Labour government went ahead and removed the VAT exemption from January 2025.[144]

This policy would not be possible within the EU, as it is specifically detailed in EU law that educational establishments must be exempt from VAT.

The Greek government attempted to introduce the same policy in 2015 and was reminded by the EU Commission that such a policy is against EU law and accordingly had to withdraw its action.[145] Council Directive 2006/112/EC of 28 November 2006 on the common system of value-added tax - Art. 132, '1. Member States shall exempt the following transactions: [..]

(i) the provision of children's or young people's education, school or university education, vocational training or retraining, including the supply of services and of goods closely related thereto, by bodies governed by public law having such as their aim or by other organisations recognised by the Member State concerned as having similar objects;' [146]

The removal of the VAT exemption for private schools was a headline policy of the Labour Party campaign, being mentioned throughout the campaign as something that they would look to introduce in short order should they win. So it is fair to say that the current Labour government campaigned on pledges that they were only able to make due to having left the EU.

49. The Return of Democracy

Brexit restored democratic control over our lawmaking to the British people and their elected representatives. We gave the power to make and scrutinise the laws that apply to us back to our Parliament and the devolved administrations so that they are now made in Belfast, Cardiff, Edinburgh and Westminster, not Brussels.

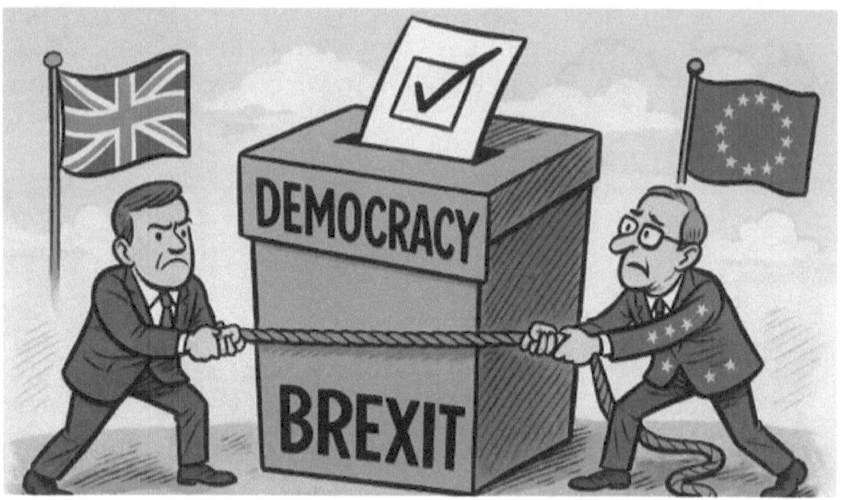

A core tenet of the democratic relationship between government and the electorate in the UK is the understanding that the government acts on behalf of the electorate, given the power to do so *by* the electorate. To quote the website of the Council of Europe – 'democracy can be thought of as power of the people: a way of governing which depends on the will of the people'.[147]

A fundamental concern with EU membership is the sacrifice of legislative control from national government over to the central control of the EU Commission and Parliament – governmental structures where the voter has either very weak or in fact no control at all in who wields that power. In March 2001, the Labour MP Tony Benn proposed five questions which should be asked by those in positions of legislative power, to determine whether they are operating in a democratic manner:

1. What power do you have?
2. Where did you get it from?
3. In whose interests do you exercise it?
4. To whom are you accountable?
5. How can 'we' (the people) get rid of you?

The British people understood that the above questions were unable to be answered satisfactorily as EU members, which was responsible in part for the growth in discontent in EU membership.[148]

Leaving the EU allowed for a core desire of the British electorate to be realised - that laws governing the UK would be decided upon and enacted by those elected to do so within the UK political structure. This includes 152 areas of policy where previously the EU had regulatory competence, where it now sits with the devolved administrations.[149]

This has a very clear tangible benefit - that the UK voter is now more empowered to enact change through their vote, making their vote more valuable and more effective.

To again quote Tony Benn MP from the same intervention in 2001: 'If you cannot get rid of the people who govern you, then you do not live in a democratic system'.

50. Approaching Artificial Intelligence, Intelligently

Advancement in AI tools and technology is improving at breakneck speed, and the EU approach to ban anything it doesn't understand is leaving it in the technological dark ages. The UK is a world leader in AI, and it is only able to be that because of leaving the EU and its antiquated approaches to the modern world.

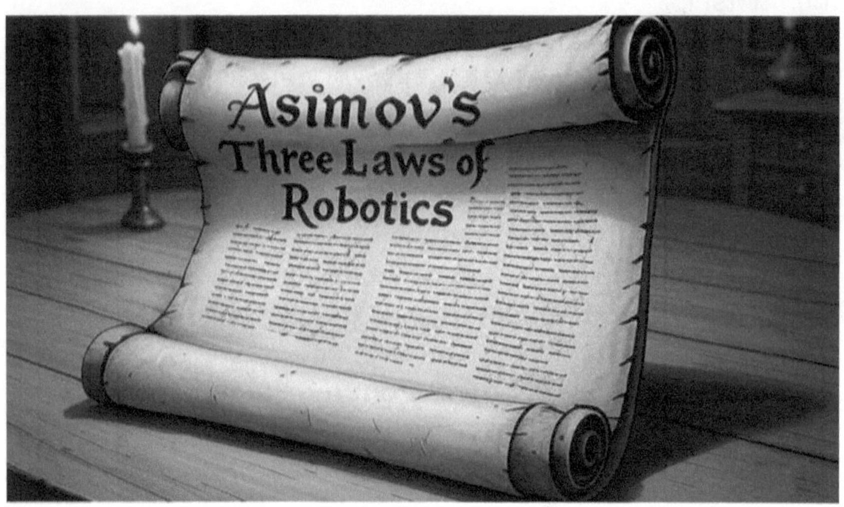

The advancement of AI tools is moving at a remarkable pace, with the benefits visible to all of us on a daily basis. Many of these tools, however, would not be available to us at all right now, if not for having left the EU. While the EU is tangled up with the heavy chains of regulation, the UK has the freedom to sprint ahead.

With Brexit having been completed in 2021, the UK is outside of the EU's AI Act, which means that UK consumers and businesses are not bogged down by the same restrictive rules and can have access to tools and features leading the market across the globe. The UK has opted to adopt a more flexible approach to AI regulation, focusing on innovation while still managing risks. This has allowed for quicker integration of cutting-edge AI like Meta AI's latest tools, which are not yet accessible in the EU due to ongoing regulatory negotiations.

ChatGPT, Apple Intelligence, Meta AI, X Grok and many more have opted to delay feature launches in the EU or even avoid the EU market completely - but the UK has had access to all of them from the outset. As the CEOs of Meta and Spotify, Mark Zuckerberg and Daniek Ek, recently stated in a joint article 'The EU risks falling behind [in AI] because of incoherent and complex regulation'.[150]

Moreover, the UK is now free to tailor its AI policies to suit its own tech ecosystem, potentially attracting more investment and tech startups looking for a less regulated environment. This could lead to a tech boom, where the UK positions itself as a global AI powerhouse, leveraging its post-Brexit regulatory flexibility. As the CEO and Founder of AI Tech Unicorn Synthesia, Victor Riparbelli, recently said in an interview on the matter - 'I think that it's positive for the UK that they're not in the EU right now. The EU is doing what they always do, which is they regulate - and so now the EU has all the regulation and none of the AI companies.'[151]

As the former UK Deputy Prime Minister Nick Clegg recently stated, in his capacity as President for global affairs at Meta, 'Europe should be the perfect place for global companies to invest, build technologies and release products. Instead, Europeans are getting access to technology later than the rest of the world.'[152]

51. Trainer, Trailer, Saver, Drive

An EU directive required all Category B driving licence holders (standard car drivers) to pass an additional driving test to tow a trailer - Brexit allowed the UK government to remove this unnecessary overhead - reducing costs for UK drivers and freeing up over 30,000 driving test slots a year for more worthwhile test activities.

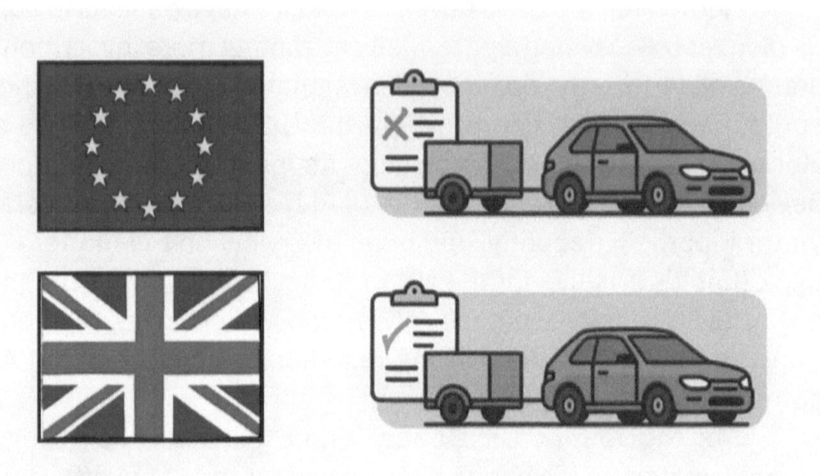

EU Directive 2006/126/EC introduced a requirement for all car drivers (category B vehicles) to pass an additional test, before being able to tow a trailer. When transposed into UK law, this took the form of making it illegal to tow a trailer without passing an additional driving test to do so, if you had passed your category B driving test after 1st January 1997.[153] This additional requirement was not only seen by UK drivers to be superfluous and unnecessary but also caused a large overhead in additional testing costs for UK drivers when none existed previously.

Following UK exit from the EU in 2021, and with a view of streamlining what had become an overly bureaucratic system, the UK government amended multiple aspects of UK driving tests - including removing the need for an additional driving test in order to tow a trailer below 3,500kg in weight (what is known as a Category BE or B+E licence).[154]

These changes came into place in December 2021 - and so all holders of UK Category B licences, unless otherwise banned from doing so, can now tow a trailer on their existing licence without additional cost and training. This not only saves UK drivers additional costs but also frees up over 30,000 driving test slots a year - to be used for other more worthwhile testing.

52. Not So Super, Super League

April 2021 saw an attempt to create a new Super League of European football, which was hated almost immediately by players and fans alike. FIFA and UEFA shut it down – but an EU court ruling in December 2023 said the actions of FIFA and UEFA were unlawful. The UK can happily ignore that court ruling from outside the EU.

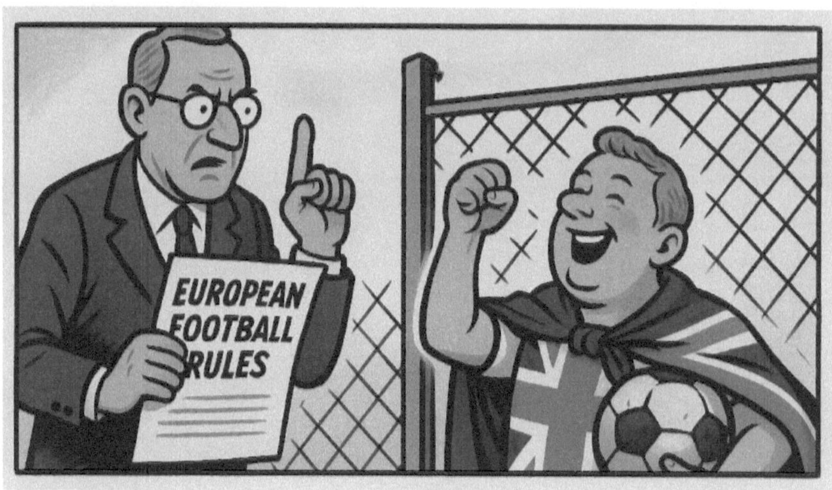

On the afternoon of Sunday 18th April 2021, the news broke that a new European Football 'Super League' (ESL) had been in the works in the background for some time, and that twelve top-flight European Football teams had signed up to take part - including six from the UK. This announcement was wildly unpopular with Football fans across the country and was even found to be a somewhat unifying topic between political parties at an otherwise fractious time.[155] Polling conducted at the time found as many as 96% of fans were strongly against the plans, which effectively removed the concept of fair play and rankings for 15 top-flight teams, who would have permanent positions within the breakaway league irrespective of their performance.[156]

Within 72 hours of the announcement being made, the plans were all but destroyed - with all six UK teams having seen such levels of anger from their fans, that they quickly U-turned and removed themselves from the ESL. This change of heart was also assisted by assurances given by both UEFA and FIFA, that their actions would not be taken lightly and their presence in the UK Premier League and ability to be eligible for the Champions League were in jeopardy.[157]

Roll the clock forward to December 2023, and the European Court of Justice (CJEU or ECJ) gave a ruling on the actions conducted by FIFA and UEFA in 2021 to prevent the Super League. The ECJ found that the actions of the regulatory bodies 'abused their dominant position' and were unlawful - despite the actions being exactly what the fans desired the governing bodies to do.[158]

Luckily for the UK and the Football Association (FA), all of this story took place after the UK had left the EU - and with it the jurisdiction of the ECJ and its formal judgements. So from the perspective of UK Football the ECJ ruling is irrelevant, as it has no standing at all in the UK. Had the UK still been in the EU and under the jurisdiction of the ECJ, the possibility of a wildly unpopular breakaway Super League would still be of concern. So, UK Football fans should be very happy that the UK is no longer a member of the EU.[159]

53. High Stakes Make or Break for Fake Steak

The UK is at the forefront of scientific research into the emerging and fast-growing industry of lab-cultivated meat products, and that is only possible due to being outside the EU. 'Leaving the EU means we now have the capability to take something to market in the UK without having to have the sign-off from every European nation'.

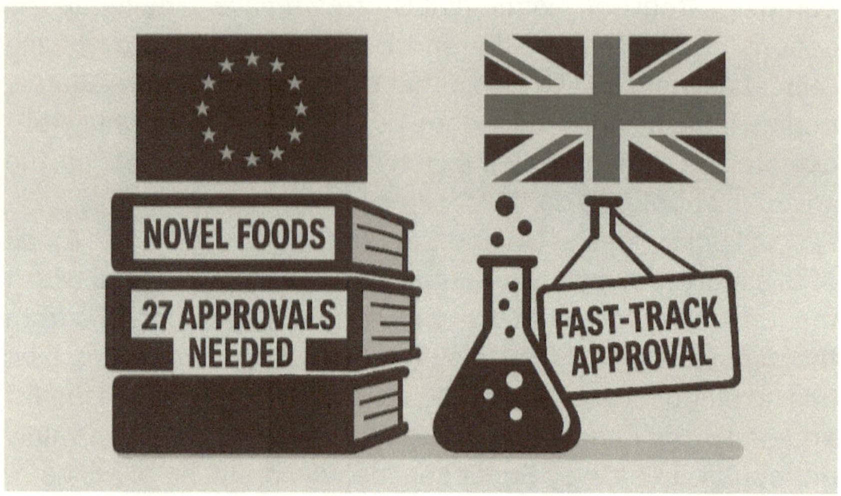

The burgeoning 'novel foods' or cultivated meats industry is set to grow massively in the coming years, to meet the increased collision between consumer tastes and consumer concerns over the eating of animals and the changing global climate.

The definition of a 'novel food' in the UK is actually that which was implemented by the EU and retained post-departure: it essentially means any food or food ingredients that were not used for human consumption to any significant degree prior to May 15th, 1997. An example of a so-called novel food would be lab-grown meat, as such a concept did not exist until very recently and was beyond human scientific ability.[160]

The UK is at the forefront of this industry from a scientific research perspective, and that is only possible due to being outside of the EU. Founder of Cambridge biotech startup Qkine,

Catherine Hyvonen, said that 'leaving the EU means we now have the capability to take something to market in the UK without having to have the sign-off from every European nation'. In stark contrast to this status in the UK, the French newspaper Le Monde recently said of the EU Common Agricultural Policy (CAP) that it 'maintains production practices that are not sustainable in the face of climate and biodiversity challenges and weakens European cohesion'.[161]

In January 2022, the UK government confirmed that they intended to make the streamlined and improved authorisation of novel foods a priority for post-Brexit regulatory amendments. They stated that the UK Food Standards Agency (FSA) would 'update the process for approving novel foods, to create a transparent and effective system that is the best in the world for innovators, investors and consumers'.[162] To achieve this, the FSA commissioned Deloitte to conduct a review of the regulatory framework in place for novel foods - a framework inherited from the EU. The findings of this review were published in a report in June of 2023, reflecting an opinion already shared in the industry - that there were significant deficiencies in the EU approach, and many opportunities for improvement.[163]

54. Respect My Authoritah!

When the UK was a member of the EU, the Competition and Markets Authority (CMA) was unable to involve itself in any mergers where the EU body was already investigating. Brexit means that the CMA is now able to make decisions in the best interests of the UK, instead of being based on the 'greater good' of the EU.

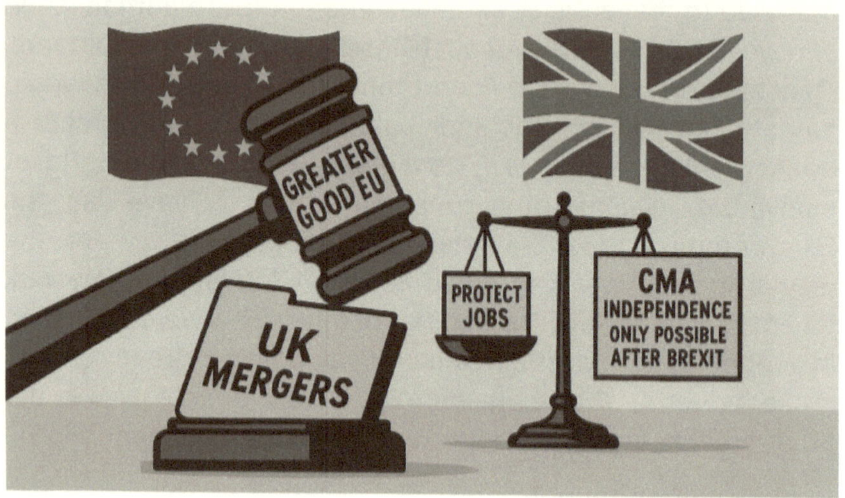

Following the United Kingdom's exit from the European Union, the UK Government has significantly enhanced the powers of the Competition and Markets Authority (CMA), the country's primary competition regulator. This strategic shift grants the CMA greater autonomy to investigate and scrutinise mergers and acquisitions that it deems relevant to the UK's economic and competitive landscape, prioritizing national interests.[164] During the UK's membership in the EU, the CMA's jurisdiction was limited; it was precluded from intervening in merger cases already under investigation by the European Commission, the EU's competition authority, which operated under a framework designed to promote the collective interests of all EU member states. This invariably meant that decisions on mergers with significant implications for the UK were made with the broader

EU market in mind, sometimes at the expense of UK-specific economic priorities or consumer welfare.

The newfound independence of the CMA allows it to focus exclusively on the UK's best interests, free from the constraints of EU-wide considerations. This means the CMA can now assess mergers based on their impact on UK consumers, businesses, and market competition, ensuring that decisions align with national economic goals, such as fostering innovation, protecting jobs, and maintaining competitive markets. For instance, the CMA can now block or impose conditions on mergers that might lead to higher prices, reduced consumer choice, or diminished innovation within the UK, even if such mergers were previously approved by the EU for the 'greater good' of the European single market.[165]

Moreover, this enhanced authority strengthens the UK's position in global markets, as the CMA can now act decisively to address anti-competitive behaviour or mergers that could harm the UK's economic sovereignty. For example, in high-profile industries such as technology, pharmaceuticals, or energy, where mergers can have far-reaching implications, the CMA's ability to intervene ensures that the UK retains control over its market dynamics. This change also aligns with the UK's broader post-Brexit agenda of asserting regulatory independence, allowing the government to shape a competition policy that reflects domestic priorities. However, this increased responsibility places a significant burden on the CMA to balance rigorous enforcement with the need to maintain the UK's attractiveness as a destination for investment, ensuring that its decisions do not deter legitimate business activity or stifle economic growth. By empowering the CMA, the UK aims to create a more agile and responsive competition framework that safeguards national interests while promoting a dynamic and competitive economy.

55. Rules Are Made to be Broken (or Made Better)

Leaving the EU has allowed the UK to simplify and refine public procurement rules, away from the terms agreed upon and designed for wider EU benefit – instead focusing on what makes the most sense for UK businesses and local authorities putting procurement opportunities out to tender

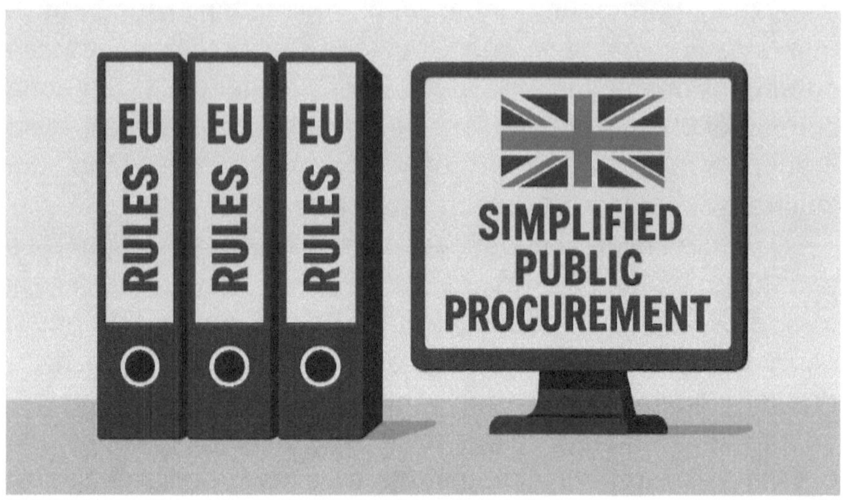

During the EU referendum campaigning in 2016, one of the attractive prospects for those involved in local and central government was the possibility of reforming and simplifying our public procurement rules so that the public sector could buy locally for goods and services. The process of withdrawal from the EU required legislation to be passed to maintain the status quo for day one, but it was not long before changes to public procurement rules were being presented to Parliament.

Firstly, the UK regained its independent seat at the WTO, and joined the WTO Government Procurement Agreement (GPA). The UK had previously taken part in the GPA under the wider EU umbrella, but the terms agreed upon were those agreed by the EU. Post-Brexit, the UK's accession to the GPA had a narrower set of commitments to those the EU signed its members up to, leaving out health, social and cultural services.

The other GPA members accepted this narrower access without objection, so the UK did not lose access to other government procurement contract bidding opportunities because of it.[166]

Second, the UK made commitments within the Trade and Cooperation Agreement with the EU (The UK-EU TCA) to ensure continued procurement access mirroring that existed between UK and EU member states prior to Brexit - but again the UK was able to narrow the scope of procurement access for EU companies to exclude those services contracts within healthcare, social services and some areas of defence.[167]

Lastly and most importantly, the Conservative government introduced the Procurement Act 2023, which came into effect in February 2025.[168] This Act represented a major overhaul of UK procurement law, and replaced EU-derived regulation with an all-new framework. The key features of this overhaul include:

Simplified Procedures: The EU has multiple procedures, which the UK has since reduced down to just two options from the EU's five (contracting authorities can choose between a 'competitive flexible' tender, and an 'open' one, allowing a more streamlined and straightforward process).

SME and Local Supplier Support: Goods and services contracts below £138,760 (central government), £213,477 (sub-central authorities) and £5.3 Million (construction throughout the public sector) can be reserved solely for UK suppliers.

Centralised Platform: A single digital platform for all tenders.

Altered Criteria for Tender Selection: The amendments allow the contracting authority to consider social criteria, not just economic (so a bid that is not the cheapest, but benefits the local area more can be selected)

Exclusion Rules: Suppliers who have a track record of non-delivery can be excluded from the tendering process.

All of these changes, and those changes that will no doubt come in the future, would not be possible were it not for the decision to leave the EU.

56. The Man with the Golden Share

Our departure from the European Union allowed the UK to once again use the notion of so-called golden shares to protect the continued operation of vital infrastructure and services when operated by the private sector – such as the deal struck for the purchase of Royal Mail in 2024.

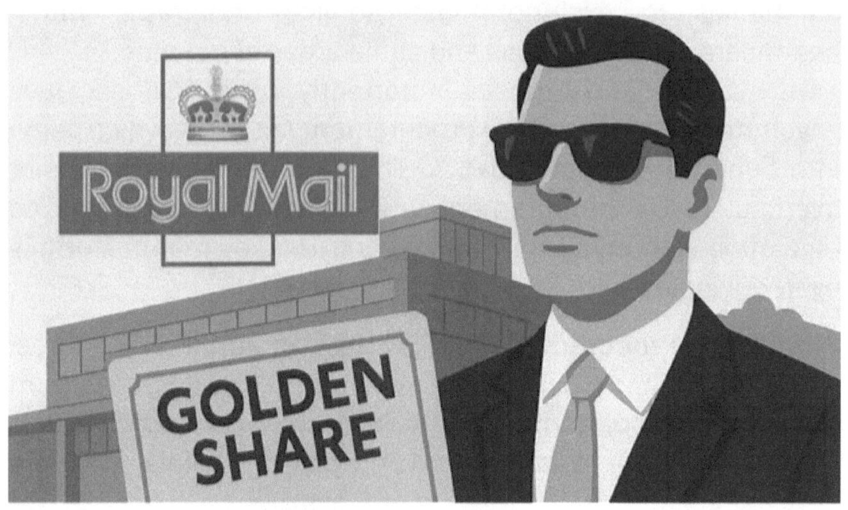

Golden shares are a special type of share in a business, held by a government or public authority, that grants the holder significant control or veto power over key decisions of the business, even if they only hold a very small percentage of the total shares. Such decisions might include changes to ownership, location of head offices, headquarters location, business residency for tax purposes, or major decisions such as mergers or dissolutions. Golden shares are typically used to protect national interests in privatised companies deemed vital to the economy, infrastructure, or security, such as utilities, defence firms, or in this particular example, postal services.

In 2024, the government approved a £3.6 Billion takeover of Royal Mail's parent company, International Distribution Services (IDS), by Czech billionaire Daniel Kretinsky.[169] The deal was finalised in April 2025 after clearing regulatory hurdles and, as a part of the takeover, the UK government secured a single golden share in the company.[170] This golden share grants the UK government veto power over several significant types of changes deemed of political significance to the UK, such as:

Ownership: Any future sale of the business would require government approval to proceed

Headquarters and Tax Residency: A hard condition was implemented that, without government approval to the contrary, Royal Mail would have to remain headquartered and tax-resident in the UK

Universal Service Obligation (USO): The new parent company, EP Group, committed to maintaining the Universal Service Obligation - ensuring letter deliveries six days a week, and parcel deliveries five days a week, across the UK at the same uniform price.

Brand: That the existing Royal Mail brand would remain in use for as long as EP Group owned the company

Dividends and Sales: Prohibiting any dividends or asset sales that could jeopardise the USO or financial stability, unless performance targets set by the regulator Ofcom are met

Employee Protections: This included the formation of a workers' group to have regular meetings with the company board, and a guaranteed share of dividends of at least 10% of the value of any paid to the owner

The golden share was seen to be a critical safeguard for allowing the sale to continue, due not only to the Royal Mail's role as vital piece of national infrastructure, but also due to concerns about Kretinsky himself and his other business ties.

But what, I hear you ask, does any of this have to do with the EU? Well, the very notion of a golden share within a business with the power for a government to veto the actions of a business undermines a core principle of the EU – the free movement of capital. The European Court of Justice (ECJ) has ruled against golden shares in several high-profile cases, having declared them to be illegal due to the restriction of investor rights.

Golden shares can be permissible in the EU, but only if they meet very strict criteria. In the case of the sale of the Royal Mail, the terms would have been deemed illegal by the ECJ as it has struck down similar deals in the past. For example the golden shares held by the Dutch government in TPG (postal services), granting prior approval rights over mergers, dissolutions, and other decisions.[171]

To summarise – the protections that the UK government deemed vital for safeguarding the continuation of critical national infrastructure would not be possible within the EU.

Section 5

Brexit Means a Better Economy

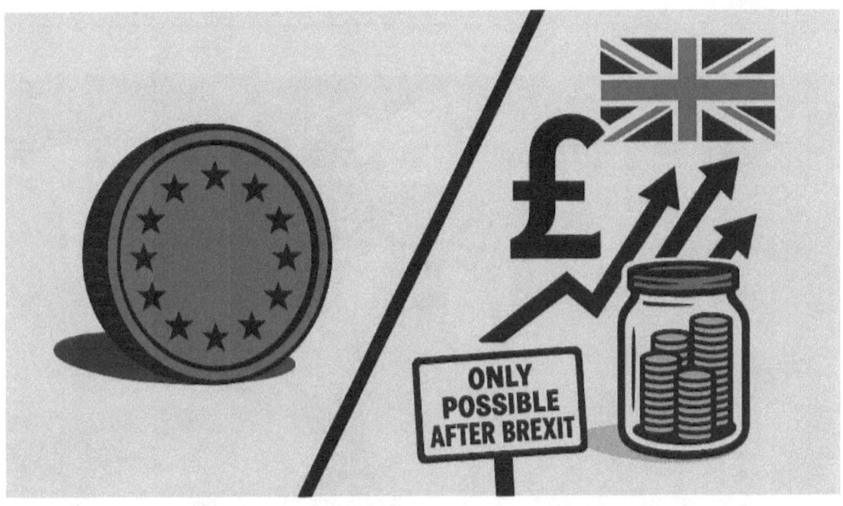

57. A Crescendo of Contactless

Contactless card is the UK's favourite method of payment, with nearly 95% of in-store payments in 2023 using a contactless card. The EU has a hard limit of €50 set in law, so many of the 1.5 billion monthly contactless card transactions in the UK would have to use slower and less convenient methods were it not for Brexit.

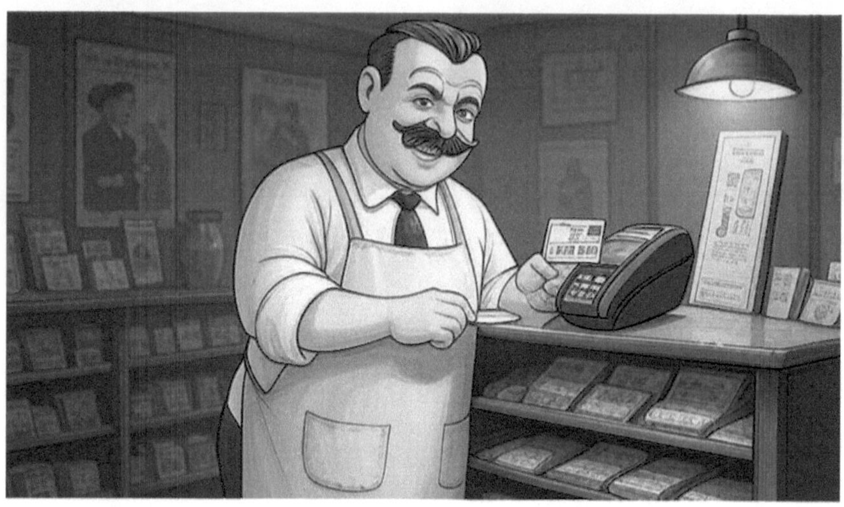

The UK's most popular payment method, owing to its speed and convenience, is the use of contactless – and with transactions using contactless taking less than one second on average to conduct, it's no real surprise as to why, despite the UK's much-advertised love of queueing. In October 2021, the FCA allowed UK banks to offer contactless card payments for transactions up to £100 - and in 2023 a record 93.4% of all in-store transactions under £100 were paid for using contactless.[172] The EU has a €50 (£42) limit on contactless card payments, so the only reason that UK banks can make payments quicker and easier for so many UK consumers and their many transactions is because the UK left the EU.[173]

The use of contactless during the Covid pandemic was seen as one of the many changes able to be made in the UK, due to the flexibility of having left the EU, which aided consumers in still being able to purchase their necessary goods whilst limiting contact and the risk of contagion. Not only is the use of contactless beneficial to the consumer through making their transactions quicker and easier, but it also allows businesses to process their customers quicker at no extra cost on a per transaction basis. There were 1.59 billion in-store contactless card transactions in March 2024 - many hundreds of millions of them were only possible at that level of speed and convenience, taking only seconds instead of minutes to transact, because of Brexit.[174]

It is important to note that this benefit is regarding the use of contactless for card payment, without the use of an intermediary device such as a mobile phone or smart watch. The limit within the EU is regarding card payments specifically, and not payments using smart devices – as these transactions are treated differently and have no set upper limit in EU law.

In 2025, the UK Financial Conduct Authority (FCA) opened a consultation with UK businesses and financial institutions on the scrapping of the £100 limit entirely, or at the very least increasing it. This intention to yet again change this limit demonstrates a core principle of the benefits of Brexit – that the UK has been able to change something twice, before the EU has been able to change it even once.[175] When you consider the level of inflation seen in the last five years, the limitations on contactless spending in the EU effectively increase with every passing year. The UK continues to revise the limitations to keep this capability relevant.

58. No No, There's No (Commodity Position) Limit!

Commodity position limits brought in as part of the EU's MiFID II financial regulations are strict, rigid and burdensome – damaging the best interests of the UK and its global leadership role in financial markets. Brexit allowed this approach to be abolished, replaced with one which is catered to the needs of the industry.

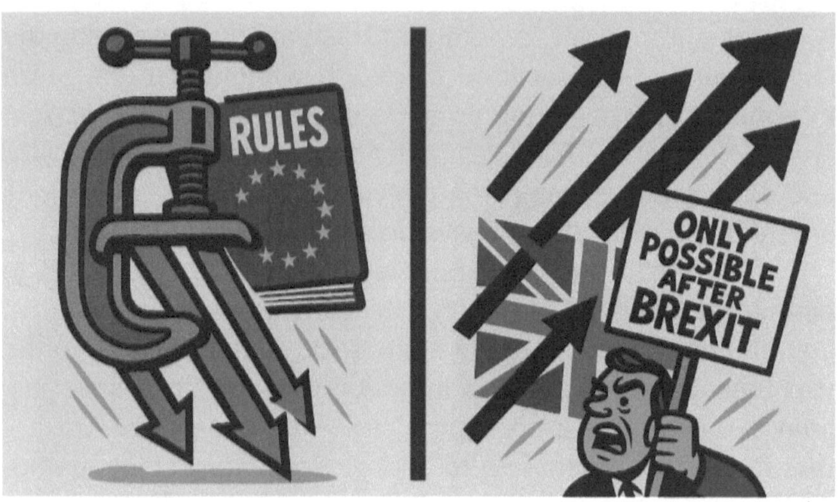

Under the EU's MiFID II financial regulations, commodity position limits were applied to market participants trading in commodity derivatives (futures, options, and swaps) on regulated markets. The position limits were set by both the European Securities and Markets Authority (ESMA) and national regulators - and were based on a rigid formula that considered the size of the market, trading volumes, the number of participants, and the nature of the commodity (whether it's critical for the economy or has volatile prices). MiFID II's position limits applied to all contracts traded on EU trading venues, as well as over-the-counter (OTC) contracts that were deemed economically equivalent to exchange-traded contracts.[176]

Post-Brexit, the UK abolished most commodity position limits for contracts traded on UK venues. Instead of mandatory limits on all commodity contracts, the new rules allow trading venues to impose limits or position management controls where appropriate. The focus shifted away from strict position limits to a more flexible position management regime, where trading venues themselves are responsible for setting and enforcing position limits based on their own assessments of the market (self-regulation). Trading venues can also grant hedging exemptions, making the system less burdensome for market participants. Additionally, the UK's post-Brexit framework eliminated the equivalent position limits that covered economically equivalent OTC contracts, reducing regulatory overhead and simplifying compliance.[177]

The move away from rigid, one-size-fits-all position limits is beneficial to market operations. Trading venues can adapt position management rules according to market conditions and participant needs, which is expected to enhance efficiency. Additionally, by reducing the regulatory burden, UK markets are more attractive to commodity traders and commercial hedgers. This attracts volume from industries like energy, agriculture, and metals, which use derivatives to manage risk.[178]

Finally, by allowing market participants to hold larger positions where appropriate, without the constraints of stringent limits, liquidity in UK markets improves. This results in deeper, more resilient markets with better price discovery.

59. Hire Locally, Higher Salary

Removing the UK from a supply of cheap labour from eastern Europe undercutting the domestic workforce allowed the central concept of supply and demand to kick in, and for the low-skilled workers of the UK to see a much-needed pay rise.

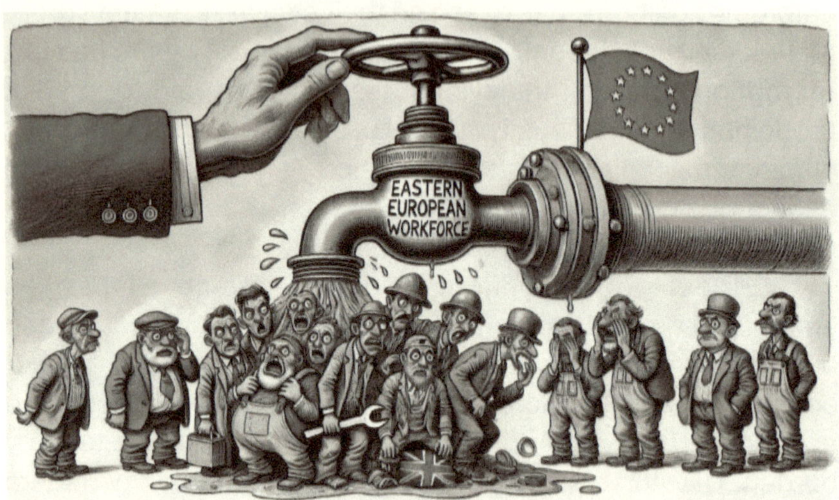

The concept of supply and demand is a demonstrable truth about the modern world and is a foundational tenet of modern economics. That market forces find a natural balance for the price of a good or service, based on how much that good or service is in demand and how much of it is available. So it was of some surprise to me that such an easily understood truth was so heavily argued against, when it came to the debate on leaving the EU and the impact of Freedom of Movement (FoM) on low-skilled workers in the UK.

As was regularly cited as a core motivation for the ending of Freedom of Movement (FoM), membership of the EU had seen an increase in what was in effect a cheaper workforce from predominantly Central and Eastern European member states – which had been said by those campaigning for Brexit to be having a downward effect on both job availability and salary levels for those employment sectors most affected, such as

Hospitality, Construction, Haulage / Logistics and Social Care. Following the UK's exit from the EU, and the end of FoM as a consequence of it, the availability of said cheaper workforce from EU member states came to an end.

As has been covered by many news articles since, the sectors heavily affected as mentioned earlier have all seen above inflation wage increases as well as improvements to job conditions, to encourage and retain the domestic workforce in these professions.[179] In the case of the haulage sector, this change was in some cases as much as a 27% increase in salary between 2000 and 2023.[180] This change would simply not have happened without the ending of Freedom of Movement, which in turn would not have happened without leaving the EU. In February 2025, the Financial Times published an article entitled 'Whatever happened to the great truck driver shortage' – where the author looked back on the arguments made about the forecasted impact of Brexit, and how in fact the impact had not come to pass. More than this though - and the author was clearly at pains to admit this – the article admits that the reduction in drivers from the EU delivered a pay bump for truck drivers.[181]

In 2023, Reuters covered how staff across the aforementioned sectors were seeing significant improvements in pay and working conditions due to the UK having left the EU. It interviewed the CEO of the high-street bar and restaurant chain Loungers as well as a number of staff from their venue in Brighton, who all agreed in their own words that Brexit had caused improved pay and conditions for them.[182]

60. The Nuclear Option

Free from the overly strict state aid rules that prevented its use, the UK can now freely use the Regulated Asset Base (RAB) financing mechanism to unlock private investment in major infrastructure projects such as nuclear power stations.

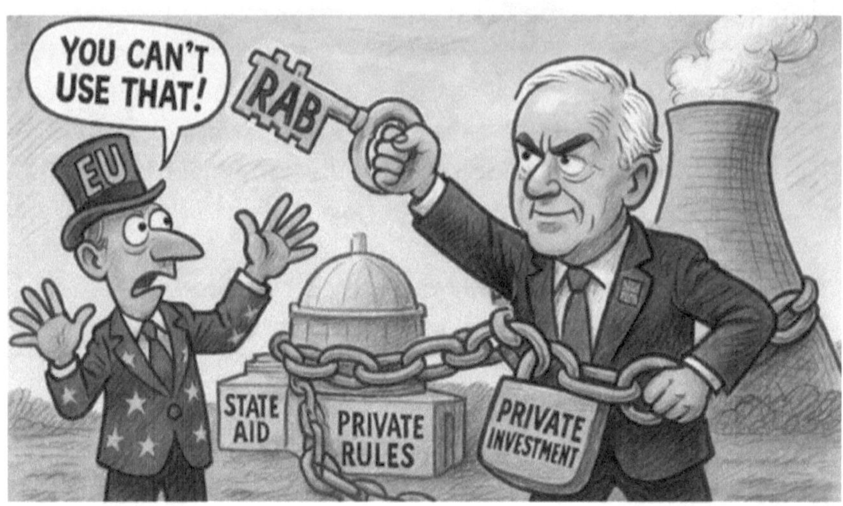

The Regulated Asset Base (RAB) model is a financing mechanism designed to encourage private investment in large infrastructure projects, such as nuclear power plants, by offering greater financial security to investors. Under this model, investors receive a regulated, phased return on their investment throughout the construction and operation phases. This approach spreads the cost and risk of financing over a longer period, reducing the upfront burden on developers.

The RAB model is central to the UK government's strategy for attracting private investment into new nuclear power stations, as outlined in the Nuclear Energy (Financing) Act 2022.[183] Before Brexit, the EU's overly restrictive state aid rules imposed significant constraints on the use of the RAB model, posing a key challenge to the UK's nuclear financing strategy. One only needs look at the evidence submitted by the Nuclear Economics Consulting Group (NECG) to the Inquiry on

Financing Energy Infrastructure in February 2019, to see this spelled out quite matter of factly – 'If the UK remains in the EU, or leaves the EU but continues to be bound by certain State Aid provisions, then most options for new nuclear power investment will be challenging.' [184]

Now free from the European Commission's stringent oversight and approval processes, the UK can offer more favourable terms to investors, including earlier cost recovery and tailored financial incentives. This newfound flexibility allows the government to accelerate critical nuclear projects, positioning the RAB model as a more effective and efficient solution for bolstering energy security in the post-Brexit era.

61. Just Be Good to Me

Brexit allowed the UK welfare system to be offered equally, instead of giving EU nationals preferential treatment over those from non-EU countries – meaning all those who are not UK citizens are treated the same, whether they come from the EU or not.

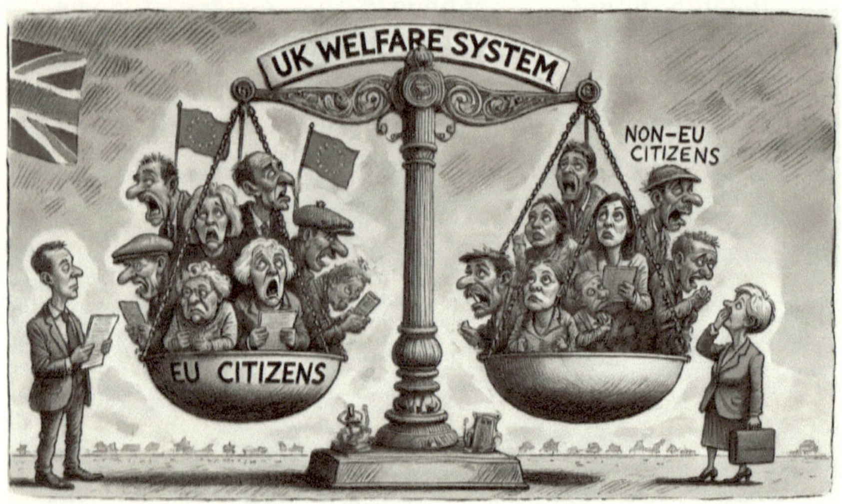

As EU members, EU citizens in the UK had preferential access to the UK welfare system compared to those from non-EU countries. Before Brexit, EU and EEA citizens enjoyed rights to live and work in the UK under EU free movement rules, which also influenced their access to welfare benefits. These rights stemmed from EU law, in particular the 2004 Citizens' Rights Directive, which allowed EU nationals to access benefits in host countries if they were deemed to be 'economically active' (workers or self-employed), 'self-sufficient,' or had a 'right to reside'. [185] The UK implemented these rules through the Habitual Residence Test (HRT) and an additional 'right to reside' test, introduced in 2004, to determine eligibility for certain benefits.

Non-EU nationals faced stricter rules. Most were subject to 'no recourse to public funds' (NRPF) conditions on visas (e.g., work, study, family), barring access to benefits like Universal Credit, Child Benefit, or housing benefits until they gained indefinite leave to remain (ILR), typically after five years.

Having left the EU, the access to the UK welfare system has now been equalised for all non-UK citizens present in the UK, irrespective of whether they happen to be from the EU or not. This equal treatment of visitors to the UK was not possible as an EU member, as EU membership required preferential treatment of EU citizens, over and above that provided to those from other countries.

62. The Revolution Will Be Subsidised

The UK's post-Brexit subsidy control regime is faster, more flexible, less bureaucratic and more aligned with UK priorities instead of the broader and differing aims of the European Commission.

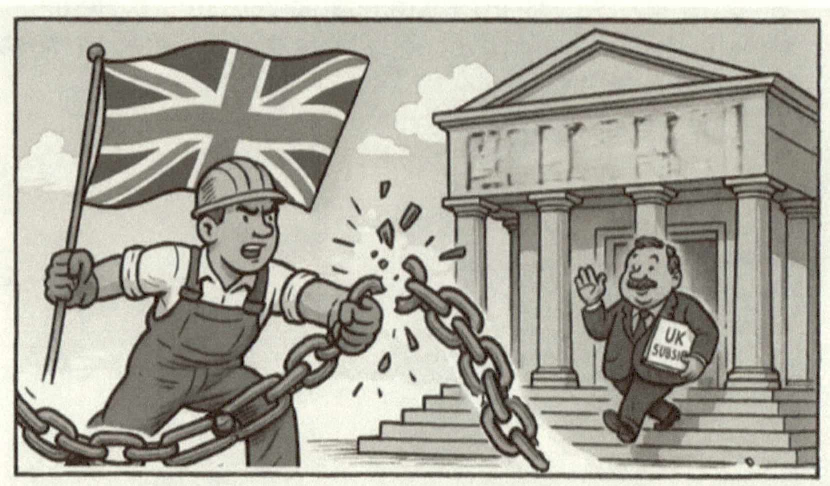

Leaving the EU has allowed the UK to roll out its own bespoke subsidy control regime, which takes into account feedback from UK industries and is able to move more quickly to facilitate decision-making. This includes a system of self-certification for smaller subsidies, with guidance as to how best to validate a subsidy as being permissible. These changes would not have been possible while a member of the EU.

The EU's state aid regime is highly centralised, with the European Commission holding exclusive authority to pre-approve subsidies. Member states must notify the Commission of proposed subsidies (unless they fall under exemptions like the General Block Exemption Regulation) and await approval, ensuring compliance with EU competition and Single Market rules.[186] The UK's Subsidy Control Act 2022 however establishes a decentralised framework. What this means in practice is that public authorities (local governments and devolved administrations) assess subsidies themselves against the seven principles outlined in the Act, such as pursuing a public-policy objective, proportionality, and minimizing trade distortions. There is no mandatory pre-approval by a central body, though the Competition and Markets Authority's Subsidy Advice Unit (CMA SAU) provides non-binding advisory reports for certain subsidies.[187]

The EU's state aid rules are rigid, with strict criteria for permissible subsidies (regional aid, R&D, environmental protection for example). These subsidies must align with EU objectives, and templates like the General Block Exemption Regulation provide certainty but limit flexibility. In stark contrast to this is the new UK regime, which allows for greater flexibility to tailor subsidies to domestic priorities, such as 'levelling up' disadvantaged regions or supporting net-zero goals. For example, the UK can define a 'disadvantaged region' more broadly, or it can offer larger subsidies for projects in such areas. The Trade and Cooperation Agreement (TCA) with the EU still sets general principles mutually agreed upon, but these are less prescriptive than EU rules.

The European Commission enforces state aid rules, with the power to investigate and order recovery of illegal subsidies - with any appeals going to the European Court of Justice (CJEU or ECJ). In the new UK system, subsidies can be challenged though a judicial review in the UK's Competition Appeal Tribunal.

With the new UK system, subsidies must be reported to a public database, with exemptions for subsidies below £315,000 over two years or up to £725,000 for Services of Public Economic Interest (SPEI). Emergency aid such as for COVID-19 support is broadly exempt, allowing more generous support than the EU's Temporary Framework. Again this is more generous than the previous EU system, with higher thresholds and broader exemptions.

EU state aid rules prioritise Single Market objectives, limiting member states' ability to design subsidies for purely domestic goals. The UK's ability to prioritise policies like 'levelling up' or broader regional aid definitions was constrained by EU criteria. For example, the UK could not have offered more generous aid to disadvantaged regions without Commission approval.

So to summarise - the UK's subsidy control regime is faster, more flexible, less bureaucratic and more aligned with UK priorities instead of the broader and differing aims of the European Commission.

63. All Around My Cap

The UK from outside the EU has been able to remove the cap on bankers' bonuses introduced by the EU in 2014, despite strong British opposition at the time - allowing London to yet again be competitive on the world stage for the best and brightest talent in the sector.

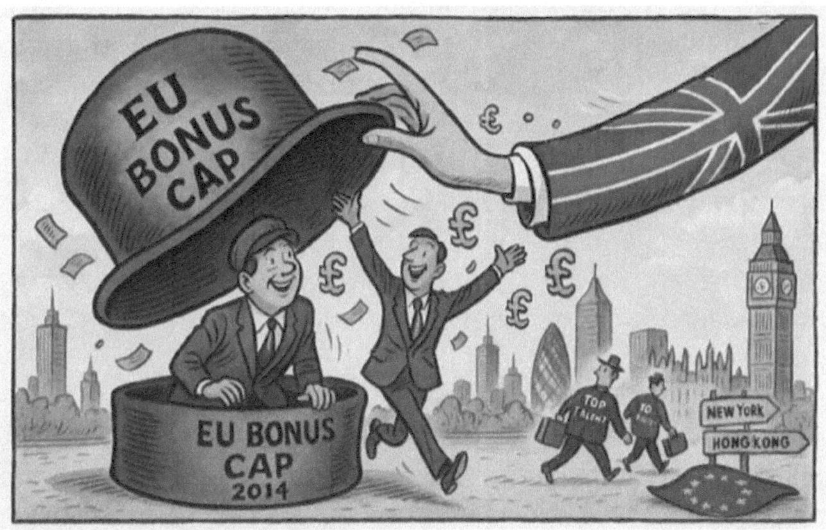

In 2014 the EU introduced a cap on the amount able to be awarded as a bonus to employees in the banking sector, despite the opposition of the UK who were the member state most affected by the legislation. This action left London (along with the other much smaller financial centres in the EU) uncompetitive on the global stage for the best talent within the banking sector.

The action was taken as part of the Capital Requirements Directive (CRD IV), enacted in response to the 2007–2008 financial crisis. Though well intentioned, the impact had both intended and unintended consequences - and as a major global financial hub (London is arguably the global financial capital), the UK was significantly affected by the changes, more so than any other member state. As the Bank of

England stated in October 2014, 'The bonus cap is the wrong policy, the debate around it is misguided'.[188]

The cap drove some talent to unregulated sectors like hedge funds, FinTechs, and digital asset firms, which offered uncapped compensation. Mark Shaw of Pinsent Masons noted a 'banking skills drain' to these sectors, as they were outside the scope of the CRD IV regime.[189] Meanwhile high-calibre bankers, especially in the investment banking sector, were lured to jurisdictions without caps (predominantly in the US and Asia) or to non-banking financial roles. US banks in London struggled to align UK pay with global practices, making it harder to deploy top talent to the City.

From outside the EU, the UK has been able to remove this cap - which allows London to once again compete with the other global financial capitals like New York and Hong Kong, but will also result in a higher amount of banking revenue being invested into public services through the tax collected on those increased bonuses.[190]

So in summary - the EU bonus cap, while well-intentioned, created competitive frictions for UK banks, pushing talent toward uncapped sectors and leaving the country for other financial hubs outside of the EU. Its removal in 2023 has enhanced remuneration flexibility and boosted talent attraction, with notable bonus increases in 2024.

Section 6

Brexit Means We Control Our Own Borders

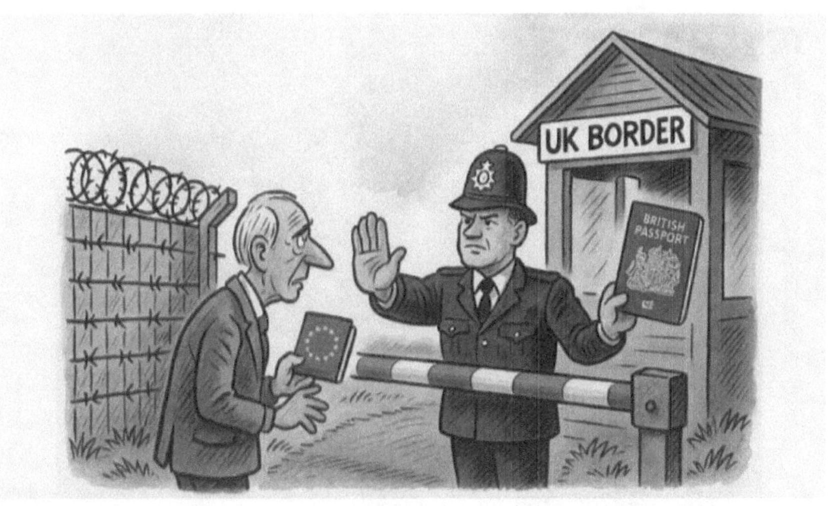

64. Go Your Own Way

Leaving the EU has allowed the UK to offer a truly fair points-based immigration policy, that does not unduly favour predominantly white Europeans over those from other nations - UK policy now treats everyone the same, irrespective of their country of birth.

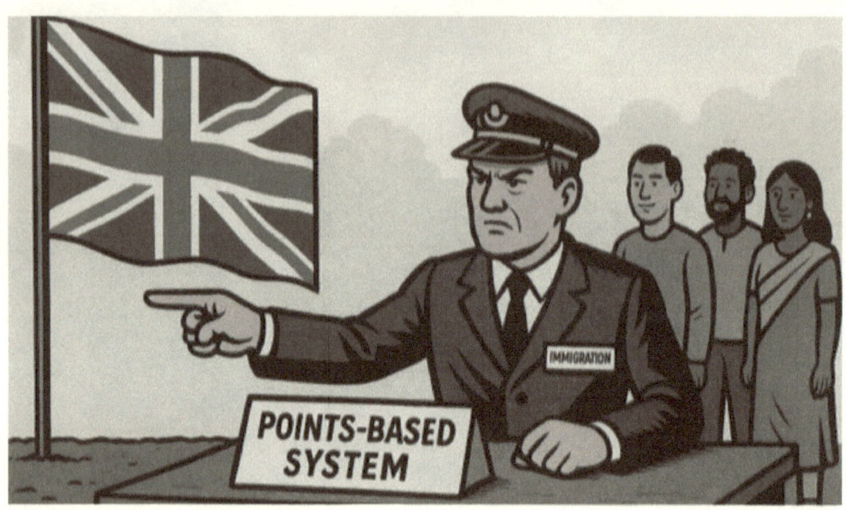

One of the major tenets of EU Single Market membership is the principle of the four freedoms: the free movement of goods, of capital, of services and of people.

Despite the Freedom of Movement (FoM) of people being something that those wishing to remain in the EU were the most vocal about losing, the UK population actually took very little advantage of it – as the UK is one of the richest nations in the world, and so leaving it to live elsewhere is not a natural desire outside of retirement to warmer and perhaps drier climates. This of course meant that more citizens of the EU27 used FoM to live and work in the UK, than in the other direction – which is of course exactly what a rational person would expect.[191] The majority of EU27 countries learn English as a second language from an early age in school, as English is the most spoken language in the world, and it is the language of business. In addition to this, the UK has many of the most highly-sought after universities in the world, whereas the EU without the UK is devoid in this respect.[192]

In 2016, there were more UK citizens living and working in Australia and New Zealand than there were in all 27 other EU member states combined.[193] Of those in the EU27, a significant number of them were in Ireland through the Common Travel Area (which for reference predates the existence of the EU and its forebears). This naturally meant that those from the EU, who are predominantly white Europeans, had an unfair advantage to live and work in the UK when compared to others from around the world.

By leaving the EU, the UK has been able to implement a truly meritocratic immigration system – one that no longer prioritises and prefers those from a particular set of countries.[194] This desire to no longer unfairly bias immigration from predominantly white Europeans also goes against the lazy and unfair characterisation of leave voters being racists.

Country or Bloc	% Emigrant UK Citizens Resident in 2017
Australia and NZ	33%
USA and Canada	28%
Ireland (through the CTA)	6%
European Union 26 (not UK or IE)	20%
Rest of the World	12%

Fig 2: British Citizens Living Abroad, 2017

65. Crime Doesn't Pay

Under EU freedom of movement rules, the UK had to allow European criminals into the country who would otherwise have been stopped and turned away - implementing equal treatment of all criminals after Brexit resulted in over 12,000 EU citizens being refused entry to the UK in both 2023 and 2024.

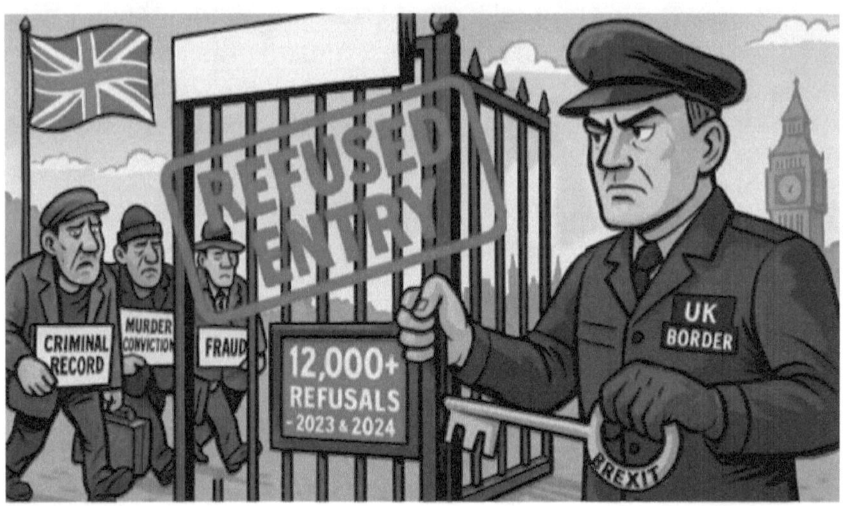

One little-known and even less understood aspect of Freedom of Movement is how little control member states can employ on the prevention of unwanted peoples entering the country – which is odd because as the saying goes, it does what it says on the tin. Movement is free within the EU, outside of very special and specific circumstances.

One of the complications that comes out of this is a very real limitation on how the UK as an EU member state could prevent known criminals from entering from another fellow member state. To quote a Home Office news story from 2020, 'EU rules currently require the Home Office to demonstrate that EU criminals present a genuine, present and sufficiently serious threat affecting one of the fundamental interests of society in order to restrict their free movement rights. This decision cannot be based solely on the criminal conviction, even if for murder or rape.' [195]

Brexit made it tougher for EU criminals to enter the UK. The ending of Freedom of Movement for EU citizens within the UK allowed for equal application of UK entry rights for both EU and non-EU citizens, including the default refusal of entry where someone has been in prison for a year or more. Under EU free movement we had to allow some foreign criminals into the country who would otherwise have been stopped and turned away. The implementation of equal treatment of all criminals contributed to a five-fold increase of over 12,000 EU citizens being refused entry to the UK in both 2023 and 2024 – who otherwise would have been likely granted entry under Freedom of Movement. [196]

66. I'm Picking Up Good Migrations

The new points-based system as implemented has resulted in the UK having a significantly higher rating as regards attractiveness for highly skilled workers from the OECD, 'owing to changes to the migration regime introduced after Brexit' - that the UK was only able to do having left the EU.

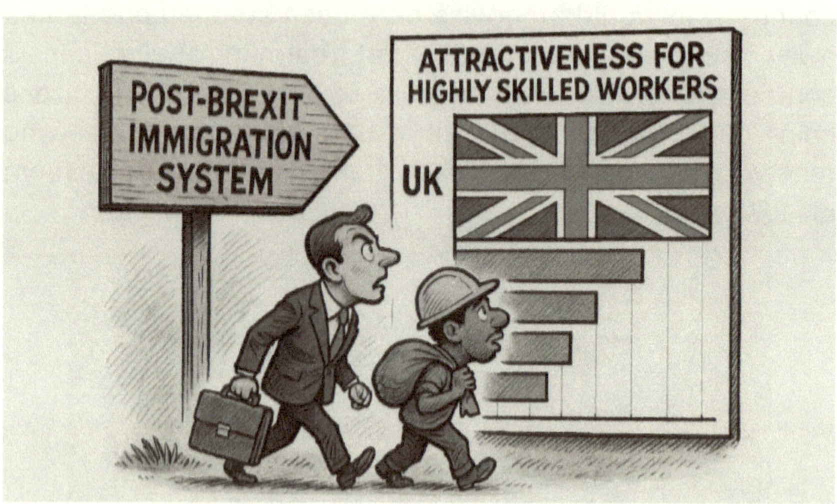

The topic of inward migration to the UK is a contentious one, and one which has often been incorrectly portrayed by the media both inside and outside of the UK when it comes to Brexit. Voters for leaving the EU have often been unfairly vilified in my view, as being completely anti-immigration without caveat or exception. My personal experience of leave voters, as well as my own view in this regard, is that leave voters wanted to see an end to uncontrolled immigration - and knew that such a desire was not possible from within the European Union.

Much has been said and written about the immigration issue since the UK voted to leave the EU, with some placing undeserved blame on Brexit for the so-called 'small boats' migration. However, the actual benefit of Brexit as regards migration has been lost through the noise of this and other legitimate concerns.

Prior to Brexit, inward migration was able to be broken down into four distinct categories:

1. Legal migration from the EU through Freedom of Movement
2. Legal migration from outside of the EU, through visas or Commonwealth ties
3. Illegal migration through smuggling or otherwise
4. Provision of asylum for those who lay claim to refugee status

The objective for post-Brexit prosperity was to reduce net migration to a manageable figure, still offering asylum to those who truly need it, and at the same time increasing the average value of those who were economic migrants by attracting highly skilled people.

Post-Brexit, the Johnson government brought in a new points-based meritocratic system of migration approval similar to that in place in other Commonwealth nations such as Australia. This system, as implemented, resulted in the UK receiving a significantly higher ranking from the OECD as regards attractiveness for highly skilled workers - which in their annual report the OECD attributed directly to 'the migration regime introduced after Brexit'. A regime that was only possible to implement, after leaving the EU. To further quote the OECD: 'The United Kingdom climbs several places in the ranking due to lower capital requirements for entrepreneurs, but also a favourable environment when considering most other aspects such as a strong skills environment and being welcoming to immigrants'.[197] These changes were not accidental - they were by design. Sadly, other changes such as those for students to be able to bring dependents were also implemented alongside them that, though also not possible from within the EU, led to a significant spike in immigration which clouded the topic and tarnished the whole endeavour in a poor light. Having a fair system of immigration, that judges all equally irrespective of which part of the world they come from, is a benefit to the UK economy and was not possible from within the EU.

67. Freeport Convention

Leaving the EU Single Market and Customs Union allowed for the UK to implement and roll out freeports across the country - not just in name only as they had been before – providing various tax and customs reliefs, simplified import and export procedures, enhanced trade promotion, and additional support for innovation.

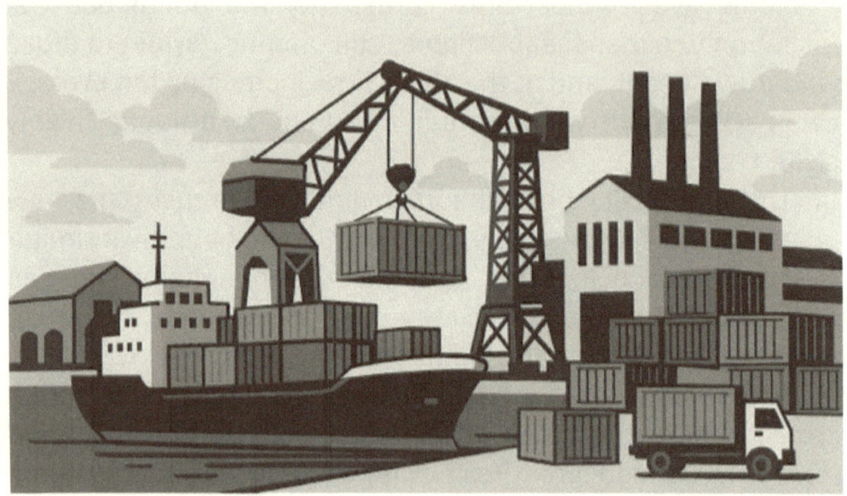

The topic of freeports, and the ability for them to exist within the EU, has been one of regular confusion within the debate regarding Brexit. There are indeed ports that are considered to be freeports within the EU - by which we mean that they are considered to be freeports by the EU, not by the rest of the world. As the Institute for Government (IfG) stated in their explainer on freeports: 'EU freeports are governed by the Union Customs Code as well as by EU rules on state aid, which stop member states using selective tax exemptions and financial incentives'.[198] Leaving the EU Single Market and Customs Union allowed for the UK to implement and roll out actual full-blooded freeports across the country - not just in name only as they had been before - providing various tax and customs reliefs,

simplified import and export procedures, enhanced trade promotion, and additional support for innovation.[199]
But what, I can hear you say, are the specific aspects of the UK Freeport model, that would not be possible from within the EU? Well, here are a few examples:

Customs Flexibilities: As previously stated, EU Freeports operate under the Union Customs Code, which standardises customs procedures across all member states. The UK implementation allows for a bespoke model that provides a more aggressive tariff inversion (where lower tariffs are paid on finished products assembled within the freeport, than would have been paid on the components used to make the finished product) along with simplified customs declarations - both of these things would not be allowed within the EU, as they would likely affect trade (incentivise companies to move from one member state to another).

Tax Incentives: EU rules on State Aid restrict member states from providing selective tax exemptions, to prevent trade distortion (see above) through what they would see as an unfair playing field. The UK's freeports offer extensive tax reliefs (full business-rate relief and enhanced capital allowances) that would not be allowed within the EU at the levels offered. Further examples would include the 10% Structures and Buildings Allowance (up from the standard 3%) and zero employer National Insurance contributions for a fixed period - both of these would violate EU state aid rules.

Regulatory Autonomy: The UK's Freeports, or to be more precise the businesses that opt to locate themselves within UK Freeports, benefit from streamlined planning and regulatory engagement (for example the Freeport Regulation Engagement Network) - this would conflict with EU regulations on both environment standards and on labour rights.

By the end of 2023, UK Freeports had attracted over £2.9 Billion in investment and created over 6,000 jobs. The long-term estimate for the whole UK Freeport scheme has over 200,000 jobs being generated.[200]

68. Fake It Til You Make It

In 2020, nearly half of all fraudulent global ID intercepted at the UK border was ID cards from EU member states. In October 2021, the UK removed the ability for many EU/EEA/EFTA ID cards to be used at the border to gain entry to the UK –- and in so doing massively reduced fraudulent ID being used to get into the country.

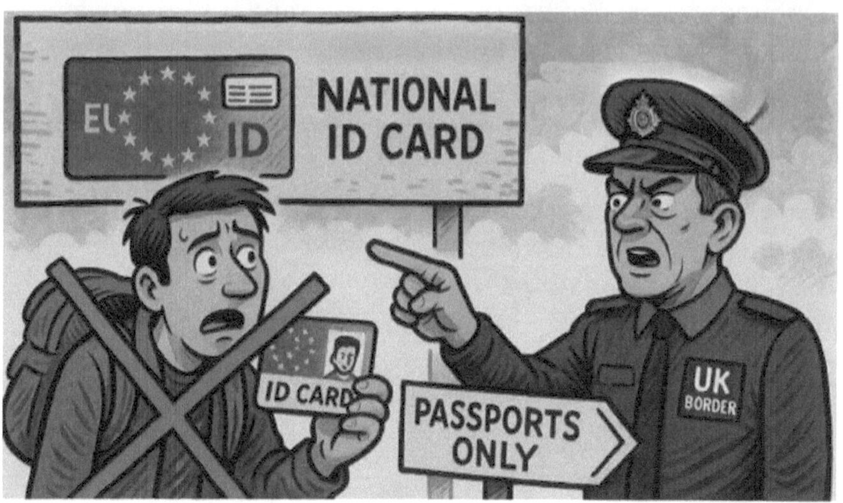

Under EU Freedom of Movement (FoM), citizens of the EU and the wider EEA could enter the UK using their national ID card, which unfortunately varied widely as regards their complexity and ease to forge. Some member states such as Italy, Greece and Romania used simple laminated cards, which were easily forged. According to the EU border agency, Frontex, the top six EU countries whose ID cards were caught being falsified were Italy, Belgium, Greece, Spain, France and Romania.[201]

Passports are of course more secure, but with EU FoM rules as they were, the UK was unable to insist on the use of passports at the border - and so had to allow the use of knowingly weak ID cards at the insistence of EU law. In 2020, nearly half of all false documents detected at UK border security were EU ID cards.

Post-Brexit, the UK was able to enforce the use of passports for entry into the UK, phasing out the ability to use EU ID Cards. In October 2021, the UK removed the ability for many EU/EEA/EFTA ID cards to be used at the border to gain entry to the UK –- and in so doing massively reduced the chances of fraudulent documentation being used to get into the country.

To quote the UK Home Office in 2021 - 'Identity cards are among the least secure documents seen at the border and ending their use will strengthen our security as the UK takes back control of its borders at the end of the transition period.' The UK Home Secretary at the time, Priti Patel, also said 'We must clamp down on the criminals that seek to enter our country illegally using forged documents. By ending the use of insecure ID cards we are strengthening our borders and delivering on the people's priority to take back control of our immigration system.' [202]

Section 7

Brexit Has Strengthened Our Defences and Our Standing in the World

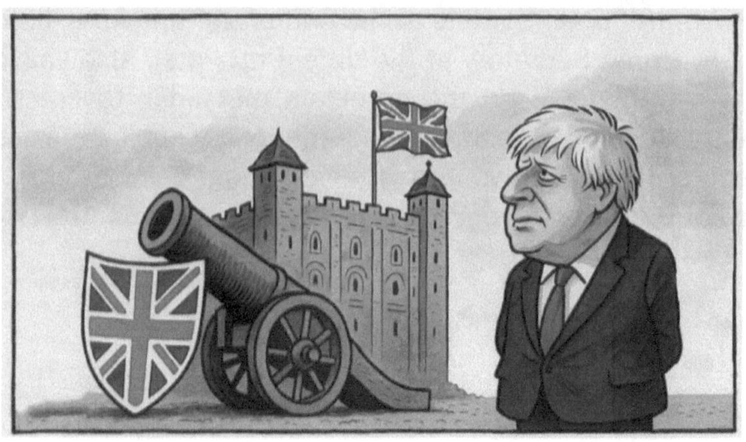

69. You Down With 'TPP, Yeah You Know Me

By leaving the EU, the UK has been able to align with those markets projecting the highest growth over the coming decades (the so-called Indo-Pacific tilt), as opposed to being tied to a bloc projected to see continued decline in relevance and stagnation. UK CPTPP accession took place in late 2024.

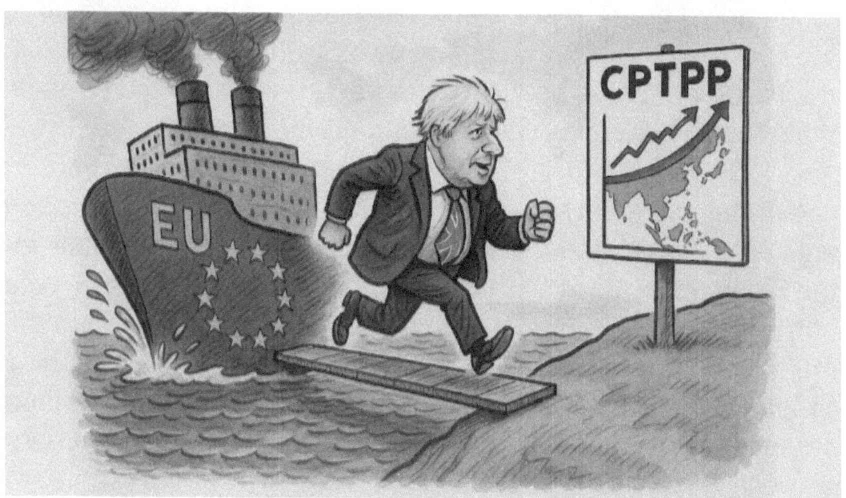

By leaving the EU, the limitations on UK alignment with the fastest growing part of the world, the Indo-Pacific have been removed. By the EU's own admittance the majority of global growth will be coming out of the Indo-Pacific in the coming decades, while the nations of the EU will collectively see a relative decline in importance on the world stage.[203]

The UK had voiced interest in acceding to the Comprehensive and Progressive agreement on Trans-Pacific Partnership (CPTPP) – a 'gold standard' trade agreement between 11 countries in the Indo-Pacific as early as 2018.[204] However, the UK could not actually start this process until after the departure from the EU had been completed as the EU retains all rights to negotiate as regards international trade on behalf of its members.

The UK began the process of CPTPP accession in February 2021, by sending a letter formally requesting membership.[205] This request was approved in July of 2023, and came into effect in December 2024.[206]

A government response to commentary on the Integrated Review states that 'Between 2021 and 2050, 54% of global growth and advances in key technologies are expected to come from the Indo-Pacific'.[207] Even a NATO report states that 'Economic figures speak by themselves'. The report goes on to say that 'two thirds of the global wealth will be concentrated in the Indo-Pacific region within the next decades, which means that Western interests will dramatically increase'.[208]

By joining the CPTPP the UK takes an important geostrategic step in securing the rules-based trading approach enjoyed by most of the world and secures a 'seat at the table' for the many accessions to the CPTPP in the future - getting a vote and a veto on every one. It is also worth noting that, despite the major benefits of CPTPP membership for the UK being geostrategic in nature, the actual terms from a free-trade perspective are also not to be sniffed at. As the UK government strategic approach document of the CPTPP was able to demonstrate, the terms of the agreement are better for the UK than all the EU's FTAs with the individual CPTPP members.[209]

The CPTPP is seen by many in the international trade community as being a potential replacement for the WTO agreements. With the UK being the first country to accede to the agreement outside of the original founder members, the UK gets to help craft and steer the CPTPP on that journey – and every country that wishes to join in the future will need UK permission to do so.

With UK accession, the CPTPP is now of equivalent size to the EU as regards global GDP and outweighs the EU at the G7. Future accessions to the CPTPP will see the now 12-country bloc quickly overtake the EU for global relevance.

In April 2025, 100,000 tonnes of Malaysian palm oil entered the UK tariff free for the first time, at the Port of Liverpool (incidentally one of the UK's new Freeports). This means that all of the products produced in the UK using this palm oil, for which there are many thousands on sale in the UK that include it as an ingredient, will now be able to be manufactured and sold cheaper than they otherwise would have been.[210]

NOTE: As of June 2025, there are seven countries queueing behind the UK who have formally requested accession into the CPTPP: China; Taiwan; Ecuador; Uruguay; Costa Rica; Ukraine; and Indonesia.

70. Service(s) With a Smile

In 2019, as a member of the EU, the UK was not even in the top ten OECD countries on their Services Trade Restrictiveness Index. In 2022, having been able to liberalise in multiple sectors outside of the EU, the UK ranked second only to Japan – a ranking retained into 2025.

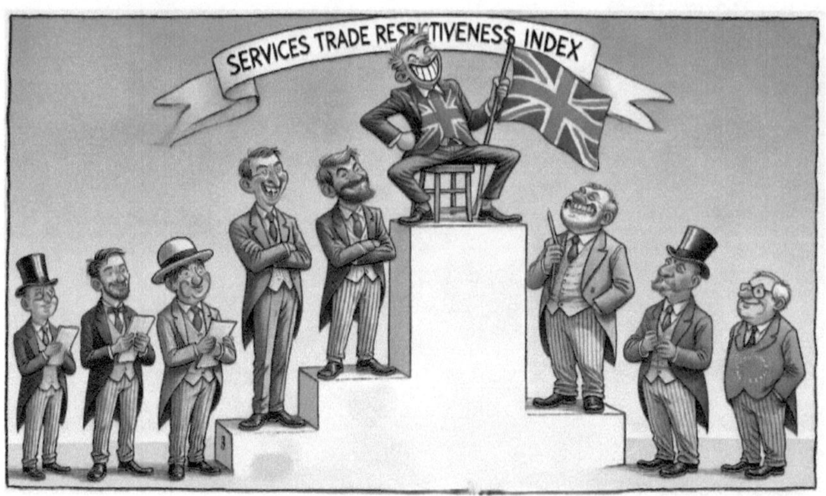

As a member of the European Union, the UK was unable to break into the Top Ten of the 37 OECD (Organisation for Economic Co-operation and Development) members, on their index of which of the world's most-developed economies were the least restrictive on their services trade – known as the Services Trade Restrictiveness Index (STRI).

In 2022, having been able to liberalise in multiple sectors following departure from the EU, the UK was ranked second out of the now 38 members (Costa Rica joined in 2021). The country ranked first out of the 38 was fellow non-EU member Japan. The OECD wrote of the change in rank for the UK, 'A large number of new legislations and regulatory amendments were introduced as a result [of leaving the EU], and some of these have implications for [the Services Trade Restrictiveness Index].

The OECD STRI report specifically calls out the Skilled Worker visa scheme; the accession to the WTO General Procurement Act (GPA); the regulatory changes to air transport services; the 'open coast' policy for cabotage; the Financial Services Act; and the abolishment of the Low Value Consignment Relief.[211]

In February 2025, the OECD published their updated version of the STRI, reflecting on global changes between the now 51 countries covered by the report - confirming that the UK retains the position of the second biggest services exporter in the world after the USA, and retained the second place spot in the ranking of the STRI, still just behind Japan.[212]

71. Slava Ukraini

Leaving the EU has allowed the UK to offer full-throated support to Ukraine from day one during their conflict with Russia, without the weeks and even months of dithering and delay that comes from EU obligations to always work in consensus with other member states,

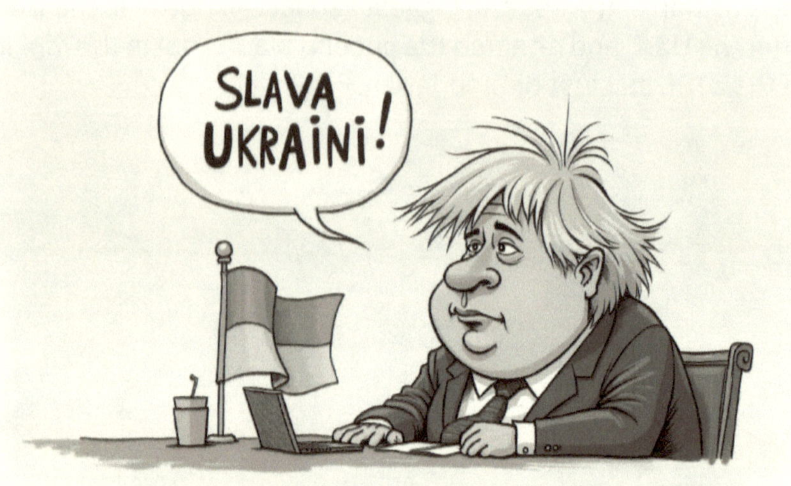

On the 24th February 2022, war returned to continental Europe, with the Russian invasion of Ukraine. What proceeded in the corridors of power in Western Europe in the days and weeks immediately following the invasion gave the world a very clear indication of whose commitments to peace and defence of their neighbours were just warm words, and who would stand with Ukraine in its darkest of hours.

According to Bate Toms, from the British-Ukrainian Chambers of Commerce, Brexit allowed the UK to cut tariffs, speed up weapons shipments to Ukraine, and move faster on targeting Russian fossil fuels than the EU. He went on to say that 'Britain is now again in its historic role protecting Europe from conquest, freed from having to get along within the EU'. 'Historically, the Duke of Marlborough, the Duke of Wellington and Winston Churchill saved Europe from itself, and the UK has this role again'.[213]

Our independence from the EU has allowed the UK to take a leading independent role in supporting Ukraine through its continuing conflict with Russia. Though EU member states have followed suit, they did so weeks later, after numerous discussions to get consensus opinion on how to proceed, which could well have been the difference between victory and defeat. It is more than possible that, without UK independence from EU dithering and bureaucracy, Ukraine could well have fallen. Even the Polish Foreign Minister, Radoslaw Sikorski, agrees that this was a benefit of leaving the EU, being able to move quicker without the commitment to work in consensus with other member states. He went on to say that 'The UK has found a niche, a very useful and honourable one, namely to take advantage of its quick decision-making. You do the right thing before others, and therefore encourage the rest of us'.[214]

In May 2022 the UK announced that it would unilaterally remove all tariffs on imported goods from Ukraine – a decision that the EU replicated some weeks later. Ukraine followed suit without need to do so, and so a two-year commitment to zero tariffs between the UK and Ukraine was put into place. In February 2024 this agreement was extended, so that it would last until at least February 2029.[215] In contrast to this, the EU made the decision to allow their tariff-free offer to come to an end in June 2025, with an intent to replace it with a 'transitional arrangement' which would drastically reduce quotas available to Ukrainians for tariff-free exports to the EU.[216] If the UK was still a member of the EU, it would have no choice but to follow suit with this reduction in EU support for Ukrainian trade.

72. How Do You Take Your Power? Hard or Soft?

Since leaving the EU, the UK has improved its score on the Global Soft Power Index compiled by Brand Finance (the world's leading independent brand valuation and strategy consultancy) and consolidated its position at the top of the leaderboard, second only to the US.

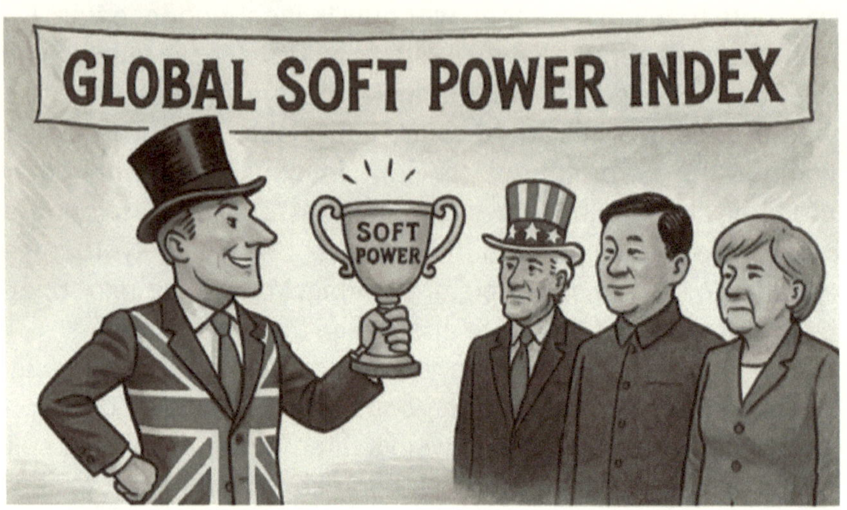

Since its launch in 1995, Brand Finance has been looking to carve a niche for itself in the exploration of the value of a national Brand. In 2020, they launched their Global Soft Power Index, which provided insight on the so-called 'Soft Power' of the brands of nations across the world. This ranking looks at multiple criteria to provide a comprehensive analysis against multiple data points and is a well-respected view on the strength of the brand of a given country or nation on the global stage. Each report is a view on nations across the world in the previous 12 months, and how the events and news that have taken place have changed public perceptions against those multiple criteria.[217]

In 2019 the UK was ranked third globally, behind the USA in first and Germany in second. The report reflects on this period with an all-too common string of words that have become

179

almost a catchphrase of the Brexiteer - 'despite Brexit'. But here is where the reports get interesting, as the results in the subsequent years show the method in what was perceived by ardent EU supporters as being madness.

In every year since the UK departed from the EU, the UK's soft power score has seen an increase. Even where some scoring criteria took a notable and significant decline (for 'friendly', the UK dropped from eighth in 2019 to 47th in 2021), the increases in other criteria were always able to offset them resulting in a net increase. Against the quality of governance metric, the year the UK left the EU resulted in a score increase - from ninth in the world to fourth. By way of explaining this scoring, Brand Finance stated that it was driven by the positive change in the UK being more 'politically stable and well-governed'.

In 2023 the UK ranked fourth in the world for the 'Reputation' metric - the highest score the UK had received against this criterion. Those advocating for remaining in the EU in 2016, consistently argued that to leave the EU would be to damage the UK's reputation on the world stage. The rankings in the Global Soft Power Index prove that in fact the opposite was true - it is through leaving the EU, that the UK has been able to improve its reputation, and the consistent top-three ranking ever since is testament to this fact.

NOTE: In the 2025 Soft Power Index, the UK dropped again to third place – not out of a reduction in UK soft power score, but an increase for the new second place, China.[218]

73. Who Ya Gonna Call?

'Brexit probably makes Britain a more important country with a greater voice on strategic security matters, because it's not about the fact that the EU is larger, it's about the fact that the EU is way behind' – Former US Special Advisor, Pippa Malmgren.

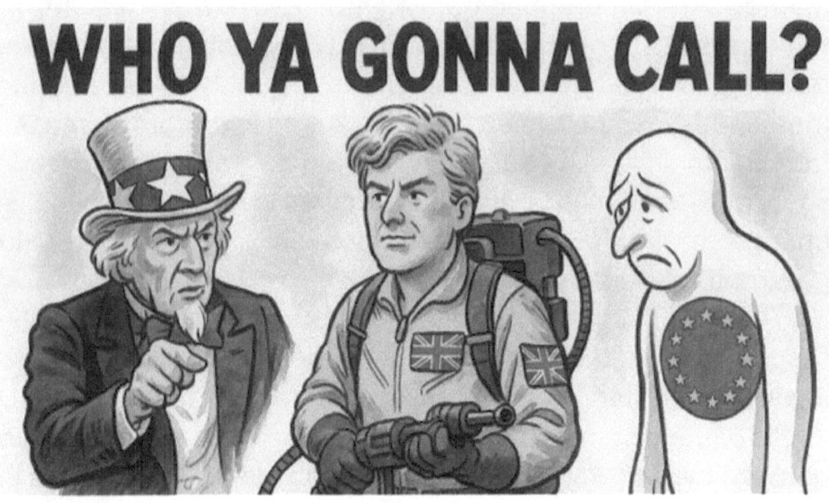

During an interview for a long-form podcast on the geostrategic importance of Svalbard to western security, the economist and former Special Advisor to the US President, Pippa Malmgren, stated the following:

'I think the way the Americans think about Britain is, you're the only one of our allies that can actually keep up and work with us side to side. Everybody else can't quite keep up, they're not as technologically advanced, they don't have the command structures, and so we just kinda view Britain as our closest of our Five Eyes partners, Five Eyes being the closest tightest security arrangement that exists in The West'.[219]

The UK remains one of Europe's few full-spectrum military powers, with nuclear capabilities, a permanent UN Security Council seat, and significant defence spending (meeting NATO's 2% GDP target and planning for at least 2.5% by 2030). Its military strength was a key asset within the EU, and continues to be so outside of it, arguably with more flexibility to deploy resources. Article 32 of the Treaty on European Union (TEU) requires member states to consult each other on any matter of foreign and security policy, to 'ensure mutual solidarity' between member states. The UK is no longer bound by that requirement.[220]

In the podcast, Pippa Malmgren went on to say that 'Brexit probably makes Britain a more important country with a greater voice on strategic security matters, because it's not about the fact that the EU is larger, it's about the fact that the EU is way behind'. The events of late 2024 and early 2025, with the EU's acknowledgement that hundreds of billions of Euros in investment were needed to bring EU member states up to a reasonable standard as regards their military defence infrastructure gives clear example of how true that statement was.[221]

A final quote from Pippa Malmgren - 'I do think in this modern era, this isn't about how many aircraft carriers have you got, it's about what's your capacity to problem solve — and I would say on that front the British are cleverer than the Americans when dealing with the Russians.'

74. Take Me Down to the Acronym City

As an EU member, the UK was bound to work within the commitments of the EU Common Foreign and Security Policy (CFSP) - something which would have prevented significant aspects of the AUKUS agreement from being signed up to by the UK, and so potentially sinking the entire agreement.

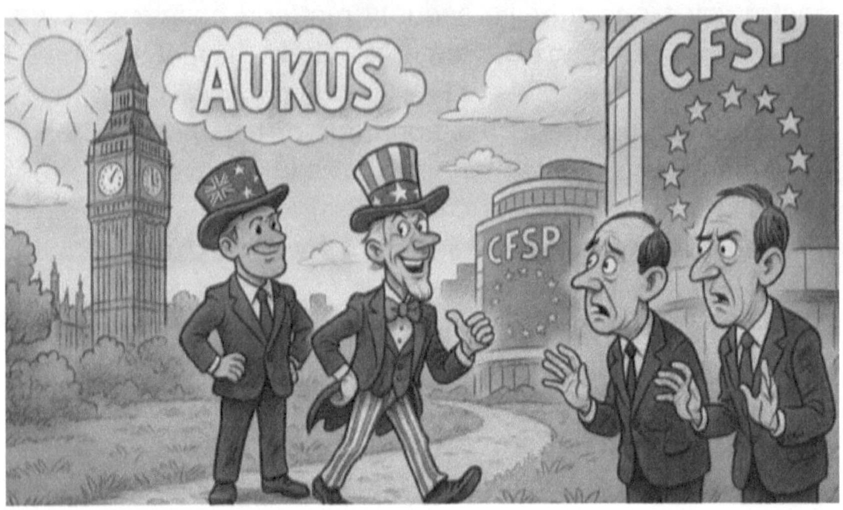

In September 2021, the United Kingdom, United States, and Australia formalised a landmark trilateral security and defence partnership known as AUKUS - a strategic initiative designed to deepen cooperation among these three nations in response to evolving geopolitical challenges, particularly in the Indo-Pacific region. The AUKUS agreement focuses on fostering closer integration of the military-industrial complexes of the three countries, leveraging their collective technological and industrial capabilities to enhance security and defence.[222] The most prominent and widely publicised component of the agreement is the commitment to provide Australia with a fleet of nuclear-powered submarines, a transformative step for Australia's naval capabilities. This initiative relies on cutting-edge British and American technology, with the submarines based on UK designs. The development process involves prototyping and initial construction in the UK, funded by Australia, marking a significant collaboration that strengthens the defence industrial bases of all three nations.

Before Brexit, the UK's membership of the European Union would have imposed significant constraints on its ability to participate in such an agreement. As an EU member, the UK was obligated to align with the EU's Common Foreign and Security Policy (CFSP), which coordinates the foreign and defence policies of member states to promote a unified European stance. The CFSP's requirements for collective decision-making and alignment on strategic priorities would have conflicted with the objectives of AUKUS, particularly given the agreement's focus on a non-EU geopolitical framework and its implications for sensitive defence technologies. For instance, the transfer of nuclear propulsion technology and the establishment of a non-EU defence pact would have been deemed incompatible with EU regulations or interests, especially since the EU has its own defence cooperation mechanisms, such as the Permanent Structured Cooperation (PESCO). These constraints would have prevented the UK from committing to the full scale of the final AUKUS agreement, potentially derailing the entire agreement and limiting the strategic alignment of the UK, US, and Australia in countering regional security challenges, notably from powers like China in the Indo-Pacific.

The AUKUS agreement has already delivered substantial economic and industrial benefits for the UK, demonstrating the tangible advantages of its post-Brexit autonomy. Australia's financial commitment to the submarine programme has driven billions of pounds in investment into the UK's defence sector, catalysing economic growth and job creation. A key beneficiary is Rolls-Royce, which has secured contracts to design and manufacture the nuclear propulsion systems for the submarines at its facilities in Derby. This work is expected to create thousands of high-skilled jobs in engineering, manufacturing, and related fields, boosting local economies and reinforcing the UK's position as a global leader in advanced defence technologies.[223] Other UK companies and supply chains, particularly in regions like Barrow-in-Furness, where submarine construction expertise is concentrated, are also poised to benefit from the programme's long-term industrial demands.

Beyond the economic impact, AUKUS underscores the UK's ability to pursue an independent foreign and defence policy tailored to its national interests and global ambitions. By partnering with the US and Australia, the UK is strengthening its strategic presence in the Indo-Pacific, a region of growing importance in global trade and security. The agreement also enhances interoperability among the three nations' armed forces, facilitating joint operations, intelligence sharing, and technological innovation in areas such as cyber defence, artificial intelligence, and quantum technologies, which are additional pillars of AUKUS. These advancements would have been far more challenging to achieve within the EU's regulatory and political framework, which often prioritised European cohesion over external partnerships.

Brexit has unlocked opportunities that are reshaping the UK's economy, security posture, and global influence, with AUKUS serving as a cornerstone of its post-EU strategic vision.

75. Through the Fire and the Flames

Post-Brexit changes to UK defence procurement rules have allowed the Royal Navy to accelerate the development and deployment of new weapons platforms such as the DragonFire LDEW by a full five years – helping to protect our armed forces and UK interests both domestically and internationally.

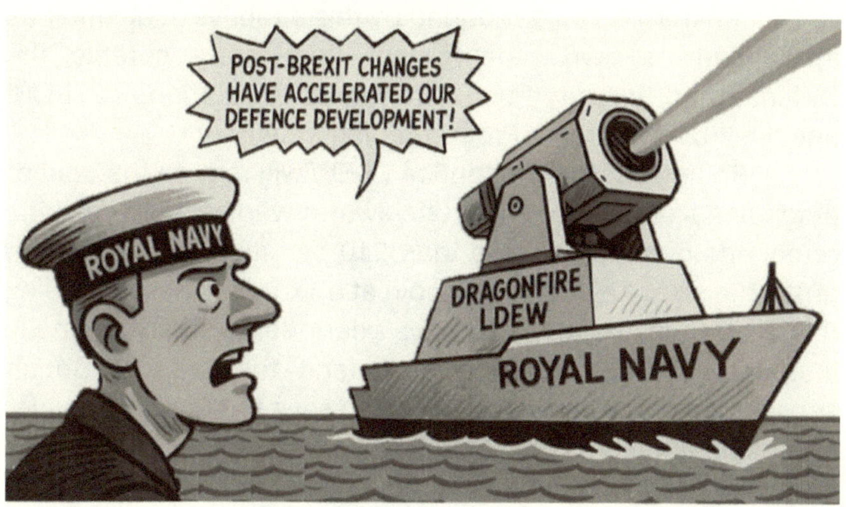

In April 2024, the UK Ministry of Defence (MoD) announced that the DragonFire laser-directed energy weapon (LDEW) - a weapon whose successful trials had been met with significant fanfare in the British press - would be installed on British naval warships in 2027, a full five years earlier than the anticipated 2032 rollout.[224] The reason for this significant acceleration? Leaving the EU.

From outside of the EU, the UK was able to introduce a refined Integrated Procurement Model, which prioritises delivering a 'minimum deployable capability' quickly and finalising the development in-service. The reforms also aim to streamline the procurement processes, involve industry earlier, and avoid issues common in the past such as cost overruns and delays.[225]

While the UK was an EU member, its defence procurement was subject to EU Directive 2009/81/EC, which governed defence and security procurement to ensure transparency, non-discrimination, and competition across member states. This directive required open tendering processes and compliance with EU single-market rules, which limited flexibility in prioritizing national industries or streamlining processes for rapid deployment.[226] Post-Brexit, the UK is thankfully no longer bound by this directive at all and has introduced its own procurement framework, notably the Defence and Security Public Contracts Regulations (DSPCR) and the 2024 Integrated Procurement Model.

Rolling out the DragonFire LDEW will reduce the cost of defending against modern drone swarm warfare from millions of pounds per shot, to less than £10 per shot - and can hit a target the size of a one pound coin at a 1km distance.[227] Having this system in theatre a full five years earlier than originally intended, will not only better defend the lives of British servicemen and women, but will also save the British taxpayer hundreds of millions of pounds in costs to replace missiles as they will no longer need to be fired.

The DragonFire LDEW is just the first in a long line of defence innovation coming down the track, to benefit from entering service years earlier than it otherwise would have been. Our armed forces will be better prepared, better defended and more cost efficient, thanks to leaving the EU.

Acknowledgements

Pulling together this book has been a labour of love for me, and a culmination of a three-year crusade that I did not initially realise I had embarked upon. The exercise of researching and writing up Brexit benefits instantly puts you in the crosshairs of the very vocal and militant 'Follow Back Pro-EU' ground troops on social media – who have been opposed to my existence from the outset. Finding reasonable voices within the social media space who can help in your quest and thirst for knowledge, be it through assistance or constructive critique, is to find veritable diamonds in the rough. So I want to focus some time on a few particular voices within the Twitter/X space, who have played a critical and up to now unsung role in providing their support and companionship – whether they perhaps realised the importance they were playing or not.

Fellow critical and thorough researchers such as Clarissa @clarescastle; Shepherdess @BaaRamEwe; Catherine @ceemacbee; Derrick @DerrickBerthel1; Joe @JoeleTax188567 and others (not in any way an exhaustive list). I've lost track of the number of times you've either found material to help support my argument, or made me aware of something that I had missed that was of interest and of use for my own research.

The members of the Conservative Democratic Organisation, who made me feel so welcome at what was my first event attendance under my Gully Foyle pseudonym and my first attendance at a political event, where I knew exactly zero people and came away with what will hopefully be life-long friendships.

Those in the political arena who have assisted in the research and polishing of this book from time to time, through tolerating my requests for their expertise on topics outside of my wheelhouse. Brian, Daniel, Alison, Julian, Claire and many more over the past six months. The book would genuinely not be what it is without your patience and assistance with this first-time author.

The political legend that is John Redwood, for honouring me with the foreword to this book, and for his expert eye over the text - an author could not ask for a more gracious offer.

Robert and the team at Bruges Group, for their support throughout the authoring of the book. For taking up a first-time author and giving the opportunity of publication. I am truly grateful for your having taken a chance on me on what was at the time a very long Twitter post and a few draft chapters of what became this book.

Those who have on occasion funded a glass or two of Rum and Coke - I drank it to your honour, and it is a privilege that you consider me deserving of your hard-earned pounds to get me a drink. I really do appreciate it.

My family and friends, who have stuck by me through this fractious period in British history where it was much easier to pick a side and shun those who thought differently, than it was to consider nuance. Sadly I have lost both family and friends through this time, and so I treasure those who are still around. Honorary mentions to Rob, Carl, Geoff, Eddie, Ryan, Jules, Jason, Mike, Panos and Harry - all brothers from other mothers, all absolute reprobates in their own ways.

Finally my wider non-political support network, some of whom know nothing at all about my alter ego. At times in life we all go through challenges, and my life has been no different in this regard. I have at times needed to reach out to strangers for support, and have found those strangers to be some of the best mankind has to offer. You know who you are.

Notes

All the below URLs were correct at the time of authoring this content and were checked and found to still be active and correct in July 2025. Please use the below QR code to be taken to an online version of this list with clickable URLs.

Section 1. Brexit Has Saved Us Billions in EU Fees and Membership Costs

Benefit 1: Same-Same, But Different
1. European Union, '*Treaty on the Functioning of the European Union: Article 3*',
   https://eur-lex.europa.eu/legal-content/EN/TXT/?uri=celex%3A12012E%2FTXT
2. Full Fact, (2018), '*How the EU works: what is the customs union?*',
   https://fullfact.org/europe/how-eu-works-what-customs-union/
3. World Trade Organization (WTO), '*Regional Trade Agreements Database*',
   https://rtais.wto.org/UI/PublicMaintainRTAHome.aspx
4. World Trade Organization (WTO), 'Regional Trade Agreements Database: EU Treaty',
   https://rtais.wto.org/UI/PublicShowMemberRTAIDCard.aspx?rtaid=120
5. L. Gonzalez Garcia (2016), '*Brexit: what trade agreements can the UK negotiate whilst being a part of the EU*', Matrix Chambers,
   https://www.matrixlaw.co.uk/resource/possible-united-kingdom-negotiate-trade-agreement-eu-ftas-third-countries-new-legal-status-within-wto-part-eu/
6. UK Government Department for Business and Trade, '*UK trade agreements in effect*',
   https://www.gov.uk/guidance/uk-trade-agreements-in-effect

Benefit 2: Emission Impossible

7.   European Commission (2023), 'Questions and Answers: An adjusted package for the next generation of own resources', https://ec.europa.eu/commission/presscorner/api/files/document/print/en/qanda_23_3329/QANDA_23_3329_EN.pdf

8.   A. Breckenridge (2024), 'The Carbon Border Adjustment Mechanism – its impact on UK competitiveness and carbon pricing', https://www.frontier-economics.com/uk/en/news-and-insights/news/news-article-i20594-the-carbon-border-adjustment-mechanism-its-impact-on-uk-competitiveness-and-carbon-pricing/

9.   European Parliament (2023), 'System of own resources of the European Union', https://www.europarl.europa.eu/RegData/etudes/BRIE/2023/751480/EPRS_BRI(2023)751480_EN.pdf

Benefit 3: The Bill Comes Due. Always.

10.   European Commission, 'Recovery plan for Europe', https://commission.europa.eu/strategy-and-policy/recovery-plan-europe_en

11.   K Körner, B Böttcher (2020), Deutsche Bank Research, 'Financing the EU's recovery: Increased budget ceiling and (new) EU revenues', https://www.dbresearch.com/PROD/RPS_EN-PROD/PROD0000000000510750/Financing_the_EU%27s_recovery%3A_Increased_budget_ceil.pdf

12.   European Commission (2025), 'Questions and answers on ReArm Europe Plan/Readiness 2030', https://ec.europa.eu/commission/presscorner/detail/en/qanda_25_790

Benefit 4: Plastic Fantastic

13.   European Commission, 'Plastics own resource', https://commission.europa.eu/strategy-and-policy/eu-budget/long-term-eu-budget/2021-2027/revenue/own-resources/plastics-own-resource_en

14.   UK Department for Environment, Food & Rural Affairs (DEFRA), 'UK statistics on waste', https://www.gov.uk/government/statistics/uk-waste-data/uk-statistics-on-waste#packaging-waste

Benefit 5: It's All About the Benjamins, Baby!

15.   European Commission (2023), 'EU budget 2024: Enabling Europe to address its priorities', https://ec.europa.eu/commission/presscorner/detail/en/ip_23_3062

Benefit 6: The More the Merrier?

16.   H. Foy (2023), Financial Times, 'EU estimates Ukraine entitled to
       €186bn after accession',
       https://www.ft.com/content/a8834254-b8f9-4385-b043-
       04c2a7cd54c8

Benefit 7: Removing the Lion, Keeping the Lion's Share

17.   M. Keep (2022), House of Commons Research Briefing, 'The UK's
       contribution to the EU budget',
       https://researchbriefings.files.parliament.uk/documents/CBP-
       7886/CBP-7886.pdf
18.   S. Sutcliffe (2022), Blick Rothenberg, 'Customs Duty receipts up by
       50% in the last year',
       https://www.blickrothenberg.com/insights/detail/customs-duty-
       receipts-up-by-50-in-the-last-year
19.   Statista, 'Customs duty tax receipts in the United Kingdom from
       2010/11 to 2024/25',
       https://www.statista.com/statistics/284363/customs-duty-united-
       kingdom-hmrc-tax-receipts/
20.   T. Kovacevic (2019), BBC News, 'EU Budget: Who pays most in and
       who gets most back?', https://www.bbc.co.uk/news/uk-politics-
       48256318

Benefit 8: Banana-Rama

21.   S. Bradley (2023), The Week, 'Why the UK and EU are fighting over
       bananas',
       https://theweek.com/business/retail/the-uks-love-affair-with-the-
       banana
22.   UK Department for Business & Trade (2023), 'The accession of the
       UK to the CPTPP: agreement summary',
       https://www.gov.uk/government/publications/cptpp-agreement-
       summary/the-accession-of-the-uk-to-the-cptpp-agreement-
       summary-web-version
23.   D. Coughlin (2025), Love Money, 'The cost of bananas in 25
       countries around the world',
       https://www.lovemoney.com/galleries/427000/the-cost-of-
       bananas-in-25-countries-around-the-world

Benefit 9: I Have a Semillon

24.   S. Neish (2023), The Drinks Business, 'Foil to be scrapped on English
       sparkling wine?',
       https://www.thedrinksbusiness.com/2023/01/foil-to-be-scrapped-
       on-english-sparkling-wine/

25. European Parliament, parliamentary question E-004993/2020, 'Capsules/foil and sparkling-wine bottles', https://www.europarl.europa.eu/doceo/document/E-9-2020-004993_EN.html

26. The Wine (Amendment) (England) Regulation 2024, https://www.legislation.gov.uk/uksi/2024/115/memorandum/contents

27. UK Government press release, 31 December 2023, 'English Sparkling Wine makers raise a glass to new opportunities', https://www.gov.uk/government/news/english-sparkling-wine-makers-raise-a-glass-to-new-opportunities

Benefit 10: Get Them While They're Young

28. Times Higher Education (2025), 'World University Rankings 2025', https://www.timeshighereducation.com/world-university-rankings/latest/world-ranking

29. C. Gallardo (2020), Politico, 'UK pulls out of EU's 'extremely expensive' Erasmus scheme', https://www.politico.eu/article/uk-students-lose-participation-in-eu-erasmus-university-exchange-scheme

Benefit 11: Bring Me the Horizon

30. UK Government press release, 7 September 2023, 'UK joins Horizon Europe under a new bespoke deal', https://www.gov.uk/government/news/uk-joins-horizon-europe-under-a-new-bespoke-deal

Benefit 12: Quads Out, Quids In

31. Judgement of the Court (Third Chamber), 4 September 2014, 'Damijan Vnuk V Zavarovalnica Triglav', https://curia.europa.eu/juris/liste.jsf?num=C-162/13

32. Motor Insurers Bureau press release, 25 April 2022, 'MIB welcomes removal of EU's Vnuk ruling from UK law', https://www.mib.org.uk/media-centre/news/2022/april/mib-welcomes-removal-of-eu-s-vnuk-ruling-from-uk-law/

33. A. Shalchi (2021), House of Commons Research Briefing, 'The cost of motor insurance: impact of the Vnuk case', https://commonslibrary.parliament.uk/research-briefings/cbp-9321/

34. Hansard (2022), House of Lords Chamber, 'Motor Vehicles (Compulsory Insurance) Bill', https://hansard.parliament.uk/lords/2022-03-18/debates/8ACA5C1A-A614-4ADA-8325-38CCA17954F5/MotorVehicles(CompulsoryInsurance)Bill

Benefit 13: Less is More

35.   UK Ministry of Housing, Communites & Local Government (2024),
       'Costs of the 2019 European Parliamentary elections',
       https://www.gov.uk/government/publications/costs-of-the-2019-
       european-parliamentary-elections/costs-of-the-2019-european-
       parliamentary-elections

Section 2. Brexit Has Returned Our Independence in Fishing, Farming, Animal Welfare and the Environment

Benefit 14: Huffin and Puffin

36.   UK Department for Environment, Food & Rural Affairs (2024),
       'Consultation on spatial management measures for industrial
       sandeel fishing',
       https://www.gov.uk/government/consultations/consultation-on-
       spatial-management-measures-for-industrial-sandeel-
       fishing/outcome/government-response

37.   Royal Society for the Protection of Birds (2025), 'Relief for seabirds
       as court rules that UK within its rights to end sandeel fishing',
       https://www.rspb.org.uk/whats-happening/news/a-huge-victory-for-
       seabirds-as-uk-and-scottish-closure-of-sandeel-fishing-stands

38.   Marine Conservation Society (2025), 'Sandeels: under threat again',
       https://www.mcsuk.org/news/sandeels-under-threat-again/

39.   J. Stone (2024), Politico, 'Brexit eel wars: Brussels accuses Britain of
       being too green',
       https://www.politico.eu/article/brexit-eel-wars-brussels-accuses-
       britain-of-being-too-green/

40.   Oceana (2024), 'Nature charities back UK pressing ahead with
       world-leading sandeel protections, despite EU legal pressure',
       https://europe.oceana.org/press-releases/nature-charities-back-
       uk-pressing-ahead-with-world-leading-sandeel-protections-
       despite-eu-legal-pressure/

41.   Permanent Court of Arbitration (2025), 'PCA CASE No. 2024-25 –
       Ruling in the matter of an arbitration pursuant to Article 739 of the
       Trade and Cooperation Agreement between the European Union and
       the European Atomic Energy Community and the United Kingdom of
       Great Britain and Northern Ireland',
       https://pcacases.com/web/sendAttach/70467

42.   A. Thompson (2025), Channel 4 News, 'How Brexit is boosting
       Britain's Puffin population'
       https://www.channel4.com/news/how-brexit-is-boosting-britains-
       puffin-population

Benefit 15: My Chemical Romance

43.   Cruelty Free International, 'Where it all began',
        https://crueltyfreeinternational.org/make-change/cosmetics/uk-
        cosmetics

44.   National Centre for the Replacement Refinement & Reduction of
        Animal in Research, 'The use of animals in cosmetic testing
        (including REACH regulation)', https://nc3rs.org.uk/use-animals-
        cosmetic-testing-including-reach-regulation

45.   Court of Justice of the European Union, 'Judgement of the General
        Court of 22 November 2023 – Symrise AG v European Chemicals
        Agency (ECHA)', https://eur-lex.europa.eu/legal-
        content/EN/TXT/PDF/?uri=OJ:C_202400725

46.   S. Braverman (2023), UK Parliament Written Statement UIN
        HCWS779, 'Regulation Update, https://questions-
        statements.parliament.uk/written-statements/detail/2023-05-
        17/hcws779

47.   Priya S (2021), People for the Ethical Treatment of Animals, 'Despite
        the Ban, Animals Tests for Cosmetics Are STILL Taking Place in the
        EU',
        https://www.peta.org.uk/blog/animal-tests-for-cosmetics/

Benefit 16: (Don't) Bring Your Daughter to the Slaughter

48.   UK Parliament, Parliamentary Bills, *Animal Welfare (Livestock
        Exports) Act 2024*',
        https://bills.parliament.uk/bills/3533

49.   Royal Society for the Prevention of Cruelty to Animals, *Live transport
        of farm animals*',
        https://www.rspca.org.uk/adviceandwelfare/farm/livetransport

50.   BBC News (2014), *Ramsgate live animal export ban unlawful*',
        https://www.bbc.co.uk/news/uk-england-kent-26371844

51.   Compassion in World Farming (2024), *Success! Ban live exports bill
        passed into law*',
        https://www.ciwf.org.uk/our-campaigns/other-campaigns/gb-live-
        export-ban/

52.   J. Crisp (2025), *The Telegraph*, *Starmer could weaken animal
        protection laws to secure Brussels deal*',
        https://www.telegraph.co.uk/news/2025/05/13/starmer-could-
        weaken-animal-protection-laws-secure-brussels/

Benefit 17: The Fin-al Countdown

53.   A. Passantino, ICES Journal of Medical Science (2014), *The EU shark
        finning ban at the beginning of the new millennium: the legal
        framework*',

https://www.researchgate.net/publication/273028198_The_EU_sha
rk_finning_ban_at_the_beginning_of_the_new_millennium_The_legal
_framework
54.   UK Parliament, Parliamentary Bills, '*Shark Fins Act 2023*',
        https://bills.parliament.uk/bills/3207
55.   UK Government press release, 29 June 2023, '*Government
        introduces law banning international shark fin trade*',
        https://www.gov.uk/government/news/government-introduces-law-
        banning-international-shark-fin-trade

Benefit 18: Skin in the Game
56.   UK Parliament, Parliamentary Bills, '*Fur (Import and Sale) Bill*',
        https://bills.parliament.uk/bills/3789
57.   PoliticsHome (2024), '*Bill to ban UK fur imports and sales to be
        introduced to Parliament*'
        https://www.politicshome.com/members/article/bill-ban-uk-fur-
        imports-sales-introduced-parliament

Benefit 19: Plenty More Fish in the Sea
58.   G. Taylor (2021), National Federation of Fishermen's Organisations,
        '*Brexit Balance Sheet*',
        https://ukfisheries.net/media-centre/brexit-balance-sheet-report-
        for-nffo
59.   UK Government press release, 21 December 2021, '*UK secures
        fishing access and quotas with Norway*',
        https://www.gov.uk/government/news/uk-secures-fishing-access-
        and-quotas-with-norway
60.   UK Government press release, 8 December 2023, '*UK secures £970
        million of fishing opportunities for 2024*',
        https://www.gov.uk/government/news/uk-secures-970-million-of-
        fishing-opportunities-for-2024

Benefit 20: Do Sheep Dream of Electric Androids?
61.   UK Parliament, Parliamentary bills, '*Animal Welfare (Sentience) Act
        2022*',
        https://bills.parliament.uk/bills/2867

Benefit 21: Poppin a CAP in Your Ass
62.   I. Johnston (2016), Independent, '*Brexit is a 'once-in-a-generation'
        chance to restore our green and pleasant land, conservationists
        say*',
        https://www.independent.co.uk/climate-change/news/brexit-save-
        wildlife-nature-rspb-wwf-farming-agriculture-a7340161.html
63.   UK Parliament, Parliamentary bills, '*Agriculture Act 2020*',
        https://bills.parliament.uk/bills/2551

Benefit 22: Wet Wet Wet

64.   Marine Conservation Society (2024), '*Campaign win for banning plastic in wet wipes*' https://www.mcsuk.org/news/single-use-wet-wipes-containing-plastic-to-be-banned/

65.   Uk Government press release, 22 April 2024, '*Uk-wide ban on wet wipes containing plastic to be put into law*', https://www.gov.uk/government/news/uk-wide-ban-on-wet-wipes-containing-plastic-to-be-put-into-law

Benefit 23: Honk Honk

66.   Legislation.gov.uk, '*Animal Welfare Act 2006*', https://www.legislation.gov.uk/ukpga/2006/45

67.   F. Murphy (2007), Reuters, '*French foie gras producers expect record year*', https://www.reuters.com/article/world/french-foie-gras-producers-expect-record-year-idUSL24202151/

68.   W. Dodds (2024), Food Manufacture, '*85% back UK foie gras import ban*', https://www.foodmanufacture.co.uk/Article/2024/08/01/85-back-UK-foie-gras-import-ban/

69.   Animal Equality press release, 20 March 2025, '*UK celebrities, lawmakers demand and end to foie gras imports*' https://animalequality.org/news/2025/03/19/uk-demands-an-end-to-foie-gras-imports/

Benefit 24: Hush Puppies

70.   Four Paws press release, 30 April 2025, '*Members of the European Parliament are shaping the fate of cats and dogs in the EU*', https://www.four-paws.org/our-stories/press-releases/april-2025/european-parliament-shaping-fate-of-cats-and-dogs-eu

71.   UK Parliament, parliamentary bills, '*Animal Welfare (Import of Dogs, Cats and Ferrets) Bill*', https://bills.parliament.uk/bills/3790

Section 3. Brexit Means Better Trade

Benefit 25: Harder, Better Faster, Stronger

72.   F. Islam (2025), BBC, '*Trump tariffs may have helped drive UK-India trade deal*', https://www.bbc.co.uk/news/articles/cn919g2v3w2o

73.   Australia Ministry for Agriculture, Fisheries and Forestry (2023), '*Interview with David Lipson, ABC RN Breakfast*', https://minister.agriculture.gov.au/watt/speeches-and-

transcripts/abc-rn-breakfast-eu-trade-talks-trade-china-national-emergency-management-stockpile

Benefit 26: How Low Can You Go?

74.   Wall Street Journal (2017), Interview with Roberto Azevêdo Director-General of the World Trade Organization, '*The WTO on Brexit and Trade*', https://www.youtube.com/watch?v=FKi4ccjwiYY

75.   UK Government policy paper, 13 January 2021, '*The UK's Integrated Tariff Schedule*', https://www.gov.uk/government/publications/the-uks-integrated-tariff-schedule/the-uks-integrated-tariff-schedule

76.   Hansard (2023), House of Commons Chamber, '*Oral Answers to Questions: Business and Trade*', https://hansard.parliament.uk/Commons/2023-05-18/debates/7B88C646-229A-4F84-AEC3-2B1D2EEC6F87/BusinessAndTrade#contribution-1065B729-4551-4243-B1AE-84E374FF8EF9

Benefit 27: Common People

77.   Independent Television News (1963), '*Clement Attlee Reflects on Lifetime in Politics: 80th Birthday Interview*', https://www.youtube.com/watch?v=SHJYLB-5fmE

78.   The Commonwealth press release, 15 October 2024, '*Record highs for Commonwealth Trade and Investment: 2024 Commonwealth Trade Review launched*', https://thecommonwealth.org/news/record-highs-commonwealth-trade-and-investment-2024-commonwealth-trade-review

79.   M. Buhari (2022), The Telegraph, '*We can make the Commonwealth a real global power*', https://telegraph.co.uk/news/2022/04/25/can-make-commonwealth-real-global-power/

80.   M. Ward (2024), House of Commons research briefing, '*Statistics on UK trade with the Commonwealth*', https://commonslibrary.parliament.uk/research-briefings/cbp-8282/

Benefit 28: Epic Berne

81.   J. Crisp (2019), The Telegraph, 'Swiss row with Brussels escalates with share trading ban', https://www.telegraph.co.uk/business/2019/06/24/swiss-ban-eu-stock-exchanges-row-brussels-escalates/

82.   London Stock Exchange Market Notice, 25 June 2019, 'Suspension of Swiss shares for trading with effect from 1 July 2019', https://docs.londonstockexchange.com/sites/default/files/documents/n0819.pdf

83.   London Stock Exchange Market Notice, 3 February 2021, 'Resumption of on Exchange trading of Swiss shares', https://docs.londonstockexchange.com/sites/default/docume nts/n0521.pdf

84.   M. Shields and H. Jones (2021), Reuters, 'Switzerland lifts ban, and London will resume trading Swiss stocks', https://www.reuters.com/world/uk/switzerland-lifts-ban-london-will-resume-trading-swiss-stocks-2021-02-03/

85.   UK Government press release, 21 December 2023, 'UK signs first of its kind financial services agreement with Switzerland', https://www.gov.uk/government/news/uk-signs-first-of-its-kind-financial-services-agreement-with-switzerland

86.   B. Lesar (2024), Herrington Carmichael, 'The Berne Financial Services Agreement', https://www.herrington-carmichael.com/the-berne-financial-services-agreement/

Benefit 29: Competency? What Competency?

87.   J. Rooke (2024), Carleton University Centre for European Studies, '*CETA Ratification Tracker*', https://carleton.ca/tradenetwork/research-publications/ceta-ratification-tracker/

88.   UK Government Guidance, 18 July 2024, '*Trade with Canada*', https://www.gov.uk/guidance/summary-of-the-uk-canada-trade-continuity-agreement

89.   M. Stoddart (2018), Politico, '*Justin Trudeau: UK-Canada trade talks can begin 'day after Brexit'*', https://www.politico.eu/article/justin-trudeau-uk-canada-trade-talks-can-begin-day-after-brexit/

Benefit 30: Through the Barricades

90.   UK Government press release, 5 September 2019, '*New service to open overseas markets for UK businesses*', https://www.gov.uk/government/news/new-service-to-open-overseas-markets-for-uk-businesses

91.   Department for Business and Trade official statistics, '*market access barriers for financial years April 2019 to March 2023*', https://assets.publishing.service.gov.uk/media/6679849688a5f8d9 390e7320/data-tables-revised-market-access-barriers-for-financial-years-april-2019-to-march-2023.ods

92.   UK government press release, 30 June 2022, '*Bonfire of the barriers to unlock new export markets worth tens of billions*', https://www.gov.uk/government/news/bonfire-of-the-barriers-to-unlock-new-export-markets-worth-tens-of-billions

93.   N. Huddleston (2023), UK Parliament Written Answer UIN 177789, '*Business: Trade Barriers*', https://questions-

statements.parliament.uk/written-questions/detail/2023-03-30/177789/

94.   UK Government press release, 9 October 2023, '*Trade Minister in Peru and Colombia to boost trade with Latin America*', https://www.gov.uk/government/news/trade-minister-in-peru-and-colombia-to-boost-trade-with-latin-america

Benefit 31: In It for the Long Haul

95.   UK Government press release, 10 May 2023, '*UK economy boosted by £1.4 billion as longer lorries roll out on roads*' https://www.gov.uk/government/news/uk-economy-boosted-by-14-billion-as-longer-lorries-roll-out-on-roads

96.   Department for Transport (2021), Impact Assessment DfT00423, '*Proposal to conclude the Longer Semi-Trailer (LST) trial and allow LSTs to enter into general circulation*', https://assets.publishing.service.gov.uk/media/631afa5e8fa8f502069e7728/ending-the-longer-semi-trailer-trial-impact-assessment-2022.pdf

Benefit 32: Feed the World

97.   European Union Trade and Economic Security, '*Generalised Scheme of Preferences*', https://policy.trade.ec.europa.eu/development-and-sustainability/generalised-scheme-preferences_en

98.   Department for Business and Trade (2024), '*Developing Countries Trading Scheme*', https://www.gov.uk/government/collections/trading-with-developing-nations

99.   M. Di Ubaldo, G. Larbalestier, M. Tong Koecklin (2023), UK Trade Policy Observatory, '*The UK's new (and improved?) Developing Countries Trading Scheme*', https://blogs.sussex.ac.uk/uktpo/publications/the-new-and-improved-uks-developing-countries-trading-scheme/

Benefit 33: Ill Customs are Seldom Forgotten

100.   UK Government press release, 27 April 2023, '*New service launched to make importing easier for UK traders*', https://www.gov.uk/government/news/new-service-launched-to-make-importing-easier-for-uk-traders

101.   HM Revenue and Customs Policy paper, 15 March 2023, '*Import Duty: ruling as to method of valuation of goods*', https://www.gov.uk/government/publications/introduction-of-customs-advance-valuation-rulings/import-duty-rulings-as-to-method-of-valuation-of-goods

Benefit 34: Perfect 10

102. C. Taylor, J. Reid, S. Meredith (2025), CNBC, '*The biggest winners and losers in Europe as Trump announces sweeping tariffs*', https://www.cnbc.com/2025/04/03/trump-liberation-day-tariffs-biggest-winners-and-losers.html

103. E. Buchwald, K. Liptak (2025), CNN Business, '*Trump announces 90-day pause on reciprocal tariffs with exception of China*', https://edition.cnn.com/2025/04/09/business/reciprocal-tariff-pause-trump

104. UK Government press release, 8 May 2025, '*Landmark economic deal with United States saves thousands of jobs for British car makers and steel industry*', https://www.gov.uk/government/news/landmark-economic-deal-with-united-states-saves-thousands-of-jobs-for-british-car-makers-and-steel-industry

105. A. Wickham, L. White (2025), Bloomberg, '*Starmer Gets Diplomatic Win He Needs, If Not the Economic Boost*', https://www.bloomberg.com/news/articles/2025-05-08/starmer-gets-diplomatic-win-he-needs-if-not-the-economic-boost

Benefit 35: Time to Make the Chimichangas

106. Financial Conduct Authority statement (2021), '*Update on the Double Volume Cap*', https://www.fca.org.uk/news/statements/update-double-volume-cap

107. HM Treasury press release, 20 July 2022, '*Financial Services Bill to unlock growth and investment across the UK*', https://www.gov.uk/government/news/financial-services-bill-to-unlock-growth-and-investment-across-the-uk

Benefit 36: Digital Killed the Analog Star

108. J. Eyal (2023), Straits Times, '*Digital economy deal unlocks vast opportunities for Singapore, UK*', https://www.straitstimes.com/world/europe/world-s-first-fully-digitalised-goods-shipment-sent-from-uk-to-singapore-as-they-boost-trade-cyber-security

109. Department for Business and Trade press release, 25 September 2023, '*World first fully digitalised goods shipment sent from Burnley in billion-pound Brexit boost for British businesses*', https://www.gov.uk/government/news/worlds-first-fully-digitalised-goods-shipment-sent-from-burnley-in-billion-pound-brexit-boost-for-british-businesses

Benefit 37: Rotterdam or Anywhere, Liverpool or Rome

110. S. Ansari (2020), Economics Online, '*The Rotterdam effect*', https://www.economicsonline.co.uk/global_economics/the_rotterdam_effect.html/

111. M. De Prez (2022), Fleet News, '*Mazda cuts lead times by shipping cars directly to UK*', https://fleetnews.co.uk/news/manufacturer-news/2022/04/05/mazda-cuts-lead-times-by-shipping-cars-directly-to-uk

112. Mazda UK press release, 4 April 2022, '*First shipment of cars arrives at Bristol Port as Mazda Uks new direct from Japan import route begins*', https://uk.mazda-press.com/news/2022/first-shipment-of-cars-arrives-at-bristol-port-as-mazda-uks-new-direct-from-japan-import-route-begins

Benefit 38: Rock, Paper, Scissors, Blockchain

113. Department for Business and Trade press release, 20 July 2023, '*UK economy to receive £1 billion boost through innovative trade digitalization act*', https://www.gov.uk/government/news/uk-economy-to-receive-1-billion-boost-through-innovative-trade-digitalisation-act

114. R. Tyler (2024), The Times, '*Fuel for wood burners benefits from bonfire of red tape*', https://www.thetimes.com/business-money/entrepreneurs/article/fuel-for-wood-burners-benefits-from-bonfire-of-red-tape-g6rj6k7gd

115. International Chamber of Commerce UK (2024), '*Seizing the moment: Unleashing the potential of trade digitalisation*', https://iccwbo.uk/wp-content/uploads/2024/04/Seizing_the_moment_Unleashing_the_power_of_trade_digitalisation_report.pdf

Benefit 39: Liberalisation, Across the Nation

116. P. Thompson (2021), Tholos Foundation, '*International Trade Barrier Index 2021*', https://atr-tbi19.s3.amazonaws.com/TBI_FullReport_2021_FINAL.pdf

117. A. Kammer (2024), International Monetary Fund, 'Europe's Choice: Policies for Growth and Resilience', https://www.imf.org/en/News/Articles/2024/12/15/sp121624-europes-choice-policies-for-growth-and-resilience

Benefit 40: A Stay of (Tariff) Execution

118. Department for Business and Trade Guidance, 19 June 2025, '*UK Trade Tariff: duty suspensions and autonomous tariff quotas*', https://www.gov.uk/guidance/duty-suspensions-and-tariff-quotas

119. S. Wingate (2024), The Independent, '*Import tariffs to be paused on 120 goods, ministers announce before SME event*', https://www.independent.co.uk/news/uk/warwickshire-kemi-badenoch-sme-government-rishi-sunak-b2513873.html

120. Department for Business and Trade press release, 13 April 2025, '*Government cuts price of everyday items and summer essentials*', https://www.gov.uk/government/news/government-cuts-price-of-everyday-items-and-summer-essentials

Benefit 41: Oh (Antipodean) Brother, Where Art Thou?

121. UK Government press release, 31 March 2024, '*UK Artists On Course For Royalty Windfall Down Under*', https://www.gov.uk/government/news/uk-artists-on-course-for-royalty-windfall-down-under

122. Design and Artists Copyright Society press release, 27 May 2025, '*First Artist's Resale Right royalty payments received from Australia following historic agreement with the UK*', https://www.dacs.org.uk/news-events/first-arr-royalty-payments-from-australia

Section 4. Brexit Means We Run Our Own Country Again

Benefit 42: Some Are More Equal Than Others

123. V. Miller (2010), House of Commons Library, '*How much legislation comes from Europe?*', https://researchbriefings.files.parliament.uk/documents/RP10-62/RP10-62.pdf

124. A. Sippitt, C. James McKinney (2016), FullFact, '*UK law: What proportion is influenced by the EU?*', https://fullfact.org/europe/uk-law-what-proportion-influenced-eu/

125. L. Macchi (2025), Statista, '*Number of the MEPS in the European Parliament in 2019, by member state*', https://www.statista.com/statistics/974861/number-of-members-of-parliament-in-the-ep/

Benefit 43: Rise of the Machines, Interrupted

126. European Union (2019), '*Regulation (EU) 2019/2144 of the European Parliament and of the Council of 27 November 2019*', https://eur-lex.europa.eu/eli/reg/2019/2144/oj

127. D. Buratti (2024), Which? Magazine, 'Car testing reveals serious concerns with MG4's lane assist technology', https://www.which.co.uk/news/article/popular-family-car-exhibits-

potentially-dangerous-behaviour-during-which-testing-
afXHU1t7gttC
128.   P. Barker (2024), Auto Express, 'Modern ADAS driver-assistance
systems can be borderline dangerous',
https://www.autoexpress.co.uk/opinion/364367/modern-adas-
driver-assistance-systems-can-be-borderline-dangerous
129.   D. Trent (2021), Bike Radar, 'Is lane-keeping car safety tech a danger
to cyclists?',
https://www.bikeradar.com/features/lane-keeping-assist-cyclists

Benefit 44: (No Longer) Arrested Development

130.   M. Lynn (2023), The Spectator, *The UK has finally chalked up a Brexit
win*, https://www.spectator.co.uk/article/the-uk-has-finally-
chalked-up-a-brexit-win/
131.   UK Government press release, 14 October 2020, *Cutting-edge
treatments to be fast-tracked to patients through international
collaborations*,
https://www.gov.uk/government/news/cutting-edge-treatments-to-
be-fast-tracked-to-patients-through-international-collaborations

Benefit 45: Running Up that Bill

132.   UK Government, 1 January 2021, *Tampon tax abolished from today*,
https://www.gov.uk/government/news/tampon-tax-abolished-from-
today
133.   UK Government Policy paper, 23 March 2022, *Changes to the VAT
treatment of the installation of Energy Saving Materials in Great
Britain*,
https://www.gov.uk/government/publications/changes-to-the-vat-
treatment-of-the-installation-of-energy-saving-materials-in-in-great-
britain
134.   Streets LLP (2024), *VAT on period products scrapped*,
https://www.streetsweb.co.uk/about/news/2024/jan/11/vat-on-
period-products-scrapped/
135.   A. Panjwani (2022), FullFact, 'Chris Bryant wrong on 0% EU VAT for
heat pumps',
https://fullfact.org/economy/solar-installations-vat-eu/

Benefit 46: I've Got the Power(s)

136.   UK Government and Parliament Petitions, Petition 41492, *Stop
mass immigration from Bulgarian and Romanians in 2014, when EU
restrictions on immigration are relaxed*,
https://petition.parliament.uk/archived/petitions/41492

137. UK Government and Parliament Petitions, Petition 29349, '*Return VAT on Air Ambulance fuel payments*', https://petition.parliament.uk/archived/petitions/29349

138. UK Government and Parliament Petitions, Petition 64331, '*End non-stun slaughter to promote animal welfare*', https://petition.parliament.uk/archived/petitions/64331

139. UK Government and Parliament Petitions, Petition 107516, '*Stop all immigration and close the UK borders until ISIS is defeated*', https://petition.parliament.uk/archived/petitions/107516

Benefit 47: Cellophane, Mr Cellophane

140. Judgement of the Court (Grand Chamber), 22 November 2022, 'Reference for a preliminary ruling – Prevention of the use of the financial system for the purposes of money laundering or terrorist financing', https://curia.europa.eu/juris/document/document.jsf?docid=268059&doclang=en

141. UK Government Policy paper, 12 March 2025, 'Economic Crime and Corporate Transparency Act: outline transition plan for Companies House', https://www.gov.uk/government/publications/economic-crime-and-corporate-transparency-act-outline-transition-plan-for-companies-house/economic-crime-and-corporate-transparency-act-outline-transition-plan-for-companies-house

142. Macfarlanes LLP (2022), 'The future of corporate transparency', https://www.macfarlanes.com/what-we-think/2022/the-future-of-corporate-transparency/

Benefit 48: School's Out for Starmer

143. UK Labour Party (2024), '*General Election Manifesto 2024*', https://labour.org.uk/wp-content/uploads/2024/06/Labour-Party-manifesto-2024.pdf

144. HM Revenue & Customs Policy paper, 15 November 2024, '*Private school fees — VAT measure*', https://www.gov.uk/government/publications/vat-on-private-school-fees/applying-vat-to-private-school-fees

145. Ekathimerini (2015), '*Commission says private school VAT breaks rules*', https://www.ekathimerini.com/news/201031/commission-says-private-school-vat-breaks-rules/

146. European Union (2006), '*Council Directive 2006/112/EC of 28 November 2006 on the common system of value added tax*', https://eur-lex.europa.eu/eli/dir/2006/112/oj/eng

Benefit 49: The Return of Democracy

147.   Council of Europe, Manual for Human Rights Education with Young People, '*Democracy*',
https://www.coe.int/en/web/compass/democracy

148.   YouTube, '*Tony Benn and the Five Essential Questions of Democracy*', https://www.youtube.com/watch?v=M0gWYmYy77o

149.   M. Keating (2022), Scottish Parliament Committee Briefing, '*Common Frameworks after Brexit*',
https://www.parliament.scot/chamber-and-committees/committees/current-and-previous-committees/session-6-constitution-europe-external-affairs-and-culture-committee/correspondence/2022/common-frameworks-after-brexit

Benefit 50: Approaching Artificial Intelligence, Intelligently

150.   M. Zuckerberg, D. Ek (2024), The Economist, '*Why Europe should embrace open-source AI*',
https://www.economist.com/by-invitation/2024/08/21/mark-zuckerberg-and-daniel-ek-on-why-europe-should-embrace-open-source-ai

151.   UKTN The Podcast, Season 7 Episode 6, '*Why the UK must not make the EU's AI mistakes – Victor Riparbelli, CEO, Synthesia*',
https://share.transistor.fm/s/3a2a58f5

152.   N. Clegg (2024), Le Monde, 'When it comes to making AI available to Europeans, EU regulators are still moving at a snail's pace',
https://www.lemonde.fr/en/opinion/article/2024/12/20/nick-clegg-when-it-comes-to-making-ai-available-to-europeans-eu-regulators-are-still-moving-at-a-snail-s-pace_6736309_23.html

Benefit 51: Trainer, Trailer, Saver, Drive

153.   European Union (2006), 'Directive 2006/126/EC of the European Parliament and of the Council of 20 December 2006 on driving licences',
https://eur-lex.europa.eu/eli/dir/2006/126/oj/eng

154.   UK Driver & Vehicle Standards Agency Consultation outcome, 25 April 2022, 'Changes to HGV and bus driving tests and allowing car drivers to tow a trailer without an extra test',
https://www.gov.uk/government/consultations/changes-to-hgv-and-bus-driving-tests-and-allowing-car-drivers-to-tow-a-trailer-without-an-extra-test/changes-to-hgv-and-bus-driving-tests-and-allowing-car-drivers-to-tow-a-trailer-without-an-extra-test

Benefit 52: Not So Super, Super League

155.   E. Aarons, Sean Ingle (2021), The Guardian, '*European Super League: Premier League 'big six' sign up to competition*',

https://www.theguardian.com/football/2021/apr/18/five-english-clubs-sign-up-to-european-super-league-report-says

156. J. Masi (2021), Express and Star, *'POLL: Is the Super League a bad idea? 96% say YES'*,
https://www.expressandstar.com/sport/football/2021/04/20/poll-is-the-super-league-a-bad-idea-96-say-yes/

157. S. Ingle, P. Walker, N. Ames (2021), The Guardian, *'European Super League collapsing as all six English clubs withdraw'*,
https://www.theguardian.com/football/2021/apr/20/european-super-league-unravelling-as-manchester-city-and-chelsea-withdraw

158. Court of Justice of the European Union press release, 21 December 2023, *'The FIFA and UEFA rules on prior approval of interclub football competitions, such as the Super League, are contrary to EU law'*,
https://curia.europa.eu/jcms/upload/docs/application/pdf/2023-12/cp230203en.pdf

159. M. Hardy (2023), CityAM, *'European Super League: Brexit means UK doesn't need to follow ECJ ruling'*,
https://www.cityam.com/european-super-league-brexit-means-uk-doesnt-need-to-follow-ecj-ruling/

Benefit 53: High Stakes Make or Break for Fake Steak

160. UK Food Standards Agency (2025), *'Novel foods authorization guidance'*,
https://www.food.gov.uk/business-guidance/regulated-products/novel-foods-guidance

161. M. Scialom (2023), Cambridge Independent, *'At last! Brexit benefit identified by Cambridge biotech as £12m new agri-hub launched in cultivated meat sector'*,
https://cambridgeindependent.co.uk/business/brexit-benefit-emerges-for-uk-as-agri-hub-launched-in-cultiv-9330499/

162. T. Dvorkis, R. Jappie (2023), Fieldfisher LLP, *'Novel Food Compliance in the UK – Finally, a Brexit Benefit?'*,
https://www.fieldfisher.com/en/insights/novel-food-compliance-in-the-uk-finally-a-brexit-benefit

163. UK Food Standards Agency (2023), *'Novel Foods Regulatory Framework Review: Executive Summary'*,
https://www.food.gov.uk/research/novel-and-non-traditional-foods-additives-and-processes/novel-foods-regulatory-framework-review-executive-summary

Benefit 54: Respect My Authoritah!

164. Competition and Markets Authority News Story, 28 January 2020, *'The UK's withdrawal from the EU – The CMA's role post Brexit'*,

https://www.gov.uk/government/news/the-uk-s-withdrawal-from-the-eu-the-cma-s-role-post-brexit

165. B. Batchelor, A. Luoma, I. Vandenborre (2021), Skadden, Arps, Slate, Meagher & Flom LLP, '*Post-Brexit, a More Demanding UK Merger Review Process*', https://www.skadden.com/insights/publications/2021/01/2021-insights/regulatory/post-brexit-a-more-demanding-uk-merger

Benefit 55: Rules Are Made to be Broken (or Made Better)

166. World Trade Organization News item, 7 October 2020, '*UK to join government procurement pact in its own right in the new year*', https://www.wto.org/english/news_e/news20_e/gpro_07oct20_e.htm

167. W. Kale, J. Harrison, J. Ellison (2021), Mayer Brown International LLP, '*UK Public Procurement from 1 January 2021*', https://www.mayerbrown.com/-/media/files/perspectives-events/publications/2021/01/uk-public-procurement-postbrexit.pdf

168. Uk Parliament, Parliamentary Bills, '*Procurement Act 2023*', https://bills.parliament.uk/bills/3159

Benefit 56: The Man with the Golden Share

169. S. Jack, N. Edser (2024), BBC News, 'Royal Mail takeover by Czech billionaire approved', https://www.bbc.co.uk/news/articles/ckg933908080

170. D. Bernard (2024), Print Week, 'Royal Mail takeover cleared, Gov't retains golden share', https://www.printweek.com/content/news/royal-mail-takeover-cleared-govt-retains-golden-share/

171. Euractiv (2006), 'ECJ rules against golden shares', https://www.euractiv.com/section/competition/news/ecj-rules-against-golden-shares/

Section 5. Brexit Means a Better Economy

Benefit 57: A Crescendo of Contactless

172. UK Finance News item, 27 August 2021, '*Contactless limit to increase to £100 from 15 October*', https://www.ukfinance.org.uk/press/press-releases/contactless-limit-increase-100-15-october

173. European Union (2018), Commission Delegated Regulation (EU) 2018/389, '*supplementing Directive (EU) 2015/2366 of the European Parliament and of the Council with regard to regulatory technical standards for strong customer authentication and common and secure open standards of communication*',

        https://eur-lex.europa.eu/legal-
        content/EN/TXT/PDF/?uri=CELEX:32018R0389

174.   UK Finance News item, 18 June 2024, '*UK reaches 150 Million
        Contactless Cards in Issue*',
        https://www.ukfinance.org.uk/news-and-insight/press-release/uk-
        reaches-150-million-contactless-cards-in-issue

175.   Financial Conduct Authority press release, 14 March 2025, '*FCA
        seeks views on removing £100 contactless limit*',
        https://www.fca.org.uk/news/press-releases/fca-seeks-views-
        removing-100-pounds-contactless-limit

Benefit 58: No No, There's No (Commodity Position) Limit!

176.   European Securities and Markets Authority, '*Article 57 Position limits
        and position management controls in commodity derivatives*',
        https://www.esma.europa.eu/publications-and-data/interactive-
        single-rulebook/mifid-ii/article-57-position-limits-and-position

177.   Financial Conduct Authority Policy Statement, February 2025,
        '*Reforming the commodity derivatives regulatory framework*',
        https://www.fca.org.uk/publication/policy/ps25-1.pdf

178.   HM Treasury News story, 1 March 2022, 'Ambitious reforms to
        capital markets regulation and listings rules announced',
        https://www.gov.uk/government/news/ambitious-reforms-to-
        capital-markets-regulation-and-listings-rules-announced

Benefit 59: Hire Locally, Higher Salary

179.   E. Nolsoe (2023), The Telegraph, '*Brexit has boosted UK wages, say
        economists*',
        https://www.telegraph.co.uk/business/2023/11/19/uk-wages-
        brexit-boost-leave-campaigners/

180.   D. Harvey (2021), BBC News, '*Brexit and Covid cause big jump in pay
        for lorry drivers*',
        https://www.bbc.co.uk/news/uk-england-somerset-57656327

181.   S. O'Connor (2025), Financial Times, '*Whatever happened to the
        great truck driver shortage?*', https://www.ft.com/content/f3202bc8-
        d53f-42a9-b434-2e6ca7be2d69

182.   J. Davey, K. Holton, D. Milliken (2023), Reuters, '*Flexible hours, sick
        pay and meals: British workers get a better deal*',
        https://www.reuters.com/world/uk/flexible-hours-sick-pay-meals-
        british-workers-get-better-deal-2023-10-02/

Benefit 60: The Nuclear Option

183.   UK Parliament, Parliamentary Bills, '*Nuclear Energy (Financing) Act
        2022*',
        https://bills.parliament.uk/bills/3057

184.   UK Parliament Business Energy and Industrial Strategy Committee (2019), '*Written evidence submitted by Nuclear Economics Consulting Group (FEI0030)*', https://committees.parliament.uk/writtenevidence/101032/html/

Benefit 61: Just Be Good to Me
185.   European Union (2004), 'Directive 2004/38/EC of the European Parliament and of the Council of 29 April 2004 on the right of citizens of the Union and their family members to move and reside freely within the territory of the Member States', https://eur-lex.europa.eu/eli/dir/2004/38/oj/eng

Benefit 62: the Revolution Will Be Subsidised
186.   European Union, Competition Policy, 'State Aid Overview', https://competition-policy.ec.europa.eu/state-aid/overview_en
187.   Department for Business and Trade Guidance, 28 March 2025, '*Subsidy Control Act 2022: Streamlined Routes*', https://www.gov.uk/government/publications/subsidy-control-act-2022-streamlined-routes

Benefit 63: All Around My Cap
188.   N. Hirst (2014), Politico, '*Bankers' bonus cap is the 'wrong policy', says Bank of England official*', https://www.politico.eu/article/bankers-bonus-cap-is-the-wrong-policy-says-bank-of-england-official/
189.   A. Roberts (2022), Pinsent Masons LLP, '*Scrapping bonus cap 'may not be enough' to attract top talent back into UK banking*', https://www.pinsentmasons.com/out-law/news/scrapping-bonus-cap-not-enough-attract-top-talent-uk-banking
190.   M. Klimes (2023), The Banker, '*What does the UK banker bonus cap scrap mean?*', https://www.thebanker.com/What-does-the-UK-banker-bonus-cap-scrap-mean-1698391634

Section 6. Brexit Means We Control Our Own Borders

Benefit 64: Go Your Own Way
191.   L. McColl (2016), Select Statistical Services, '*EU Freedom of Movement: What are the numbers?*', https://select-statistics.co.uk/blog/eu-freedom-movement-numbers/
192.   I. El Atillah (2024), Euronews, '*Oxford named world's best university in Times' 2025 rankings. Where else in Europe came out top?*',

https://www.euronews.com/next/2024/10/13/oxford-named-worlds-best-university-again-what-other-universities-ranked-the-highest-for-2

193. J. O'Leary (2017), FullFact, *'Brits abroad: how many people from the UK live in other EU countries?'*, https://fullfact.org/europe/how-many-uk-citizens-live-other-eu-countries/

194. Uk Government Promotional material, 25 February 2022, *'The UK's points-based immigration system: an introduction for employers'*, https://www.gov.uk/government/publications/uk-points-based-immigration-system-employer-information/the-uks-points-based-immigration-system-an-introduction-for-employers

Benefit 65: Crime Doesn't Pay (You Entry to the UK)

195. Home Office news story, 21 October 2020, *'Home Office announces tougher criminality rules for EU citizens'*, https://www.gov.uk/government/news/home-office-announces-tougher-criminality-rules-for-eu-citizens

196. L. O'Carroll, M. Goodier (2023), The Guardian, *'Fivefold rise in number of EU citizens refused entry to UK since Brexit'*, https://www.theguardian.com/uk-news/2023/nov/25/fivefold-rise-number-eu-citizens-refused-entry-uk-since-brexit

Benefit 66: I'm Picking Up Good Migrations

197. Organisation for Economic Co-operation and Development (2023), *'Migration Policy Debates'*, https://web-archive.oecd.org/2023-03-09/652850-What-is-the-best-country-for-global-talents-in-the-OECD-Migration-Policy-Debates-March-2023.pdf

Benefit 67: Freeport Convention

198. J. Keane (2019), Institute for Government, *'Trade: freeports and free zones'*, https://www.instituteforgovernment.org.uk/article/explainer/trade-freeports-and-free-zones

199. A. Panjwani (2019), FullFact, 'What's a free port, and does the EU have them?', https://fullfact.org/europe/free-ports/

200. Department for Levelling Up, Housing and Communities Guidance, 19 December 2023, *'Freeports delivery roadmap'*, https://www.gov.uk/guidance/freeports-delivery-roadmap

Benefit 68: Fake It Til You Make It

201. Migration Watch UK (2022), *'Fraudulent documents presented to Border Force'*,

https://www.migrationwatchuk.org/briefing-paper/501/fraudulent-documents-presented-to-border-force

202. Home Office News story (2021), *'Insecure ID cards phased out as travel document to strengthen UK borders'*, https://www.gov.uk/government/news/insecure-id-cards-phased-out-as-travel-document-to-strengthen-uk-borders

Section 7. Brexit Has Strengthened Our Defences and World Standing

Benefit 69: You Down With 'TPP, Yeah You Know Me

203. European Union External Action (2021), *'EU Strategy for Cooperation in the Indo-Pacific'*, https://www.eeas.europa.eu/eeas/eu-strategy-cooperation-indo-pacific-0_en

204. Department for International Trade Consultation outcome, 20 July 2018, *'Trade with the Comprehensive and Progressive Agreement for Trans-Pacific Partnership'*, https://www.gov.uk/government/consultations/trade-with-thecomprehensive-and-progressive-agreement-for-trans-pacific-partnershipcptpp

205. Department for International Trade News story, 1 February 2021, *'Formal Request to Commence UK Accession Negotiations to CPTPP'*, https://www.gov.uk/government/news/formal-request-to-commence-uk-accession-negotiations-to-cptpp

206. Department for Business and Trade News story, 29 August 2024, *'UK to join CPTPP by 15 December'*, https://www.gov.uk/government/news/uk-to-join-cptpp-by-15-december

207. UK Parliament (2024), Special Committee Report, *'Tilting horizons: the Integrated Review and the Indo-Pacific – Government Response to the Committee's Eighth Report of Session 2022–23'*, https://publications.parliament.uk/pa/cm5804/cmselect/cmfaff/630/report.html

208. North Atlantic Treaty Organization (2022), *'Regional Perspectives Report on the Indo-Pacific'*, https://www.act.nato.int/wp-content/uploads/2023/05/regional-perspectives-2022-07-v2-1.pdf

209. Department for International Trade (2021), *'UK Accession to CPTPP: The UK's Strategic Approach'*, https://assets.publishing.service.gov.uk/media/61728409e90e071977182a5d/dit-cptpp-uk-accession-strategic-approach.pdf

210. Borneo Bulletin (2025), '*Malaysian palm oil enters UK market duty-free under trade CPTPP agreement*'
https://borneobulletin.com.bn/malaysian-palm-oil-enters-uk-market-duty-free-under-trade-cptpp-agreement/

Benefit 70: Service(s) With a Smile

211. Organisation for Economic Co-operation and Development (2023), '*OECD Services Trade Restrictiveness Index: Policy trends up to 2023*',
https://issuu.com/oecd.publishing/docs/stri_policy_trends_up_to_2023_final

212. Organisation for Economic Co-operation and Development (2025), '*OECD Services Trade Restrictiveness Index: Policy trends up to 2025*',
https://doi.org/10.1787/9953845b-en

Benefit 71: Slava Ukraini

213. E. Casalicchio, Leonie Kijewski (2022), Politico, '*Did Brexit help Britain help Ukraine?*',
https://www.politico.eu/article/brexit-britain-help-ukraine/

214. B. Kielak (2024), The Telegraph, '*Brexit has let UK respond quickly on Russia and Ukraine, says Polish foreign minister*',
https://www.telegraph.co.uk/world-news/2024/05/18/brexit-has-let-uk-respond-quickly-on-russia-and-ukraine/

215. Department for Business and Trade press release, 8 February 2024, '*UK extends tariff-free trade with Ukraine until 2029*',
https://www.gov.uk/government/news/uk-extends-tariff-free-trade-with-ukraine-until-2029

216. A. Kudrytski, L. Pronina (2025), Bloomberg, '*EU Seals New Trade Deal With Ukraine as Tariff-Free Regime Ends*',
https://www.bloomberg.com/news/articles/2025-06-30/eu-seals-new-trade-deal-with-ukraine-as-tariff-free-regime-ends

Benefit 72: How Do You Take Your Power? Hard or Soft?

217. Brand Finance, '*Global Soft Power Index*',
https://brandirectory.com/softpower/

218. K. Jagodzinski (2025), Brand Finance, '*Global Soft Power Index 2025: The shifting balance of global Soft Power*',
https://brandfinance.com/insights/global-soft-power-index-2025-the-shifting-balance-of-global-soft-power

Benefit 73: Who Ya Gonna Call?

219. These Times Podcast, 'The Race for the Arctic',
https://open.spotify.com/episode/0BParnQTGOheaXhLGBgf6D

220. European Union, 'Consolidated Version of the Treaty on European Union',
https://eur-lex.europa.eu/resource.html?uri=cellar:2bf140bf-a3f8-4ab2-b506-fd71826e6da6.0023.02/DOC_1&format=PDF

221. C. Caulcutt (2025), Politico, *Macron: EU needs 'hundreds of billions' in defense spending as US pivots away*,
https://www.politico.eu/article/europe-needs-defense-investment-spending-hundreds-billions-emmanuel-macron/

Benefit 74: Take Me Down to the Acronym City

222. UK Prime Minister's Office, 15 September 2021, *'PM Statement on AUKUS Partnership: 15 September 2021'*,
https://www.gov.uk/government/speeches/pm-statement-on-aukus-partnership-15-september-2021

223. Rolls-Royce press release, 21 March 2024, *'Rolls-Royce welcomes Australian investment in AUKUS preparation plans'*,
https://www.rolls-royce.com/media/press-releases/2024/21-03-2024-rr-welcomes-australian-investment-in-aukus-preparation-plans.aspx

Benefit 75: Through the Fire and the Flames

224. Royal Navy News, 12 April 2024, *'Powerful laser to be installed on Royal Navy warship by 2027'*,
https://www.royalnavy.mod.uk/news/2024/april/12/240412-powerful-laser-to-be-installed-on-royal-navy-warship-by-2027

225. Ministry of Defence Policy paper, 28 February 2024, *'Integrated Procurement Model: driving pace in the delivery of military capability'*,
https://www.gov.uk/government/publications/integrated-procurement-model-driving-pace-in-the-delivery-of-military-capability

226. European Union (2009), *'Directive 2009/81/EC on the coordination of procedures for the award of certain works contracts, supply contracts and service contracts by contracting authorities or entities in the fields of defence and security'*,
https://eur-lex.europa.eu/eli/dir/2009/81/oj/eng

227. C. Langford (2025), UK Defence Journal, *'Britain's destroyers to get laser weapons'*,
https://ukdefencejournal.org.uk/britains-destroyers-to-get-laser-weapons

Advance Valuation Ruling Service (AVRS), 90-91
Advanced Therapy Treatment Centres (ATTCs), 117-118
Aesop's Fables, 31
Algeria, 19
alternative medicines, 17
Andean Community, 33
Animal Aid, 50
animals
    breeding, 58-59, 67-68
    cruelty, 65-66
    fur, 4, 54-55, 58-59
    rights, 47-48, 49-51, 52-53, 58-59
    sentience, 58-59, 65
    smuggling, 67-68
    testing, 11, 47-48, 82
    welfare, 11, 49-50, 58-59, 65-66, 67-68, 122,
Antwerp, 99
Apple Intelligence, 130
Argos, 85
Artificial Intelligence (AI), 129-130
Artist's Resale Right (ARR), 108-109
Asia-Pacific, 52
Attlee, Lord Clement, 75-76
AUKUS, 183-185
Australia, 70-71, 108-109, 161-162, 166, 183-185
Austria, 113
Auto Express, 115

bananas, 33-34
Bank of England, 158-159
banker bonuses, 158-159
Barclay, Steve, 36
Barrow-in-Furness, 185
Belfast, 127
Belgium, 34, 113, 169

beneficial ownership, 123-124
benefit tangibility, 10
Benn, Tony, 127-128
Berne, 78
Berne Agreement, The, 78
Bike Radar Magazine, 115
Binding Customs Valuation Information (BCVI), 91
BioNTech, 117-118
BirdLife Europe, 46
Blick Rothenberg, 32
blockchain, 101-103
Bloomberg, 93
Bosnia, 19
Bowles, David, 51
Brand Finance, 179-180
Brighton, 150
British Isles, 49
Brunner, Ariel, 46
Brussels, 2, 46, 81, 127,
Buhari, Muhammadu, 76
Bulgaria, 113, 122
bullfighting, 58-59

Cambridge, 135
Canada, 79-80, 161-162
Capital Requirements Directive (CRD IV), 158
Carbon Border Adjustment Mechanism (CBAM), 21-22
carbon emissions, 21-22, 84-85
Cardiff, 127
cats, 54-55, 67-68
Channel 4 News, 46
Channel Islands, 49
ChatGPT, 130
child benefit, 154
China, 52-53, 54-55, 82, 174, 180, 184,
chinchillas, 54

Churchill, Winston, 178
Clegg, Nick, 130
Colombia, 33
commodity position limits, 147-148
Common Agricultural Policy (CAP),
    60-62, 136
Common External Tariff (CET), 73,
    105,
Common Fisheries Policy (CFP), 46,
Common Foreign and Security Policy
    (CFSP), 183-185
Common Market, 2, 75-76
Common Travel Area (CTA), 162
Commonwealth, The, 75-76, 166,
Compassion in World Farming
    (CWF), 50
Competition and Markets Authority
    (CMA), 137-138, 155-160,
Comprehensive and Progressive
    agreement on Trans-Pacific
    Partnership (CPTPP), 4, 33, 91,
    97-98, 172-174
Conservative Party, The, 68, 140, 188
contactless card payments, 145-146
corporate ownership, 123-124
cosmetics testing, 47-48
Costa Rica, 174, 175
Council of Europe, 127
covid pandemic, 10, 23-24, 118,
    145-146, 156
coyotes, 54
Croatia, 113
CueTheBBQ, 102
cumulation, 72, 88,
customs revenue, 31-32, 74, 90-91,
    167-168
customs union, 2, 4, 18-20, 31-32,
    82, 90-91, 98, 103, 104-105, 106-
    107, 167-168,
Cyprus, Republic of, 113
Czech Republic, 113, 141

dark pools, 95-96
Deadpool, 95

Deloitte, 136
Denmark, 45, 113
Department of Business and Trade
    (DBT), 74, 83, 106
Department of International Trade
    (DIT), 81,
Derby, 184
Design and Artists Copyright Society
    (DACS), 109
Developing Countries Trading
    Scheme (DCTS), 86-89
Digital Market Access Service
    (DMAS), 81-83
Dogger Bank, 45
dogs, 54-55, 67-68
double volume caps, 95-96
DragonFire LDEW, 186-187
driver-assist technology, 114
ducks, 65-66
dynamic alignment, 11

Ecuador, 33, 174
Edinburgh, 127
education, 125-126
Ek, Daniel, 130
elections, 43, 68, 71, 125
Electronic Trade Documents Act
    (ETDA), 101-103
Emergency Lane-Keeping Systems
    (ELKS), 115
Emissions Trading Scheme (ETS), 3,
    21-22
Environmental Land Management
    Scheme (ELM), 60-62
Erasmus / Erasmus+, 37-38
Estonia, 113
European Chemicals Agency
    (ECHA), 47-48
European Commission, 46, 77, 137,
    152, 155-157,
European Community (EC), 2, 37
European Court of Justice (CJEU or
    ECJ), 41-42, 123-124, 133-134,
    141-143, 156,

European Economic Area (EEA), 153,
169-170
European Economic Community
(EEC), 75, 86,
European Free Trade Association
(EFTA), 169-170
European Securities and Markets
Authority (ESMA), 147-148
European Super League (ESL), 133-
134
European Union (EU)
accession candidates, 29-30,
122
budget, 18-32
ever closer union, 8, 37
expansion, 29-30
foreign aid, 28
grants, 23-24,
issuing of bonds, 23-24
loans, 23-24
net contributors, 23, 27,
net recipients, 23, 29-30
Member of European Parliament
(MEP), 43, 111-113
own resources, 22, 24, 31,
parliament, 35, 43, 111-113, 121,
127-128
Everything But Arms (EBA), 86,
Exmoor, 62

Fédération Internationale de
Football Association (FIFA), 133-
134
Financial Times, The (FT), 29, 117,
150
Financial Conduct Authority (FCA),
95-96, 145-146
financial services, 72, 78, 95-96,
175-176
Finland, 54, 113
FinTech, 72, 159
fish or fishing
access rights, 11, 45-46, 52-53,
56-57
demersal, 56-57
pelagic, 56-57
quotas, 11, 45-46, 52-53, 56-57
Five Eyes, 181
flood prevention, 60-62
foie gras, 59, 65-66
Food Standards Agency (FSA), 135-
136
football, 133-134
Football Association (FA), 133-134
Four Paws, 67-68
Fox, Sir Liam, 19
foxes, 31, 54-55
France, 3, 34, 52, 65-66, 113, 169
Free Trade Agreements (FTA),
freedom of movement, 9, 149-150,
161, 163-164, 166, 169,
freeports, 167-168, 173,
Frontex, 169
FTSE100, 96

geese, 65-66
gene editing, 11
Generalised Scheme of Preferences
(GSP), 86-89
Geographical Indicators (GI), 72
Germany, 3, 5, 33, 113, 179
Global Soft Power Index, 179-180
golden shares, 141-143
Government Procurement
Agreement (GPA), 139-140, 176
Great Britain, 49-50, 60
Greece, 54, 113, 169
Greenland, 71
Greenpeace, 52
greenwashing, 21
Greggs, 85
Grok AI, 130
Gross Domestic Product (GDP), 5,
27, 173, 181
Gross National Income (GNI), 24
Gulf Cooperation Council (GCC), 71

Habitual Residence Test (HRT), 153
haulage, 84-85
    driver shortages, 149-150
hedge funds, 159
HM Revenue & Customs (HMRC),
    31-32, 77-78
HM Treasury, 32
Home Office, 48, 163, 170,
Hong Kong, 159
House of Lords, 42
Horizon Europe, 39-40
HSBC, 72
Huddleston, Nigel, 74
Humane Society International (HSI),
    54
Hungary, 113
Hyvonen, Catherine, 136

immigration, 9, 122, 161-162, 165-
    166, 170
India, 4, 71, 82, 88, 93
Indo-Pacific, 91, 172-174, 183-185
Indonesia, 82, 88
Institute for Government (IfG), 167
International Chamber of
    Commerce (ICC), 101-103
International Distribution Services
    (IDS), 141
international law, 46
International Monetary Fund (IMF),
    104-105
Ireland, Republic of, 33, 50, 113
Islamic State of Iraq and Syria (ISIS),
    122
Isle of Man, 49
Israel, 71
Italy, 113, 169

Japan, 70-72, 175-176

Kentucky Fried Chicken (KFC), 82
kittiwakes, 45-46

Kretinsky, Daniel, 141-143

Labour Party, The, 62, 66, 68, 75,
    107, 125-126, 127-128
Lancashire, 82
Latin-America (LATAM), 83
Latvia, 113
lawnmowers, 41-42
Least Developed Countries (LDCs),
    86-89
Liberal Democrats, The, 68
Lisbon Treaty, 58
Lithuania, 113
Liverpool, 99, 173
livestock, 11, 49-51
London, 78, 158-159
London Stock Exchange (LSE), 77-78
Loungers, 150
loveMONEY, 33
Low Income Countries (LICs), 86-89
Low Middle Income Countries
    (LMICs), 87
low skilled labour, 149-150
Lumley, Joanna, 50
Luxembourg, 113

Macfarlanes LLP, 124
Malaysia, 173
Maldives, 71
Malmgren, Pippa, 181-182
Malta, 111-113
Marine Conservation Society (MCS),
    64,
Markets in Financial Instruments
    Directive II (MiFID II), 95-96, 147-
    148
Marvel Cinematic Universe (MCU),
    95
Mazda, 99-100
mergers, 137-138, 141-143
Meta, 130
Mexico, 33, 71
MG, 115

microplastics, 63-64
Ministry of Defence (MoD), 186-187
mink, 54, 58-59
mixed competency, 79-80
Monde, Le, 136
Mongolia, 82
Montenegro, 19
Morrisons, 85
motoring
    driver assistance, 114-116
insurance, 41-42
    test, 131-132
    towing a trailer, 131-132
motorsport, 41-42
Moy Park, 82
Multiannual Financial Framework
    (MFF), 32

National Federation of Fishermen's
    Associations, (NFFO), 56-57
National Trust, The, 60-62
Netherlands, The, 99, 113
New Vehicle General Safety
    Regulation (GSR2), 114-116
New York, 159
New Zealand, 70, 76, 162
NextGenerationEU (NGEU), 23-24
no resource to public funds (NRPF),
    153
non-tariff barriers, 81-83
North Atlantic Treaty Organization
    (NATO), 173, 181
Northern Ireland, 49, 61, 116
Norway, 56, 88,
novel foods, 11, 135-136
Nuclear Economics Consulting
    Group (NECG), 151
nuclear power, 151-152, 183-185

Obama, Barack, 93
Office of the US Trade
    Representative (USTR), 92

Organisation for Economic Co-
    operation and Development
    (OECD), 165-166, 175-176

passports, 169-170
People for the Ethical Treatment of
    Animals (PETA), 50
period underwear, 120
Permanent Court of Arbitration
    (PCA), 45-46
Permanent Structured Cooperation
    (PESCO), 183-185
Peru, 33
pesticides, 61
petitions, 121-122
Pinsent Masons, 159
plastic packaging waste, 25-26
Poland, 54, 63, 113
Politico, 46
Portugal, 52, 113
poultry, 3, 82
procurement, 139-140, 176, 186-187
Project Orbis, 118
puffins, 45-46

Qkine, 135-136
quad bikes, 41-42
Qualifying Full Bank (QFB), 72
quotas, 56-57, 86-89, 178

raccoon dogs, 54
Ramsgate, 50
razorbills, 45-46
REACH, 47-48
ReArm Europe, 24
recycling, 25-26
Regulated Asset Base (RAB), 151-
    152
Renault, 115
Reuters, 150,
Riparbelli, Victor, 130
Rolls-Royce, 184

Romania, 113, 122, 169
Rotterdam effect, The, 99-100
Royal Mail, The, 85, 141-143
Royal Society for the Prevention of
    Cruelty to Animals (RSPCA), 50-
    51
Royal Society for the Protection of
    Birds (RSPB), 45-46, 60-63
Rules of Origin (RoO), 72, 74, 87-89
Russia, 177-178, 182

sandeel or sand eel, 45-46
sanitary and phytosanitary
    regulations (SPS), 11
sanitary products, 119-120
Schengen, 8
Scotland, 49, 61
seals, 54
shark finning, 52-53
Shaw, Mark, 159
Sikorski, Radoslaw, 178
Singapore, 70-72
Slovakia, 113
Slovenia, 41-42, 113
small boats migration, 165
smoking ban, 10
solar panels, 119-120
South Korea, 71
Southworth, Chris, 104
Spain, 33, 52-53, 54, 113, 169
Spectator, The, 117-118
Spotify, 130
Standard Chartered, 72
state aid, 151-152, 155-157, 167-168
Stobart, 85
Strasbourg, 8
students
    further education, 37-38
    tuition fees, 37-38
    vocational training, 37-38
sub-Saharan Africa, 33
subsidy control regime, 155-157
Sutcliffe, Simon, 32
Sweden, 113

Switzerland, 71, 77-78
Synthesia, 130

Taiwan, 174
tariffs,
    applied, 73-74, 76, 92-93
    bound, 73-74
    liberalisation, 73-74, 104-105
Thanet District Council, 50
Tholos Foundation, The, 104-105
Thompson, Alex, 46
Toms, Bate, 177
Trade and Cooperation Agreement
    (TAC), 46, 140, 156,
trade continuity, 19, 80
Trudeau, Justin, 80
Trump, Donald, 92-93
Tureci, Ozlem, 118
Turing Scheme, 37-38
Turkey or Turkiye, 71,

Union of European Football
    Associations (UEFA), 133-134
Unilever, 82
United Nations (UN), 87,
    UN Conference on Trade and
    Development (UNCTAD), 97
United States of America (USA or
    US), 4, 92-93, 105, 159, 162, 176,
    179, 181-185
university rankings, 38
UK-EU Summit, 11
UK Global Tariff (UKGT), 73-74
Ukraine, 174, 177-178
Uruguay, 174

Value Added Tax (VAT), 3, 119-120,
    122, 125-126
Vere, Baroness (of Norbiton), 42
Visitor International Stay Agreement
    (VISA), 72
Vnuk, 42

Volvo, 115

Wales, 6, 49, 61
Westminster, 81, 127
wet wipes, 63-64
Which? Magazine, 115
Wildlife Trusts, The, 60
wine, 35-36
World Bank, 87,
World Trade Organization (WTO), 19,
    73-74, 76, 139, 173, 176,
World Wildlife Fund (WWF), 60

YouGov, 66

Zuckerberg, Mark, 130

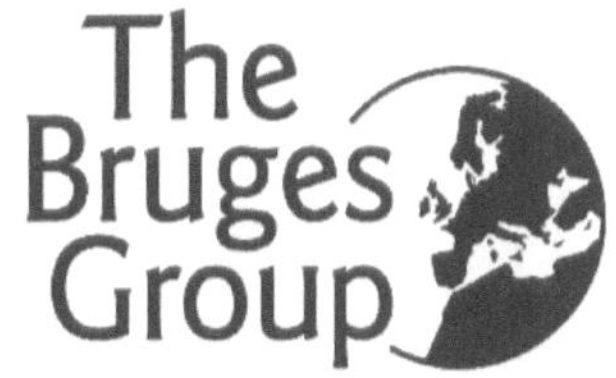

www.brugesgroup.com

www.ingramcontent.com/pod-product-compliance
Lightning Source LLC
Chambersburg PA
CBHW022131050726
47590CB00002B/503